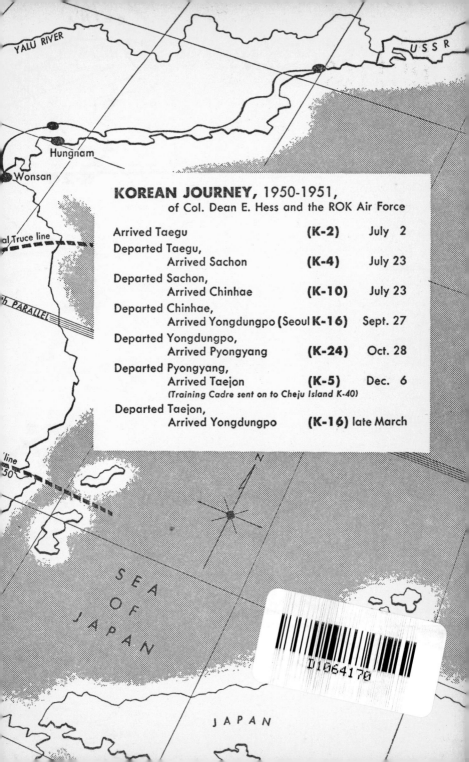

YALU RIVER

USSR

Hungnam

Wonsan

al Truce line

h PARALLEL

'line
50

KOREAN JOURNEY, 1950-1951,
of Col. Dean E. Hess and the ROK Air Force

Arrived Taegu	**(K-2)**	July 2
Departed Taegu, Arrived Sachon	**(K-4)**	July 23
Departed Sachon, Arrived Chinhae	**(K-10)**	July 23
Departed Chinhae, Arrived Yongdungpo (Seoul **K-16**)		Sept. 27
Departed Yongdungpo, Arrived Pyongyang	**(K-24)**	Oct. 28
Departed Pyongyang, Arrived Taejon	**(K-5)**	Dec. 6

(Training Cadre sent on to Cheju Island K-40)

Departed Taejon, Arrived Yongdungpo	**(K-16)**	late March

N

SEA OF JAPAN

JAPAN

BATTLE HYMN

BATTLE HYMN

Dean E. Hess
COLONEL, USAF

McGraw-Hill Book Company, Inc.

NEW YORK   TORONTO   LONDON

Library of Congress Catalog Card Number: 56-11716

Published by the McGraw-Hill Book Company, Inc.

Printed in the United States of America

To Those We Could Not Save

I wish to acknowledge the special contributions of a few persons of the dozens who have helped me so much and in so many different ways:

Gen. Earle E. Partridge and Maj. Gen. Edward Timberlake, who were a constant source of inspiration and encouragement and tolerant of my unorthodox procedures over the many months in Korea.

Charles Grayson, whose help in preparing this book for publication proved invaluable.

My wife, Mary Lorentz Hess, whose faith in my activities at war and in peace never wavered during my long years away from home.

ILLUSTRATIONS

i

Sometimes in the air over Ohio I used to think of the skies as a white-tufted blue quilt tucked over the world. It was the same kind of sky on this December morning in 1944. But these were cold, clear German skies, the clouds were flak bursts, and I wasn't jogging a little rented plane between the three towns where I preached in separate churches on those crowded but happy Sundays. Now I was on a fast-flying seven-ton gun mount called a P-47, on my way to deliver destruction rather than a sermon. I meant that destruction to be loud and vehement, just as years before I had meant my sermons always to be quiet and gentle.

The mission was to be another signpost, more cruelly bloodied than most, on the road I had begun to travel when Pearl Harbor had been attacked and which I have followed ever since. To many it has seemed a strange path for a minister. But I have tried to pursue it, according to the dictates of my conscience, as a combatant for our country and, above all, for God.

We were an element of two aircraft that morning over Germany in 1944. Capt. Bill Myers, the flight leader, and I had separated from the rest of the squadron for wider coverage and had continued on armed reconnaissance. Reaching the marshaling yards at Kaiserslautern, we found a pair of trains. Since we were in fighter planes, we each carried only two 1,000-pound bombs—one under each wing. Strafing the cars, Bill went into a run for one locomotive. I started down after the other train, pushing the release button. Just as with Bill, only one of my bombs hit its target; the other failed momentarily to fall. I could tell immediately, because one wing lifted and the plane turned slightly. Then its release mechanism worked, and the second bomb let go—past where I had intended.

Pulling out of the dive into a sharp bank, I looked back over the wing and saw the second bomb falling toward a brick building of six or seven stories at the edge of the yard. It seemed to be suspended for an eternity against the tall structure. Then a little hole appeared in the wall from the penetration of the bomb casing, and a moment later the insides of the building spilled out. The rush of the plane carried me away from the rocking explosion, and I could see no more.

Later I learned that this was an apartment building being used as a day school for hundreds of children of warworkers employed in the vicinity. I was visiting the town, driving around it in a jeep, and saw that many of its buildings were blackened shells. One of these especially drew me. I stood looking up at it, trying to keep my eyes away from the black hole where my bomb had entered; but it seemed to stare at me like some malevolent eye. I could hear the special "Crump!" of the explosion, and to my nose came the suggestion of acrid clouds of dust and cordite fumes. I wondered if beneath the piles of bricks a few small bodies still lay, as yet undiscovered.

Years later still, a writer in the *Air Force Times* conjectured that guilt stemming from this incident may have been partially responsible for the aid I rendered Korean orphans in the airlift that became known as Operation Kiddy Car. I do not know. Certainly we all are sympathetic to the needs of children, and when I was told that that building in Kaiserslautern was a day school and orphanage, that particular mission over Germany left a mark in my mind like a brand. But at the time of the bombing it seemed like just another mission, accomplished with a degree of success because at least one bomb had found its intended target in the railroad yard.

With our bombs gone, we started back to our base at St. Dizier in France, looking for other targets of opportunity—any potential enemy conveyance or weapon on which we might use the rest of our ammunition. As we flew, I wondered if Bill was having thoughts like mine. Mine were of two kinds, as they always were flying home from a mission. Had I killed anyone? If so, whom? And why had I been his particular nemesis? But these were only speculations in addition to my primary concern: Had the enemy felt the blow of the mission? Had I justified my being in the aircraft, done my best *as a fighter pilot?*

I looked down at the countryside, seeing again its similarity to the rolling, neatly cultivated hills of home. I felt the old flash of wonderment that I should be here as Captain Hess, USAAF. And again it seemed that I should feel as different from Reverend Hess as a pilot's uniform differs from a pastor's robe. But I did not; I knew that I was where I was supposed to be, doing what my conscience dictated.

I had been flying missions like this for months now, escorting B-26s and flying fighter-bomber missions against AA guns, rail lines, and bridges, and the anesthesia had set in which protects those in this ghastly work from reactions which can destroy them. There can be no giving way to remorse on this job if one is to stay on it. If I was suffering, it was in some remote and subconscious part of my mind; for when I became a combatant, it was with the full knowledge that I had to accept killing in behalf of the way of life I had sworn to protect.

My first direct encounter with this fact had taken place several months before, shortly after my arrival at the airfield in St. Dizier in October, 1944, to join the 511th Fighter Squadron. Our duty was to provide close air support for ground forces and to go behind the lines to hit enemy installations. My first combat run was almost my last.

Our mission was to dive-bomb the Delmi Woods, near Metz. The squadron commander, Maj. Jake Abraham, placed me in the last position of the last flight of aircraft. I promptly proved his wisdom by showing my inexperience.

We were to start our run on the woods from 10,000 feet and drop our bombs at 5,000. Concentrating on flying correctly, I made a beautiful run. But when I pressed the button on top of

3

the control stick, my bombs did not fall. Of the three major steps to be taken before a bomb run, I had forgotten one—to turn my bomb-release switch on. Coming out of the dive, I radioed the leader that I still had my bombs. He allowed me to go back and discharge them over the woods.

My heart was hammering and my right palm, grasping the stick, was wet, but I knew that in this baptism of fire lay the moment of decision on which future ones must hinge. I turned the plane around and started another run. As I dove lower than before into the range of the antiaircraft guns, I was more curious than concerned at the puffs of antiaircraft shells bursting like orange golf balls all around me. (After a few more missions, my curiosity was replaced by acute respect for those lethal bursts.) But now I was concentrating with single-minded intensity on my target in my desire to prove myself. And this time my bombs found their mark —a thicket hiding enemy troops that were stopping our Third Army near Metz.

I started back to base, hardly realizing that at last I had crossed the barrier. It had all come and gone so quickly. It was difficult to believe that I was past the point of no return for which I had been conditioning myself since the day I had entered flight training. I had anticipated qualms of conscience and revulsion the first time I tore a man into pieces by the mere pressure of my thumb. Now I was committed. My hands were stained, albeit for a cause.

But where was the disgust and remorse I was sure that I, like all men after initial combat, must suffer? Shouldn't I, who had dedicated years of my young life to the ministry, suffer an especially sharp pain? Didn't those enemies have a love for life? Didn't they also have families and loved ones? True, I had resolved long ago that I had chosen the lesser of two evils: to fight, rather than to allow fascism to overrun the world. But now, though I was sure that men had died from my own efforts, it seemed impersonal, detached. I was disturbed because I felt no sense of guilt; rather, I was elated and content, eager for the next mission. Had I lost in one morning all sense of the value of human life?

4

The answer was to come only after many more missions. Men at war lose their identity as individuals and become integral components of a war machine defending a way of life. When another ideology propounds intolerance, oppression, and destruction of a civilized world, one cannot and should not try to escape a vehement hatred of that system—or for the individuals who foster and enforce it. This hatred for the system and its leaders should, of course, be offset by a profound love for the people, the masses, caught and tortured in such a system. But in combat this hatred, partly engendered by fear, is an emotion which makes for self-preservation. You fight your best when full of hatred for the enemy, coldly intent, your excitement just beneath the surface. When the threat is gone, the man killed, how quickly the feelings turn to sorrow—sorrow that it was, sorrow that it had to be.

But that revelation was to come later. Back at the airfield after my first mission, alone in my shack, I was still tormented by my satisfied and self-confident feeling when I saw my bombs drop squarely on the target. I recalled the conviction with which, months before, I had met the incredulous elders of my church to tell them of my intention to enter the war as a combatant. "If we believe our cause is just and necessary," I had declared, "how in all conscience can I ask others to protect it—and me—while I keep clean of the gory mess of war?"

Doc Baxter's knock on the door aroused me from my lethargy. The squadron flight surgeon had missed me in the ramshackle club where the pilots met before going to the evening meal. I avoided his inquiring, worried glances but agreed to walk down to the club with him.

The club was a building some 50 feet square, with an arched roof and slanting walls of prefabricated panels scrounged from some abandoned German warehouse. The interior walls were a mosaic of paperboard packing salvaged from .50-caliber-ammunition boxes. The bar, stove, chairs, and tables were crudely improvised, but the place was full of the rowdy, frontier cheer of men who live close to death.

5

They were generous with handshakes and backslaps for my successful entry into combat. These veteran pilots, having learned of my former work, had been watching to see how I would react the first time out. Now I welcomed these overtures of friendship and tried to join in the excitement and chatter. But while I was accustomed to the aggressiveness and crudity of their stories, tonight I was particularly aware of them:

"Wow—did I cut down those two bastards!" . . . "You were just lucky. . . . But did you ever see anything as funny as that Kraut with his pants on fire with napalm? . . ."

I wondered—how soon would I be speaking of my exploits in such inhuman terms? Were these the famed American fighting men—husbands of American girls, fathers of little children? The more I watched and listened, the more it seemed that they were acting roles in which they were ill cast. The psychology of war demands acute response to every primitive instinct, and these young fellows—as warriors have done through the ages—were trying to overcome innate fears by descriptions of their own bravado and superiority. They talked viciously about the enemy to quiet their own fears and to justify their killing. They were already mentally facing tomorrow's mission.

Behind their callous remarks I saw men who were tired, afraid, lonely, homesick—men who were begging for spiritual consolation in the promise of life and trying to turn their backs on the imminence of death. Though some comments were made to me which suggested this groping for something of spiritual value, I was hesitant to speak of religion in any of its formal trappings. Besides, now I was one of them—not a minister. In the face of my own feelings of indifference toward the men killed by my bombs, I was hardly the one to give their hearts ease.

But after dinner a young officer—one who had used as much invective and harsh language as the boldest—awkwardly and hesitantly told me that he got down on his knees every night to pray before going to bed. He hadn't done this since he was a little boy. Though this was but the first of many such admissions made to me in the course of two wars, this first was the most revealing. He shed for me a light by which I could discern the real character of these men who were living with death—mission after mission after mission. Listening to his hesitant confession, I silently blessed him. In his faith was renewed strength for me.

In much the same way other men helped me find myself. There was a tall, sandy-haired lieutenant, Arnold "Moon" Mullins, in our outfit, with a particularly direct way of speech. He was an aggressive pilot, thoroughly combat-trained, always on the prowl for targets to strafe. One Saturday he asked me if I was going to chapel the next day. I answered that I was, right after I returned from the morning mission.

"That's a hell of a time to go," he said.

I shrugged and turned to walk away, when he stopped me. "If you don't mind," he said, "I'd like to go with you."

Several nights after Moon and I knelt and prayed together, I had a dream which helped even more—a dream so vivid, so strong, that after all these violent years I remember its every rich detail. I was being conducted into an enormous palatial hall, dressed in old and shabby clothes. Ragged, dirty, and barefoot, I was led on either side by persons in white robes. They were gently urging but not compelling me toward a flight of stairs which led to a level platform encircled with rich red curtains hanging from a canopy of gold. Everything was bathed in golden splendor—gold with overtones of red—and a mystic light emanated from above.

At the top of the stairs before a thronelike seat stood a figure of a man in a glorious white robe. Was it Christ? Was that a crown of gold or of thorns on His head? Hands outstretched, smiling, He was beckoning me to ascend to Him. To His left sat another Person, smiling. All around the foot of the stairs to my left and to my right stood people similarly dressed in royal robes. Their peaceful countenances were like none I had ever seen—so warm, so filled with compassion.

Despite the gestures and urging I would not, could not, climb the stairs. I was too begrimed, unkempt, ragged, and unworthy to

7

ascend to Him Who was waiting. I stopped, kneeled, and bowed my head before Him, overwhelmed by the force of His love and sympathy. The dream faded. That night I grew up, matured— spiritually. The next morning I awakened with a kind of sad, inward peace alien to all my previous emotions.

Like most people I am skeptical of dreams. But be it what it may —a figment of my imagination, a flight of fancy, a manifestation of some subconscious concern, or a true spiritual experience— others can accept this vision only in the light of their own experiences. I can only accept it in the light of mine.

From that moment my doubts and fears were dispelled. My sense of the relationship of life and death took on a new complexion. I did not feel that I was invulnerable in any sense of the word—only that, if I were killed, it would be no terrible thing. It had happened to others with whom I had served; they remained part of me, and I of them. I had broken through the barrier that separates life and death, and on the other side I had found a promise.

From then on the task was easier—easier still as the missions mounted over fifty. Although my airplane was hit incessantly by flak, I escaped physical harm, as though I were being fortified by powers beyond my own. Credits were being added to my combat record. It came to seem in our flights over eastern France and deep into Germany that "The Preacher," as I was called (against my wishes), was earmarked to deal with most of the personnel targets —troops on the road, AA installations, truck convoys. They bobbed up before my guns with unaccountable persistence, and always with the same ending: the enemy, people whose terrified faces I could sometimes see, falling broken on the ground. Through it all I struggled to keep my faith.

When I was a small child visiting at my grandmother's, I was sent on an errand to a candy store. Someone asked if I was afraid to go by myself. I answered no, that God would protect and take care of me. The benediction of that belief continued with me,

8

lending credence to the claim painted on the cowling of my plane: "By Faith I Fly."

During my training period in the States a sergeant had brought me a little crest on a piece of paper. I had inscribed it with the motto: "Per Fidem Volo." It seemed uniquely appropriate in that it combined the two great impulses of my life. In France I had it put on my P-47, and years later it was to appear, this time in Korean symbols, on the F-51 I used in the Far East. A correspondent saw it, inquired into my background, and wrote an article for *The Saturday Evening Post* with the terrible title "The Pious Killer of Korea." Though I'm afraid there was little piety in my actions in either of those theaters of war, in 313 combat missions no scrap of metal touched me. The good Lord divined that there was still piety in my heart.

In all that slaughter and noisy confusion I only knew that I had taken a step which was irrevocable and which I must continue to repeat. As I saw it, combat was the lesser of two evils, which in most instances is the only choice given to man. At times—as when I learned of the children's lives I had taken at Kaiserslautern—I wished to offer the petition of David in Psalms: "Deliver me from bloodguiltiness, O God, thou God of my salvation; and my tongue shall sing aloud of thy righteousness. . . ."

But mostly, when I let myself remember, I could only think of how far away and how long ago it was to the quiet, tree-lined streets and slow-moving rivers of Marietta, Ohio.

ii

Marietta, the town of my happy boyhood, is like many Middle Western towns of twenty or thirty thousand people, with the usual neat hub of stores, churches, and tree-lined streets of old houses. Beyond range the rolling farmlands which sustain it. Even today, with its 121-year-old college campus, it resembles a New England town, and in fact it was one of the first settled communities in the Northwest Territory. Rufus Putnam, the Revolutionary War hero, built a fort there.

In the woods and fields, at school, and in the neighborhood gang, I was looked down on as the smallest and youngest, with the result that I forced myself to duplicate most of the bigger boys' activities, to accept my share of dares, no matter how frightening. I would whoop away as loudly as any of the rest from a pushed-over backhouse on Halloween.

Once a week we would pool our resources so that everyone would have a nickel for the Lyric. We would go in a body to that dingy theater to be enthralled into uncharacteristic silence by the good cowboys in the white hats triumphing over both the bad cowboys in the black hats and the hordes of savage Indians.

I was lucky that my particular friend was a boy named Everett Jett, one of the leaders of the gang, with whom I shared a Mark Twain boyhood, singing and roasting corn and potatoes by the river. He was interested in religion and had a pronounced sense of right and wrong even when young. When I became more deeply involved with it, he was always ready to discuss God, Christ, resurrection, and the hereafter. As we grew older, he encouraged my gradual leanings toward the ministry. Of all the people who later might be unsympathetic toward my taking up arms, it disturbed me most to think that Everett could be among them.

My boyhood idol, Charles Lindbergh, I viewed from a distance. Nothing in all my childhood compared with the excitement I, ten years old at the time, felt over his flight. From the moment I heard my mother and father talking about his start across the Atlantic, I was in an agony of suspense. When he reached his destination, I was wild with elation. It seemed to have a particular significance that he should engage in this brave venture alone. I thought of him continually—a tiny speck in the sky over that huge waste of waters, a solitary man daring all—until he became fixed in my mind as a symbol of flight.

I was inspired to make a plane of my own. Assembling an orange-crate fuselage on a pair of abandoned baby-buggy wheels, with a board for wings, I took the invention to the top of a hill and started down, fully expecting it to fly. It came apart on the incline, and I almost with it. I had to wait until I was old enough to earn some money raking grass and cutting lawns before I at last managed to get into the air.

With two dollars laboriously scraped together from working on lawns and carrying papers, I went to the local airport and bought a ride in a taxi plane. From the moment the tiny tandem Piper Cub took off until the end of my short ride sitting behind the pilot I was exalted, though we were flying at no more than 60 miles per hour. I had no fear nor nervousness—only a supreme sense of being perfectly at ease, an elated sensation of the earth's leaving me unshackled, as we took off. I knew with complete conviction that I would be airborne whenever possible from that time on.

This was not to happen often during my adolescence; opportunities to make money don't abound in small towns, and there were many family needs for any I might scrape together. We lived in a comfortable enough five-room frame house, and my father's work as an electrician provided for our basic needs; but luxury was a rare visitor to our house.

11

We belonged to the Christian Church, one of the town's twenty-three denominations. A fundamentalist sect which holds that there is no creed but Christ, no book but the Bible, its simplicities seem particularly appropriate to Middle Western sections like that in which we lived and in which it has its greatest popularity. Mother and Dad were not regular churchgoers; yet, oddly enough, my two elder brothers, George and Tom, my younger sister, Ethel, and myself were. The eldest, George, quiet and serious, set the pattern for us; being of German descent, the preeminence of the first-born influenced me to follow his example. Our parents urged us to attend, but it seemed more to the point that George did so faithfully —that he appeared to enjoy it, and that he looked very impressive singing in the choir.

My father was given to strong discipline, but, like many with direct ways and manners of speech, this rough exterior covered a softer nature. Gruff as he may have been—and now I love him for it—he at no time sought to frighten his brood. Instead he fostered in us a feeling of independence, encouraging us at all times to make our own decisions. When later I had to choose between fighting and preaching, I loved him the more for giving me the courage to make my decision cleanly and then stand by it.

During a lengthy period of illness of my mother's, I was looked after by a woman named Molly Hess, a warm-hearted neighbor unrelated to us. Molly, with her great capacity for loving people, was constantly giving little presents and sending flowers to both the well and the sick. She would often say that she sent flowers to the well because she wanted them to see the beautiful things in life rather than receive them after they had passed on. I marveled at her dedication to others, and it did much to make me receptive to spiritual values.

My father's father, another memorable influence, was a giant of a man and, in my eyes, a true adventurer. Raised around Marietta, he had gone west to become a cowboy, then to Mexico, and finally down to South America. For a number of years he had worked in the jungles with teams in search of oil wells. He had returned to

Marietta like the legendary elephant going home to die, and I spent much time with him. He taught me to shoot, and his fireside tales of hunting and drilling and wandering filled our little living room many a night with images of a fascinating world beyond its walls.

I was never what one would call an accomplished social performer. My first teen-age date was for a party at the Hi-Y Club—the only one to which I belonged. It had taken considerable self-bolstering to bring myself to the point of asking the girl. After combing my hair until my scalp stung, I presented myself at her home stricken mute, a condition which lasted the whole evening. Only her admission of hunger brought me partially out of my hypnosis. I raced out and bought ten candy bars with the fifty cents I had been saving. All evening, in lieu of conversation, we chewed on candy bars. She looked a little green by the time I took her home.

Always a steady attendant at Sunday school and active in Christian Endeavor, I often went to the church on weekdays to sweep, dust, paint, or do whatever there was to be done. In these menial chores I felt that I was rendering practical service to certain ideas that I was coming more and more to believe in. In a boyish, unquestioning way I had accepted the teachings of service to God and man. I had no money to give, no genius or even wisdom to impart, but I considered it a privilege to sweep out the church. I felt a great satisfaction in being there alone in the quiet church, a nearness to God that I was later to feel often when alone in an airplane.

When I was in the tenth grade, a new minister came to the church. Robert Updegraff was an affable and intelligent young man of twenty-eight—big, attractive, and with a ringing voice. Though my father was not usually interested in ministers, this one proved the exception, and Bob became a close friend of the family's. We spent many companionable evenings around our kitchen table playing poker for matches and arguing about God.

A great teacher by example, Bob would frequently take me in

13

his Model A on his calls to members of the congregation. He smoked cigars and often used to break the ice by taking out a fat black stogie and asking for an ash tray. He never refused food, and charmed more than one church lady by exclaiming over her lemon-meringue pie. He was perfectly at ease with all types and varieties of people—the rich and urbane, the poor and simple.

I remember one such parish call. We had scarcely arrived when the family learned by telephone that their daughter had just been killed in an automobile accident. Quietly Bob expressed his deep sympathy to the stunned parents and asked if there was anyone they wished to have told about the tragedy. Much to my surprise, we then left, without his saying anything more. He must have sensed my disappointment that he hadn't offered more in the way of consolation. "There are times when a minister's presence can do more harm than good," he explained as we drove away. "I'll be back when it won't be such an intrusion on their grief."

Years later in bomb-wrecked Korea, while ministering to mothers suddenly made childless and children suddenly become orphans, I was to understand the wisdom of his approach.

It distressed me that, for all the effort he put into his mission in life, Bob's material rewards were so slight. The specter of the grocery bill always hung over him. He supported his wife and two children on twenty-five dollars a week—without the usual free parsonage. It seemed wrong that a man of his ability, sincerity, and assiduous attention to his congregation should be forced to live on a standard so much lower than many of the people to whom he ministered. Why should he not be provided with at least the necessities of life? I had yet to learn how prevalent this condition is in ministerial work.

Bob kept an eye on the way I conducted the various youth services in the church. Once when I told him in a fit of brag-gadocio that I didn't think he could high-jump as well as I could, he answered quietly that he'd like to see me try to preach a sermon. I accepted the challenge, and within a few days he announced in church that on Easter night I would be the guest preacher.

14

As the hour approached, I became increasingly uncertain that I would be able to say anything worth listening to; but a buoying excitement carried me into the small auditorium and onto the platform. My first impression was one of disappointment: the empty pews. Carefully counting the house, I estimated that about forty people had gathered. At the back, near the wall where the coats hung, a man sat conspicuously alone. I heard later that he had had a few drinks and didn't want the guest preacher, at his tender age, to get a whiff of his breath.

I looked down at the faces of the congregation, all inspecting me with an air of anticipation, as if waiting for a performance to begin. My hands felt awkward; I had to struggle to keep them out of my pockets. Then I heard my voice begin to speak, and I realized that I was giving my first sermon. What I actually said that Sunday evening I cannot remember—probably a series of platitudes, interspersed with quotes from the Scriptures, that didn't amount to a hill of beans. But I was uplifted by a strength that came from without—as might any sixteen-year-old be who knows with tremendous certainty that he has found his proper place.

This was the first of many sermons I gave as a teen-age guest "minister." One in particular I shall never forget was in a small church in a disreputable neighborhood in Marietta. It was the first time I preached to a congregation not of our denomination, and a sprinkling of prostitutes was among those who had gathered to hear this oddity, a boy minister. I was uncertain how they would receive me, but I plowed through a sermon full of simple ideas and scriptural references. When I finished, I was deeply pleased, if a little uncomfortable, when some of them came to thank me, for I realized that they were reaching out to God for healing. Even so incapable and inexperienced a pastor as myself could give them a bit of comfort and guidance. I never failed to be impressed by the response of those who, like the prostitutes of Marietta, were most badly in need, and this as much as anything reaffirmed my determination to go ahead with the work.

I was accustomed to quiet worship in the churches of my own

15

denomination. The first time I led a prayer in another, more evangelical church, someone in the back of the room hollered, "Amen!" I was like an actor given the wrong cue: I lost my place and went all to pieces. But after preaching there several times, the roof could have fallen in and I wouldn't have faltered. I was learning that there are many different kinds of religious expression, and that someone in his shirt sleeves in the back of the church hollering, "Amen!" can be a better worshiper than a town father or a bank president nodding in the front pew.

I once had to share this pulpit with an evangelist. After I had delivered what I thought was a rational elucidation of the good Word, he followed with an angry tirade directed at me for trying to be practical in my faith. We must have seemed an odd pair— the tyro and the veteran shouter. Yet even in my embarrassment I was perhaps touched by the beginning of wisdom: I realized something which grew more important to me as time went on— the harsh folly of berating another form of belief or another individual, especially from the pulpit.

We often hear about when and how the call to the ministry comes. I heard no voice from the burning bush nor saw any blinding light on high. But after I had conducted several services around Marietta, a strong urge was born within me to continue with the work—to work with people. In the beginning just delivering the message—the idea of communicating from the pulpit with my people—brought a great deal of satisfaction. In later years I found need of a different and broader means of expression. I came to feel that people must be spoken to not only in church but elsewhere too; within them are requirements which cannot be fully satisfied by formal sermons or pastoral calls. But the holy persuasion, as I was to discover, finds its own climate and place.

Bob Updegraff left Marietta, and the gentle Reverend Mozena replaced him in our church. He was a fine old gentleman in whom I felt a dedicated singleness of purpose. Though our discussions did not follow strict ecclesiastical pattern—they were often about the weather and gardening—I felt a rare communion with this older

16

man. He taught me what I can only call the "common touch"—the realization that all human beings have so much to share and are so much alike. This oneness is the greatest value in my life. I feel a strong sense of the common bond of humanity which exists between me and everyone I meet, the unbreakable links between us all—people of all races, all nations.

During my last two years in high school I had to work afternoons and in the summertime. But college confronted me with a much greater financial problem. My father told me somewhat gruffly that he would be unable to help me—that if I wanted to go to college, I would have to do it on my own. Now I understand that he was so sensitive to my wants and to his inability to fulfill them that he took this negative attitude. However, I nursed a deep conviction that I would be able to attend Marietta College—that I would eventually complete the work and enter the ministry.

At the end of a summer of pumping gas, cleaning windshields, filling tires, and checking batteries, despite saving every nickel I could, I still did not have nearly enough money to go on with my schooling. I decided to work for a year.

As so often happens, it turned out for the best. It's rare that a man meets his future wife in a gas station. It's rarer still when he hides behind a pump upon her arrival. I managed both.

Edgar Lorentz, who worked with me, had on several occasions mentioned that he had a sister, Mary, in Lowell, a small town 10 miles away, whom he would like me to meet. When she drove into the station one afternoon, I knew at once that it was she and that he was going to call and introduce me. A fit of shyness struck me, and I hastened off to occupy myself behind the gas tanks. When she was gone I reappeared, already regretting my behavior and feeling like a fool. But fortunately I was to have another chance.

Mary—quiet, shy, lovely Mary—returned on another afternoon, and this time I was braver. Downright bold, in fact, because five minutes after Edgar introduced us, I found myself asking her to a dance. Perhaps I sensed that her shyness was as great as mine. On the night of the affair (my third date and first dance) I borrowed my brother's car—a Model-A Ford. It was the beginning. From that time on there was never anyone else for either of us. At first I saw her only once a week, then more often. It was almost a month, though, before I asked her if I could kiss her good night. I don't think I even opened the front gate that night —just walked right over it. That first kiss foretold my future as accurately as my first sermon or my first flight.

During this year of filling gas tanks, I continued my preaching in various churches in the community and in smaller ones in such rural villages as Paw Paw. Here, beneath giant oak trees, sat the little frame church, with its single-ringing bell and its shaded cemetery. Perhaps thirty people would come of a Sunday morning— most of the population for miles around—in their 10- and 15-year-old cars. They would come in family groups, these self-sufficient farmers whose small produce was consumed at home, with a little left over for "money crops" to be sold in town, and they would sit quietly in the pews, listening and praying. No experience in later life thrilled me so much as ministering to that small rural church in Paw Paw on a quiet, clear Sunday morning in April.

But while the sermons seemed well received, I felt that there was so much more to be said. Ideas which I was unable to express swirled about in my mind. Looking down at the bowed and humble heads, I felt keenly my own inadequacy. These people deserved a deeper spiritual guidance than I could give with my vague and general sermons. And that is why I clung so tenaciously to the idea of a college education.

One of the churches was even smaller and more rural than the others—so poor that its services had to be held in a schoolhouse. But the farmers who made up the congregation were sturdy, sincere people, most of the men in overalls, the women in plain cotton dresses. They paid rapt attention.

There was no collection plate, so a hat was passed. The hat we used that first Sunday had a hole in it, and some of the coins fell on the floor. Someone produced another, and as it was passed, it

18

finally reached an old fellow who dropped in a fifty-cent piece. He evidently changed his mind, for he grabbed the hat back and pulled out some change. I trust he didn't take more than he put in.

Another old fellow sat apart from the rest back near the door. During the sermon I kept hearing an unusual sound. I was almost finished before I realized that he was chewing tobacco. Every so often he would have to spit, and though the door was ajar, his aim was not always true. The sound I heard was tobacco juice hitting the bottom of the door.

Though these people were crude in one meaning of the word, they were refined in the spiritual sense. Here was as great a spiritual wealth as in any group I've ever encountered anywhere. As they bowed their heads in prayer, I would sense the communion they felt with God. It was perhaps more sincere than in some of the better-off churches in town, where the congregations seemed more concerned with the social activities of the church—the church suppers and socials, the card parties and dances—than with the service. Many times I could detect in the eyes of some of the more stalwart male members of the congregation a gleam that wasn't precisely heaven-sent as they looked at the younger girls in their summer dresses. But such was not the case in my little country churches.

These are some of the things that a pastor sees in a congregation. He can almost read the minds of his people, and he knows if they are with him or not. I have often been disturbed by the number of people who obviously were not in church to gain spiritual strength. Too often convention dictated church attendance rather than conviction. None of this was evident among my parishioners in the modest schoolhouse church.

I hated the fact that only by donations could I make my weekly visit. To take their offerings, so hard come by, seemed shameful. I felt that their coins had been contributed in the spirit of Christian charity, and that they might better be used for that purpose within the community than to pay for religious services which

gave me immeasurably more satisfaction than they gave these people. But there was no other way to manage even my limited expenses. To keep the candles lit in tiny, makeshift churches in scattered villages, like country pastors before me and the legion of
those who, God willing, will seek them out in the future, I had
to accept those pittances.

iii

When the year I had allowed to build up my funds to enter college had passed, I found to my dismay that I still had a total of only eighty-six dollars. But I was so anxious to get started with the ministry as a full-time profession that I could delay my education no longer. With a minimum of money and a maximum of hope I entered Marietta College.

My years at Marietta drastically changed my life. The study of man through the ages in philosophy, the study of the interior man in psychology, the sense of the timeless history of the earth that grew out of studies in geology and mineralogy—I encountered all these and more. I also learned to fly. It was this last that led me ultimately to the strangest career of all—that of professional killer.

I came to admire greatly the dean of the college. Dr. Schoonover, as bald as he was brilliant, had lost parts of two fingers at his hobby of cabinetmaking. He probably did more for me spiritually than any other person on earth. I was his one-man Greek class, and we met at seven o'clock in the morning three days a week. The second year I was showing enough progress to begin the task which was my primary aim in taking the course—translating the New Testament. In searching out new interpretations for myself, I sought to come closer to its true meanings.

When I encountered a passage that wasn't clear, Dr. Schoonover would discuss it—not the dry, academic details, but its spiritual and moral implications. He once asked what I thought about the resurrection of the Body of Christ—whether I interpreted it in the realistic sense or as a resurrection of the Spirit. I felt that, while the

21

Body might have left the grave as the Bible says, it was the resurrection of the Spirit that was of the greater importance. Schoonover agreed with wry humor. At least he *hoped* it was the Spirit and not the Body that was resurrected. "I don't want to come back with this bald head and these chopped-off fingers," he said.

I went back to pumping gas at the filling station after school and on Saturdays and Sundays. I would be there from six o'clock at night until six in the morning, go to my classes until four o'clock in the afternoon, and sleep on weekends and in class. My salary of ten dollars a week didn't leave me much for mad money. I missed out on dances, dates, and parties which other undergraduates were enjoying. But that didn't bother me; what did trouble me was that lack of time forced me to give up my Sunday sermons. The seven-day-a-week hitch prevented me from even attending church, much less preaching regular sermons. I had to settle for making an occasional guest appearance, my fingernails still black from the gas station, my eyes ringed from lack of sleep.

Once, in more desperate straits than usual, I asked Grandpa if he would loan me fifty dollars. It was the only time I had ever tried to borrow, and my embarrassment was acute. He said gruffly that he would give it consideration and that I was to come back the next day. When I did so, hesitantly, he handed me a rolled-up bill, saying that all he could spare was five dollars. While that in itself was a windfall, for a moment it scarcely seemed worth giving my pride such a beating. But upon reaching home, I took out the crumpled bill and found that it was fifty dollars. It was a lesson for me: Never judge people prematurely or let yourself be motivated by quick disappointment or avarice.

Working the clock around, my fatigue became such that I often fell asleep in the college classrooms. The notes I was taking would blur before my eyes, wavering hypnotically like the slow movement of deep-sea life. I would put up a hand to support my drooping head, doze off, and awaken with a start when my pencil slipped from my fingers and hit the floor.

This was most common in afternoon classes—particularly one

conducted by a fine, amusing professor of history whose strictness matched his academic skill. He had a habit of entering the room with a sort of brisk absorption, marching to his desk, and adjusting his lecture papers before suddenly addressing us. One day I stopped at his desk to imitate this daily routine before he appeared—but not early enough, for he caught me at it.

"Quite accurate," he said dryly as I wheeled in alarm. "Let's see if I can do as well with you, Hess." Taking up a pencil, he sat down at his desk and lowered his head onto his hand, eyes closed. The pencil dropped, and he came erect with a violent jump. The class roared with laughter, and I tried harder than ever to stay awake thereafter.

I was seeing Mary regularly, though my persistent lack of funds restricted our activities pretty much to an occasional picture show. For four years neither of us ever dated anyone else. Since both of us were spare with our words, we never talked of marriage. We didn't need to. Come to think of it, I have never proposed to Mary to this day.

Marietta College had one of the few civilian-pilot training programs subsidized by the government. In this course students were taught to fly Piper Cubs and other light planes at no expense to them as a part of the college curriculum. The actual flight instruction was given at Parkersburg Airport across the line in West Virginia, 10 miles from Marietta—the only available flying school in that part of the country. I was fortunate to be accepted for this training, and the feeling of elation which had remained dormant in me ever since the Lindbergh flight and my own first sorties off the ground flamed up again.

Several years had passed since my first flight; now actually to fly a plane rather than be a mere passenger brought back that exultation wed to suspended peace, the soaring freedom, which only the airborne can know. Mountain climbers contend that there is nothing like gaining the top of an unconquered peak—standing where no man has ever stood before. Flying must be an extension of this sense of immaculate isolation. Pilot and plane are one, alone

23

in limitless space, the downpull of earth's gravity broken. And for me the sensation of flight, especially when alone, brought me many times closer to God.

There is something else that comes quickly and absolutely to airmen, and that is a sense of identification with one's plane. In the school's tiny aircraft I felt a communion that was to reach its fullest degree with the F-51 in which I was to fly more than 100 missions during the Korean War. Switching on the Cub's engines, I sensed their eagerness to get into the air. Their struggle to be airborne, as I pushed the stick forward and then back, and the ground fell away beneath us, was the personal response of a living creature. They recognized that those trees at the end of the runway were dangerous, and they would pull up and over them almost scornfully.

It was almost with regret that I received my civilian-pilot's license, for with the end of the course ended my flying. Now the only occasions when I could go up would be those made by the kindness of the people in charge of the program. I remained a familiar figure at the field, lovingly loitering near the planes and looking about longingly for free rides.

The distance out to Mary's home was a problem. I either had to walk it, hitchhike, or borrow a car on those rare occasions when I had an evening off. Coming back late at night, there usually was no traffic on the highway. I would end by hoofing the 10 miles back to Marietta in all kinds of weather—rain, sleet, even one night in a blizzard.

These treks were so hard on shoe leather that I never forgot them. Years later I was reminded of them one evening in Korea with Madame Syngman Rhee. We were in the residence at Chinhae, where she and the President were living after their flight from Seoul. Knowing of her love for flowers, I asked her to show me the garden. She said that while she would be pleased to, she first must put a piece of paper in her shoe, which had a hole in it. As with the dress she wore, she had no others, and the gravel on the paths hurt her foot unless she used this makeshift protection.

24

It amused this gallant lady to hear how I had done the same thing on those Ohio roads.

I often did not see how I was going to make it through college. I owed them so much in tuition that I sometimes was reluctant to go from one class to another, worried that I would be met at the door and told that I was going to have to drop out. The college officials were wonderfully considerate of my problems—but I seemed an almost impossible case. While I never was able to pay the full amount until years later, I would always scrape up a couple of dollars to put down on account. Over my shoulder hung the constant threat of a notice from the registrar's office that I must leave. Yet even at my lowest period I had a sustaining feeling of certainty that I was going to graduate and be ordained. It had to be! The officials of the college remained extraordinarily kind and considerate in helping me. Dr. Harry K. Eversull, the president, used to call me in to ask how I was doing. Did I have a job that would see me through? Was there any way in which he could help me develop a work-and-study program? One of my professors, a particularly strict disciplinarian, rescheduled an exam for me one morning when he saw that my head was nodding. To these people I shall always be grateful.

During these years, 1937–1941, the international situation was becoming more grave. War appeared frighteningly inevitable. When the draft began in 1939, it never entered my mind that I, a theological student, would be going into military service, much less flying a fighter plane in foreign skies. Men were drafted, sent out to training camps. The war worsened in Europe.

I developed a kind of subconscious restlessness. Something wasn't quite right as far as my duty to my country was concerned, but the desire I had lived with for so long—to become a minister—obscured the reason for my restlessness. Everything else was secondary. Then in June of 1941 I achieved this goal. I graduated at last from Marietta College, and was ordained in the Christian Church in a ceremony conducted by our local board of deacons and elders.

They had known for a long time that I was going into the ministry. The interrogation of a candidate is ordinarily an arduous routine consisting of a series of rigid examinations. But now the chairman of the board announced that, in view of my background, previous preaching experience, and obvious dedication, they would waive all formal examinations. There was the official laying on of hands, the inspiring delineation of responsibility, the warm, heartfelt congratulations. At last I had reached the doorway to my future.

I still needed money badly. I had to borrow ten dollars to pay for my diploma, already owing about three hundred to the college. Though they generously had let me graduate with this debt outstanding, I wanted to pay it as soon as possible. It might be some time before a pastorate would open for me, and I could not tax their patience indefinitely.

A telephone call from my first sponsor in the church, Bob Updegraff, brought the answer. Bob had gone to Cleveland to continue his ministerial career on a part-time basis, going to work for Republic Steel and conducting services on Sunday. But now he had given up the terrible financial struggle and withdrawn from the ministry.

He wanted to know what I was going to do. Hearing that I needed money to pay my debts and a job to tide me over until a pastorate became available, he offered me a room in his home and the assurance of a job with his company if I would come to Cleveland. Undoubtedly Bob's quitting the ministry had something to do with his and his wife's extraordinary kindness to me; my determination to follow the work he had been forced to abandon touched him deeply. And it seemed a wonderful chance to pay my obligations before taking a full ministerial assignment.

The personnel man at the plant was startled when I stated my preference for a labor shift over office work. My intention was to meet and know as many kinds of people as I could to prepare myself for my life work. I knew my inadequacies only too well. I was young and had led a relatively sheltered, small-town life. If I was

26

going to be able to minister wisely to the people who in future years would make up my congregations, I must have more knowledge of them. When still in my teens, I had preached to workingmen, but I had never sweated alongside them. In the bleakness of the mill and the cluster of grimy buildings where its employees spent their working lives I hoped to find experience far more valuable than my wages.

I was not disappointed. These were rough men—some intelligent, some not. Mostly they were of foreign extraction—Polish, German, Italian—and to my surprise I learned that many had well-articulated philosophies, good and bad, which helped them to endure their menial work—the drudgery of the steel mill, the monotonous operation of the same machine, the identical movement of the hand, day in and day out, year after year.

It was a good choice to come among them, for they were men that a small-town boy would not ordinarily encounter. They had strong convictions, which they stated with vigor. One was certain that Hitler was on the right track. "People go for a strong leader; they are like cattle who want to be led," he would insist, with a thrust of whiskery jaw. Another was a pintsized Italian with a tolerant "live-and-let-live" attitude which prompted him to view with a special understanding those who thought and did differently from him. A third and fourth lived for their children ("They're gonna have all the advantages we ain't had") and took enormous family pride in the accomplishments of a piano-playing daughter (she would be a concert pianist) and a football-playing son (he would get an athletic scholarship to college). Still another was a lathe operator who could discuss Goethe and Dante from a fund of self-acquired knowledge. For the most part they were men of personal probity, though there were a few typified by a diemaker who contended that no one should trust anybody. "Get what you can how you can," he would snarl. "Doesn't matter, just so long as you get it." But I noticed quickly that nobody trusted him—especially when this grimy Casanova talked about his hobby of having affairs with the wives of his friends. Proud accounts of his sordid

27

exploits, particularly one with his neighbor's wife, revolted me. I was looking forward to a life of love with Mary as something to be treasured; to hear this aspect of marriage spoken of in his terms degraded it to sickening animalism.

On the night shift I had some problems at first. I was given the job of supervising the maintenance of ten enormous boilers. Under me were a number of men who had been with the company for years; but they could not pass a written examination and so had to remain helpers. At first they resented my coming in to supervise them. They had the know-how and the seniority; they should have had the job and the salary that went with it. They gave me the "silent-contempt" treatment. They did things that I directed them to do with insolent slowness and mean looks. I particularly recall a swarthy German who adjusted the valves on the boilers to keep the water at a certain height. He knew perfectly well how to do it, in fact had been doing it without mishap for years. But because I, a younger and less experienced man, was now supposed to supervise his doing the job, he stopped performing the function entirely until I told him to; then he went about it slowly and sloppily. I took him aside for a talk. I admitted that he knew the job better than I. I told him that it was ridiculous for me to supervise him, that I wasn't going to do so, and that he was on his own. From that moment on we worked in harmony, and he did his job as I never could have done it. This was another lesson for me. Men pride themselves on their abilities and their independence. The best boss keeps his hands off whenever possible.

At night, with the boilers fired, there would be times when there were no pressing duties. One or two of the men would look me up, and we'd sit together in the boilerhouse talking. None of them knew that I was a minister, but it was not unusual for us to talk of our religious and spiritual beliefs, our faiths and values in life. These men had a poor choice of words, and smatterings of profanity ran through every sentence they uttered; but many had a deep sense of searching for spiritual values and were very practical in their approach.

One of the most frequent questions was, "Do I have to go to church to be a good Christian?" It was one I answered carefully, leaving the decision up to them. But I always added that it was an unusual person, mankind being so vulnerable to temptation and error, who could retain a strong spiritual side without any church association. Also, regular church attendance has always seemed to me to be a kind of cement that keeps families together, an important spiritual experience that parents and children should have in common.

From them I learned so much more than they from me. I found out that almost every one of us aspires to life on a higher level. We are constantly searching for spiritual values—actually seeking excuses whereby we may discuss them with one another in places outside church. Many nights in the boilerhouse we talked only of matters pertaining to faith.

With my job as boiler foreman going well, I informed the chairman of the Church Board in Cleveland that I was available for Sunday services. He sent my name to outlying churches, and the need was such that soon I was visiting three different churches every Sunday—one in the morning, another at noon, and an evening service in a third. To make my satisfaction complete, I could occasionally rent an airplane from one of the local people at nominal cost. Feeling rather like a circuit preacher of the old days, I thoroughly enjoyed the satisfying combination of flying and bringing the Word to these good people who might not otherwise have received It.

As winter came on, I was slowly getting out of debt. Mary's loving letters from Marietta continued to encourage and sustain me, though I was rarely able even to visit back home. Working in the mills on weekdays and visiting my churches on Sundays absorbed all my energies and attention.

Then, on December 7, 1941, I was walking with Bob Updegraff after attending a church service in Cleveland when a man, a complete stranger, drove up to the curb and stopped to tell us that the Japanese had bombed Pearl Harbor.

Like many other Americans that fateful Sunday I just barely knew where Pearl Harbor was. But I understood precisely what the news meant.

It was as though the vehicle of my plans had run into a stone wall. I had just been able to bring my life under control; its path for the first time lay clear and direct. I would pay off my debts, get married, find a church of my own. All these hopes were now swept away on a little puff of excited words. There was a sickening void in my stomach, and a bewildering sense of shattered plans engulfed me.

But as my shock subsided, a wave of certainty began to crest in its place. A moment more and I knew what I had to do.

iv

The branches of the trees scratched against a leaden sky as Bob Updegraff and I walked silently in the city park. Weeks before, classified 4-D as an ordained minister, I had put in an application for the Chaplain Corps. Now I was tormented by doubt. Was this the kind of service I wanted? Had my brief experience in the ministry prepared me for it? Bob sensed that I was far from satisfied. I finally turned to him and said, "You know what this means, don't you, as far as I'm concerned?" Always the good listener, he asked what I planned to do.

As I talked on, sorting my thoughts, it turned out that I didn't really know.

On one hand there was my compelling desire to go on with the ministry—to remain here and work, pay off my obligations to the college, and get married. On the other hand was the surety that these things meant nothing now that our country had been attacked. It was clear that I must go. But I was unable to give voice to my feeling that I could not serve as a chaplain—that, even if I had wanted to, I wasn't experienced enough. My work in the mills had drawn me closer to the world of active men; I had learned much from it. I was capable of offering the routine solaces required in a parson's normal rounds; but what could I give to shaken, wounded, dying men? To men who every day, perhaps every hour, faced the imminent possibility of a violent, painful death? How could I give them reassurance unless I knew what they were undergoing?

Alone I continued to wrestle with the dilemma throughout the afternoon. Finally I went back to one of my three churches, in Hanover, Ohio, to give the evening service. While conducting it, I saw, looking down at the faces in the congregation, a need that I wasn't able to satisfy. Everyone in the church was visibly disturbed by what war meant to him or her personally.

Many there had sons in the service. Sitting there in church, they could foresee their sons being shipped out, wounded, even killed. Why did this war have to come? And what did it mean now that it was here? I should have had answers for them, but I had none. They were wondering—they needed some kind of strength or bolstering. Many looked depressed; others were puzzled and subdued. Regrettably, a few seemed to be elated because we were in the conflict. Numbly I mouthed some words, then called for silent prayer. I felt a closer bond with them in silence as each communed with himself and considered the days and the dangers to come.

After the prayer I asked them to sing a hymn which has always been a favorite of mine—"The Battle Hymn of the Republic." I had never heard a congregation sing it with more gusto than on that evening. As I sang the grand, sonorous words with them, a feeling of certainty and conviction spread through me; I knew what I must do. After a closing benediction I told them that this was to be my last service for the time being. I was putting down the Book. Then, watching their amazed faces, I added that, while I had applied for a chaplain's commission, I felt unable to serve in that capacity. I would join the men who were going as combatants.

There was absolute silence as I walked down the aisle. At the door, as I shook their hands for the last time, each in turn wished me well. I was prepared for resistance, amazement, even anger, but there seemed little of it. These good people, still in a state of shock on this December 7 evening, had their own sons and fathers and brothers to worry about.

The next day I quit the job at Republic Steel. There my decision was admiringly received. The company was manufacturing war materials, and it was a rarity for an employee to want to use some of it rather than accept a draft exemption to help make it. My back was slapped and my hand shaken, often with puzzled looks from some of the smarter boys, but there was deep sincerity written on the faces of many of my old cronies in the labor gang, the natural philosophers, as I shook their calloused hands.

I wrote two letters to Marietta telling what I was about to do. One was to Mary. She immediately telephoned in answer. Why? I replied as best I could that active combat seemed where I could be of most value. I had given her a heavy shock, I knew, but her voice strengthened. I must do what I thought best, she reassured me; I must always do what I thought best. Her resolute cheerfulness was a hand in the dark. It has been always, will be forever.

My mother's reaction to the letter I sent her was not so heartening. She was tearful. Why was I being so rash, so hotheaded? What of Mary, of my hopes for the ministry? She had expected that because of my classification I would never be called into the service. My haste seemed childish to her. If I must take part, why at least didn't I wait for the chaplain's commission?

I could only answer that there are some things which can't be fully explained, and that this was one of them. "When you can no longer reason you must feel," Thomas Aquinas said, and I sought to convince her how true that was now. I didn't succeed. I, her son, was accepting—no, requesting—danger, and I guess no mother can ever be fully persuaded that this is the wisest course.

I next notified the supervisor of our Church Board in Cleveland. Immediately he called me in to meet with a conclave of local ministers. These were the men who previously had submitted endorsements for me to become a chaplain.

My decision was a shock to them, obviously, but my resolve was so strong that no resistance or criticism could have altered it. Yet no such negative reaction was initially apparent when they began to question me as to why I wanted to become a combatant. The war had come so suddenly that even for most of them there was

33

no absolute course of conduct. They sat in the quiet room, expressionless for the most part, listening attentively while I sought to make an explanation.

I began by asking if they thought it was necessary for us to defend ourselves. They all agreed that it was. I replied that this was the key to my decision. The only reason that I would not ordinarily be taking up weapons was the fact that I was an ordained minister and consequently excused from acts of violence. Yet by stating that we had to defend ourselves, we in essence were shoving other young men forward and saying, "You get the blood on your hands. You accept the guilt; we'll stand by while you do it and pray for you."

No one said anything. I went on that it seemed to me a more important obligation, if my faith was firm and if I considered that my country must defend itself, to seek out the most difficult and dangerous path rather than any other. Finally, in all conscience I could not ask others to do for me that which I was perhaps better spiritually qualified to accomplish—fight for my beliefs.

As I finished, I was looking directly at one gray-haired elder whose expression throughout can only be described as condescending. On his bland face I could see, if not a rejection of what I had said, a dismissal of me as one too young to know the full meaning of religion. I was not surprised when he cleared his throat and asked, "Don't you think that, if you pursue this intention, you will be violating our thesis that the most formidable force is Christianity?"

I answered briefly, "No. Men have fought for Christianity before, and they will again."

I had said all that I had to say. Feeling as I did, and with my mind firmly set, I had no wish either to discuss theological principles or to defend myself further. I said good-by, quietly and respectfully I hope, and left. Outside two of the ministers caught up with me and in warm emotional tones wished me well. It was the last time we were ever to meet.

34

The next day I went to the Marine recruiting station. I wanted to get into the fight at once, and I had heard that the Marine Corps would see to it. A sergeant looked at the form I had filled out and, seeing that I had a college degree and was a licensed pilot, asked why I didn't apply for Marine Corps Aviation. I told him I'd be pleased to, but how? He explained that Marine Aviation drew pilots from the Navy; thus I could sign up with the Naval Air Corps, and later be assigned to the Marines. Though he gave me careful directions to the Naval recruiting station, I couldn't find it. I asked help from a postman, who told me it was in a building across the street on the tenth floor. I went there—to find a sign on the door which said, "U.S. Army Air Corps Recruiting Station." So O.K., I thought, they fly and they fight. What difference does the color of a uniform make?

This is the way great decisions are made.

On a tense and unhappy Christmas Eve I returned to Marietta. It was apparent that my folks were deeply disturbed by the step I had taken, as was Mary. She did her best to hide it, even when I revealed that our marriage must be postponed once more; one couldn't enter the Cadet Corps as a married man or as one even planning to be married. For four years we had been approaching marriage at a snail's pace, and by now it was beginning to look like a mirage. First it had been financial considerations, then education and the ministry, and now war. But somehow Mary, with that wonderful faculty that women possess and men can't even comprehend, adjusted her views once more to our new and uncertain future. She would wait; she would have faith.

An ominous feeling rode with me in the train as it passed across the fields and through the woods of my native state, heading toward Maxwell Field at Montgomery, Alabama. Was I doing the right thing? It was the same thought that I was to have so often in the months to come. I spent two of these months at Maxwell Field with the other civilians who had been thrown into military clothes, given crew haircuts and told, "You're a cadet!" I then

35

received orders sending me to a primary training school in Douglas, Georgia, and from there on to Shaw Field at Sumter, South Carolina.

At Shaw word got out that I was an ordained minister. I was invited by the chaplain to conduct a service for the cadets. Though I agreed readily enough, I found the preparation of this sermon more difficult than that of any other I had ever worked on. I ended by plagiarizing from here and there practically everything I said. I had no original ideas because as yet I didn't feel myself an integral part of the activity in which I was involved. Furthermore, my mind was oriented toward flying, not sermonizing. When a man is preaching regularly, everything he sees or hears is potential material for a sermon; he actually thinks in terms of preaching. Now I was thinking in terms of flying, and having to revert suddenly to my role of minister was peculiarly jarring.

But that sense of belonging in my strange new world did come, though slowly. I began to respond automatically to the regimentation. The word "duty" lost its ministerial meaning and took on the military look. I even became "one of the boys," learning to "goof off" with the others. I remember lying under a bed with another slaphappy cadet during air-raid drill, both of us laughing like monkeys, instead of going to a shelter. If the church deacons could only see me now, I thought. I found a perverse pleasure in a meaningless breaking of the rules just for the sake of flaunting authority in some minor way. By the time I finished basic and went confidently on to Napier Field at Dothan, Alabama, for advanced training, I was even using the best air-force jargon. I felt completely in my element.

Mary meanwhile was demonstrating her love and loyalty in letters of the kind to fill lonely nights, encouraging me ceaselessly in my conviction that I had made the right decision. When at last I was ready to be commissioned, I wrote to ask her to come and see me get my wings—after which, I added in a postscript, we would be married. She responded happily, and off I went—again airborne, but on the ground—to the post exchange for a wedding

36

ring. The sixty dollars it cost cleaned me out, but it was the greatest bargain I ever made.

Father and my sister came from Marietta with her for the dual ceremonies—graduation from flight school in the morning, and our marriage in the afternoon in the Methodist church in Dothan.

My father seemed particularly proud of me on that day. If I ever pleased him, it seems to have been then, in my new role of officer and husband. Others still had reservations about my desire to be a combatant, just as earlier they had had doubts about my becoming a minister. But I felt that Dad understood many things which they did not—notably that a man must, in the privacy of his own heart and soul, make his own decisions.

Three of my classmates stood up for me during the ceremony. When it was over, they kissed the bride with considerable enthusiasm and then tactfully disappeared. I had grown a bit nervous about my dual role as bridegroom and host to my family so many miles from home. I wondered if they had decided to stay for a few days. At the bus station I at last got my sister off, headed for Ohio. Now only Dad remained. But he gave no indication of leaving. I began to think he intended coming back to our hotel room with us for a social chat.

When my nervousness had built up to just short of the explosion point, Dad suddenly announced that he had a hankering to see the Gulf of Mexico. "Guess I'll take a little run over to Panama City," he added with a grin, and jumped on the Florida bus. Later I learned that the sly old dog already had his bags checked on the bus; his delaying tactics were only to tease me. But at that moment I was so relieved to see him go, however inexplicable his hasty departure, that he never looked more lovable than when waving good-by—and leaving me, finally, alone with my bride.

I was retained at Napier Field, much to my initial disappointment, as a flight instructor. Once resigned to the fact that another few months still separated me from combat, I found a profound satisfaction in seeing my young cadets develop into polished pilots.

37

Deeply impressed by the dedication and intelligence of these boys, I attempted to impart to them a little more than just the mechanical skills of flying. I had given more thought to the necessity and meaning of our work than most of them. The killing we were preparing for was evil in itself, but it was a lesser evil than the one we were fighting. No matter how terrible the means we were to use, it was still the lesser evil. This was a conviction which was to support me in the days and years that lay ahead—a conviction which I constantly reexamined but from which I have never wavered.

A newly assigned Protestant chaplain had not yet arrived at the field, and when Father Paul Cuddy, the Catholic chaplain, learned that I was a minister, he asked me to take on these duties in addition to my regular work. This time, well adjusted to the new life, I was happy to pick up the strings of the old.

Immediately I was shocked to find that the Negro boys had to have their chapel services in the gymnasium. I would go there to conduct their service and thence to the chapel to conduct the one for the white boys. I hated the arrangement; it was the worst kind of segregation. I discussed it with Paul, only to be reminded of what I already knew: that we were in the Deep South, where mixed services were taboo. He didn't have the same problem because there were no Negro Catholics on the field.

I answered that the Negroes should at least have their services in the chapel—at a different time if it couldn't be helped, but in the chapel, built as a house of God, and not in a gymnasium.

One of my superior officers, an older man who had no connection with the chaplains' duties, heard about my plan and disapproved vehemently. I couldn't let those niggers worship or use that chapel! As for himself, he would refuse to sit in the same pews that they had used! If I went ahead, he would see to it that reflection would be cast upon my judgment as an officer.

In a bitter private interview I heard and rejected his arguments, ignored his threats, and went ahead with my plan. Happily, no one else objected when the colored boys started worshiping under the same roof as the white. My ultimate wish—to have them join in worship at the same hour—was never realized. However, I am happy to say that today all personnel in the services are totally integrated in worship.

During the subsequent months, though thousands of miles from the fighting front, I was introduced to the tragedy of war. Beside conducting regular services and performing marriages, I took care of the chaplain's duties in the event of a crash. I particularly remember two cases which were typical of the heartbreaks peculiar to war and to a chaplain's responsibilities. The sadder was the death of a young flyer on a night training mission. His wife of a few months was living in town, and when I was asked to inform her of the tragedy, I took a medical officer with me in case what I had to say might be too heavy a shock.

The landlady at the boardinghouse in which she was staying summoned her. A robe thrown quickly over her nightdress, this veritable child came hurrying down the stairs, her eyes wide with alarm. My presence at this hour told her that something was wrong, and I didn't give her the mental anguish of waiting. I told her quickly that her husband had been killed two hours before. She looked at me, stricken, then faltered, "Why wasn't I told before?"

This was a reaction I hadn't expected. I explained that it had been necessary to make sure that he hadn't parachuted to safety, and also to identify him. I added that he had not suffered, for death had come instantly. The landlady led her back up the stairs, stiff with shock, her mind a blank—still minutes or perhaps hours before the flood of tears.

As acting chaplain my duties had just begun. Back at the base I obtained the address of the boy's parents and telephoned them at their home in Michigan. His father accepted my message, quickly given, with a sort of despairing valor. I would arrange, I told him, to have the body brought home for burial. The widow had a brother in a nearby encampment, and I obtained a leave for him to take the girl back to Michigan.

Before she left, she insisted time and again upon seeing her husband's body. We had to say no. Then she asked to go to the place where the plane had fallen. I took her to the spot where it had bored deep into the ground and left her standing beside it. In a few minutes, when it seemed that her emotions were getting out of control, I went back and tried to offer some small consolation.

On the way into town she asked if she might have his wings—"He worked so hard for them." I had to tell her, cruel though it seemed, that he hadn't earned them yet. But I gave her a pair of mine.

I was to hear more about this tragic young wife in a letter from her brother. Upon arriving in Michigan, the casket was taken to the parents' home. Hearing a noise during the night, they came downstairs to find the girl with a screwdriver, trying to open it. Eventually I learned that she had given all her husband's insurance money to a university for a scholarship in his name because he had always wanted what the war had robbed him of—a college education. And this with her three months pregnant!

It was this sad case more than any other which convinced me that I had acted wisely in refusing a chaplain's commission. I felt so helpless, so unprepared to offer solace and spiritual aid to those crushed by sudden tragedy.

Another incident, also tragic but with certain humorous aspects, offered me more opportunity to play a constructive role. One day I saw a cadet squadron leader (picked by rotation) marching a group of men. I looked again—he was wearing cowboy boots! Stopping the squadron, I asked, "You, mister—what part of the West do you come from?"

"Brooklyn, sir!"

He gave us all a laugh, then and on other occasions, but in the air he lost all the cocky confidence he seemed to have on the ground. He was a miserably poor flyer. I gave him three check rides, hoping to be able to pass him, but the last was as rough as the first, and I again had to take the controls.

Before being dismissed as a flyer, a cadet must be given a "washout" ride by his group commander. This man was a severe disciplinarian not famous for having the patience of Job, and on his washout flight the cadet was more inept than ever. The commander tongue-lashed him while still in the air, grabbed the controls, and made the landing himself. Then he came down on the boy hard, finishing his angry remarks by saying that he was the worst flyer he had ever seen, after which he stalked disgustedly away to the control tower.

For a few moments the crushed cadet remained immobile, realizing that this was the end of his pilot's career. He was one of those boys who wanted to fly more than anything else in the world and had set his heart on becoming a pilot years before. Suddenly, wild with grief and disappointment, he jumped back into the plane and took off. He zoomed up, rolled over, and buzzed the field; then he performed a slow roll over the runway, almost knocking down the flagpole.

In the control tower the commander, by now beside himself, started yelling on the radio that the cadet was to come down or be court-martialed. Hearing his voice, the cadet cried that he was coming down all right—right at him! As he started to dive the plane toward the tower, the commander scrambled down the ladder in terror.

With his first stunts I realized that the boy had gone out of his mind, temporarily at least. Running for a plane, I called to him as quietly as I could on its radio, "All right, you've had your fun. You put on a good show. Now go land at the auxiliary field and get back here—on the ground."

He finally agreed, his voice more subdued, and swung away. I flew over to the auxiliary field to see if he had followed my order; but he wasn't here. Further search didn't turn him up anywhere, and we had to report a missing aircraft. I suspected that he had flown out over the Gulf and gone into the drink.

Then a report came in from New Orleans: he had gassed up there and continued on. The next news came from Corpus Christi: our Brooklyn cowboy had landed on the range and had been found

41

sitting under his plane's wing by a Texas policeman. Later I learned that he had headed for the Gulf, intending to commit suicide by running out of gas over the water. But he had started doing acrobatics out there and had grown confused as to his position, and his stunting had spun him back to land. Seeing that he was getting low on gas, he had spotted the New Orleans field, landed there, obtained fuel, and taken his lacerated pride off again. By this time he was determined to show that he could fly as well as anyone, but near Corpus Christi his hard-pumping adrenalin glands had begun to slow down, and he had landed the plane, ready for whatever came next.

The commander, now more confused and relieved than angry, came hurrying to the hospital to talk to him, anxious to get the full details for his report. The cadet, still stung by disappointment over his failure and by humiliation over the accompanying bawling out, flung a chair at his hastily retreating CO. Father Cuddy asked me to go in and talk to him. Expecting the same reception, I stood uneasily in the doorway. "Good show," I told him. "You did just what I've always wanted to do—buzz headquarters."

He smiled. It was a weak effort, but the tension had passed. After he had been in the hospital for several days, he was well enough to be sent to a military installation in Brooklyn. He eventually was certified for return to duty—but not in an airplane.

Though most of the cadets prepared for what lay ahead without much soul searching, one came to me one day to say that he had decided he did not wish to go into combat. He obviously was not prompted by fear, for he said that he was willing to fly transport or reconnaissance in flimsy Cubs right over the front lines; it was the idea of killing which now troubled him. He stated it in the simplest terms: "Isn't it wrong according to the Bible?"

I answered that, so far as I knew, Christ had never said explicitly not to fight—that in talking to the centurions He had said, "Obey your commanders and accept your wages." I told him that this was an obligation which *someone* had to fulfill, and that he and I, having come this far, were committed to it. Moreover, I told him, in a state of war everyone is equally culpable of bloodshed who contributes in any way to the death of an enemy. Those who give money to make weapons, those who manufacture or deliver armaments, must share the responsibility with the man who fires the fatal bullet.

It was reasoning in which I believed wholeheartedly myself, and it seemed to quiet the conscience of the cadet. He returned to his training, and ultimately I had the satisfaction of seeing him become an expert B-25 pilot.

While I was still at Napier, our first son, Larry, was born, on October 22, 1943. Despite the boundless joy he brought to Mary and me, and despite my deeply felt responsibility for my growing family, I still wanted more than anything else to fly in combat.

Time after time I applied for overseas duty, and time after time the same superior officer who hadn't wanted the Negro boys worshiping in his "white" chapel refused to act upon it. He said to my face that he would never let me get out of the training command. He seemed to think that I was some sort of dangerous character whom it was his duty to supervise for the duration.

But at last he made a technical mistake. He gave me additional duty when my son was born, and when I asked him about it called it "disciplinary action." I served the extra duty hours and then went to the field commander and told him that I had been given disciplinary action without regard to my rights under Number 104 of the Articles of War, or court-martial. Therefore, my accuser was guilty of a misdemeanor for which he could be court-martialed himself.

Most men didn't have to blackmail their way overseas, but I was determined that this officer was not going to stand in my way. I continued to press my case, and, sure enough, one day he called to ask if I still wanted to go into combat. I hesitated not an instant. Alongside the prospect of joining battle with the enemy our private war was picayune. I asked him to prepare the orders.

43

v

A little over a month later I was in France in the cockpit of a P-47, a combat plane with which I was entirely unfamiliar, virtually wondering which way to work the throttle to make it take off. I had traveled from the port of embarkation, New York, straight to the Eighth Air Force in England. The Eighth had done a thorough job of cleaning enemy aircraft from the skies, and now their task was almost finished. Although missions were still being flown, some pilots had gone out on as many as fifty without firing a gun. In these clear skies I was able to log sufficient time in the fighters they were using, P-51s, to be checked out as combat-ready.

Then I requested and obtained assignment to the Ninth Air Force, which was heavily engaged in air-ground operations in France following D Day. Paris had just been liberated, and was in a state of chaotic and hilarious disorganization. I was billeted in a former girls' school with other pilots, where we were to wait for distribution to our various groups. As the place was already teeming with troops, the only available quarters were in the latrine. It wasn't very pleasant, as the facilities were still being used.

Six of us decided that we would go to a hotel, and a solicitous sergeant offered to take us to his favorite one. Ordinarily American military personnel at this time were not allowed to go to hotels, but we chanced it, wanting in the worst way to get out of that latrine.

When we checked into the hotel, I might have guessed by the lengthy conversation between the sergeant and the proprietress that something special was being discussed. Showing me to my room, she said in broken English that I had not stated my wishes for the night. I didn't know what she meant; I had what I wanted —a clean place to sleep. She finally made it clear, mostly by gestures, that I, like the others, ought to have a companion. She was so obviously desirous of being accommodating that I didn't want to offend her. After trying all manner of excuses, I finally yawned widely and explained that I was tired, and she grunted away, surely doubting my virility. After barricading the door, I went to sleep. Early the next morning I went back to my cot in the latrine.

A week later, assigned to the Nineteenth Tactical Air Command, a reconnaissance car was taking me through France toward St. Dizier. The countryside was astoundingly quiet, though all around were signs of war's devastation. Occasionally the shell of a house peered through blank eyes at the road. German vehicles, tanks, and gunpieces lay in the fields. We passed battlegrounds where heavy bombardment had taken place. Piles of empty shell cases were stacked along the roadside.

As this was only a few miles from the front lines, I was surprised by the lack of activity. I had anticipated a sort of metallic beehive, but there were only silence and the still graves of Germans, marked by rude crosses—a couple of sticks tied together and a helmet on top. I wondered who they were—wondered about the families waiting for them to come back. What kind of lives had been theirs before they had ended here?

Darkness and rain descended before we reached St. Dizier. There were blackout conditions on the field, and we stumbled across a sheet of mud to the tent of Colonel Delashaw, the group commander.

I noticed his perplexity as he checked my flight record, Form Number 5. I was alarmed to hear him speculate in a brief discussion with another officer as to whether I should be sent back to England for transition training. I immediately protested; if I needed transition work, couldn't I do it here? I must have put up a convincing argument, for he finally smiled and assigned me to the 511th Fighter Squadron.

45

A jeep took me to its area and drew up in front of a soaking tent. Inside I was greeted by one of the squadron pilots, Charlie Nation, and the flight surgeon, Capt. Edward Baxter. Baxter seemed cordial enough, but I sensed a curious coolness from Nation. Baxter told me I could use the third cot in the tent. It belonged to a pilot who was in England on recuperation leave at the time. When he returned, I would have to give it up, but for the time being I could bunk here.

I went to bed depressed. Nothing here was conducive to high morale—the mud, darkness, and cold; the commander's doubts about my qualifications; and not even a bed of my own.

In the morning my misgivings increased. Through the cold rain I now could see the flight line; it was lined with P-47s, a type of aircraft I had never flown. In concern I went to the squadron commander and told him about my dilemma, explaining that I had thought I was coming into a P-51 outfit. Evidently a mistake had been made. Colonel Delashaw had told him that my flight record showed no experience with P-47s but that I was to stay around for a few days anyway before a final decision would be reached. The chances were that I would have to go back to England to check out in P-47s.

My spirits sagged still further. Then I thought, I am here now and I am going to stay. I repeated it to myself over and over all day long. I hung hopefully around the flight line, trying to gather as much information as I could about the unfamiliar plane. The very next day, with undisguised envy, I watched twelve airplanes take off on a mission. These men knew so much more about their craft than I ever would. In two hours they reappeared in the sky, and suddenly the amplifying system spoke up, asking for the "sheet-metal men." In answer to my question someone told me that they were needed to patch up the bullet and flak holes in the arriving planes. It seemed a cold welcome for the returning "heroes," as I saw them, to call for a repair man. When only eleven of the twelve planes returned, it struck me forcefully how different this mission was from the mock missions we'd flown back home.

Like Charlie Nation the other pilots of the squadron at first appeared oddly aloof. I wondered if this was the treatment accorded all newcomers or if news of my ministerial experience had gotten around. It turned out that there was some resentment simply because of my rank of captain. These men had preceded me into the organization, and my coming into it as a captain prevented the lieutenants from moving up as fast as vacancies occurred. Also, as with all groups in combat, theirs was a clannishness based on shared dangers and *esprit de corps*, and quite understandable as such.

My insecure status plagued me night and day. Absorbing as much information about the P-47 as I could on the ground, I finally went to the squadron commander and persuaded him that I was able to fly one. He gave me a short briefing and sent me out for a test flight around the area. I managed it well enough for him to decide to let me build up some transition time there at the field, after which I could be assigned to combat. I was elated; once again I was going ahead rather than back!

I built a little shack from scrap lumber, found an old German stove, and made myself quite comfortable. Presently the pilots were dropping in during the evenings. After that first mission over the Delmi Woods, despite the fact that I'd forgotten to set the release mechanism and had had to make a second run, the ice was broken. Men working in an operational organization have a bond which prevents them from accepting an outsider until he has proven himself. Now I had been through the fire and was welded into the group. The question of my skipping ahead of some of them on the table of organization was solved, tragically, by combat losses.

Doc Baxter, the flight surgeon, became a close friend. This quiet fellow of forty-five, with his gray-black hair, his mustache, and his omnipresent pipe, developed a deep affection and concern for the pilots. In one of my talks with him I finally revealed my background. Previously I had been reluctant to admit that I was a minister, wanting to be considered only as a military man. I did not want the presence of a minister in the club or on the flight line to inhibit the other pilots, to make them self-conscious about their language or restricted in their conversation. But Doc Baxter didn't show any particular surprise upon learning about my previous work. He said he had suspected it might have been that, but he was only surprised that none of the men knew. When I revealed why I had not spoken about it, he replied that it would be a good thing for the outfit if I did. "These kids," he said, "aren't as tough as they seem."

He proceeded on this assumption that it would help the pilots to know about my background as a minister. Again some of the men became aloof, though in a different way this time. When they spoke to me, they would choose their words carefully; they would break off in the middle of a joke which they felt wasn't fit for tender ministerial ears. They didn't invite me to parties in town which promised an element of rowdiness. More than ever I was disturbed to feel the line of demarcation between a man of the cloth and these fighting laymen. I had long admired the ability of the Jesuits to break through this barrier, perhaps more readily than practitioners of other faiths. Now I wanted particularly to stand on my merits as a military man. It is a terrible feeling to fight side by side with men who stand aloof.

Only after many combat missions over Germany did the fighter pilot triumph over the minister in the eyes of my companions. Gradually the men drifted back to me. Increasingly during our discussions in the shack in the evenings matters of religion would be brought up. These discussions would be devoid of argument, prejudice, or hostility of any kind—and at first devoid of gaiety. Each month we would get a bottle of Scotch, a bottle of gin, and two or more of champagne as liquor rations. During our evening discussions I could see that my guests were getting a little dry. Finally after much hesitation they would ask me if it would be all right for them to drink, and I assured them that it would. Sometimes I would take a glass of champagne when they offered it to make them more comfortable. It was my misfortune that I didn't like the stuff, but my desire to make them see that a minister was not different or an "odd ball" was stronger than my distaste for liquor. My own liquor ration I passed on to the enlisted men, who received not a single drop through official channels.

While I attended chapel whenever a mission did not interfere, it wasn't until Thanksgiving that "The Preacher" was called upon to use his ministerial training. Our meal was to be at the end of the day, with all men convened in the mess tent. As Doc Baxter and I walked in, the men were sitting at their places talking. Their dinner was before them, but they hadn't started to eat. Doc suggested that they might be waiting for someone to say grace and asked if I would mind doing it.

I offered a blessing and concluded with the Lord's Prayer. You could have heard a heartbeat throughout the tent. Afterward some of the men came, one at a time, to thank me. I was particularly affected by this, the occasion of my first battlefield prayer, and by the shy and hesitant way these men manifested their need for spiritual communion with God.

The enlisted men had worked up a club in an old prefabricated building, and at Christmas they invited me to have dinner with them. Again I was asked if I would deliver a prayer for them. Being especially aware of the strong religious atmosphere which generates at Christmastide in combat areas, I was happy to. Yet I didn't want the squadron to lose sight of the fact that I was a combatant like themselves. It was a short service consisting of a few Christmas carols, a hymn or two, and a prayer.

Before I could finish the meal, Doc Baxter and the squadron commander came for me. They wanted me to perform the same service at the officers' mess—something which had never been done before in the history of the outfit.

I almost said no. It seemed as if I was about to become a chaplain after all. Then, disgusted by my own doubts and fears, I quickly changed my mind. When I entered our mess tent and found it charged with the same sort of hopeful expectancy which had characterized that of the enlisted men, a wave of happiness swept over me. The tent looked as usual—the wooden tables, the old boxes and crates to sit on, the dirty canvas. But because it was Christmas and because I could bring them closer to God by a few traditional words they so wanted to hear, all the crudities of that dismal enclosure were washed away. I recognized that my fellow pilots looked toward me with a degree of strangeness. They were so used to Hess, the pilot, that it seemed odd to see me standing there with a Bible in my hand. But when the fine old songs lifted in the cold French night, I had not a single doubt that I was doing the right thing, that I was somehow bridging the gap between my old profession and my new. I read passages from the New Testament pertaining to the birth of Christ and led them in prayer. Two congregations in one day—it was like old times!

A couple of nights later one of the pilots came to my shack with the blunt announcement that he had a confession to make. He had never been a praying man. Did I think it was wrong that now, when he was in danger, every night before going to bed he said a prayer? He seemed to be concerned about it because, as he phrased it, "Fear is driving me to religion."

I was deeply moved. I assured him that it was a matter between God and himself. If he felt sincerely moved to pray, either consciously or subconsciously, then there would be a communion. Putting that communion, basically an appeal, into words was certainly nothing to be ashamed of, and he should be uninhibited in revealing his emotion.

Actually prayer had become an outlet for him because he feared combat as anyone fears the unknown, and he was purging himself of the omnipresent, hovering specter of his being shot down. Kneeling to pray was his way of attempting to cope with fear. He was ashamed of his feelings because he thought they indicated weakness. I sought to persuade him that they were his strength.

The officers would occasionally invite the army nurses over to their club for parties compounded of two elements: dancing, and their standard drink, gin and grapefruit juice. Rightfully envious of the gaiety, the enlisted men decided to follow suit.

Two of them came to my quarters. Cpl. Sam Weinberg, a versatile promoter with a fine gift for language, was their spokesman. He asked if I would speak to the commanding officer and see if it would be all right for them to have a party in the enlisted men's club. They would have to get local French girls, since the nurses were officers and not allowed to socialize with the enlisted men.

The commander was receptive to the idea and delegated me, "The Preacher," to handle it as a sort of "morals" officer. Sam and I went into St. Dizier and told the mayor what we wanted, assuring him with gestures and in two languages that the men would be on good behavior.

The mayor "lined up" (as the boys termed it) twenty girls, and they were brought out to the installation in trucks. No group was ever received with more propriety. The men were so anxious to create a good impression that threats of mayhem were directed at anyone who got rowdy or out of line. Behind the cleaned and decorated club they had erected with particular solicitude a special latrine with a guard posted near it, the patch lighted and marked with French signs.

At first there was considerable stiffness between American enlisted men and French demoiselles, but it dissolved in the music of a small dance band. Everything went smoothly and it looked like a highly successful party until a member of the arrangements committee came to me with an expression of extreme harassment. He reported that the girls, instead of using the latrine, were just stepping outside. He asked me if I would tell them to go

51

where they should. This was a problem I hadn't encountered before in either my ministerial or military capacities. I answered that I didn't have at my command the French vocabulary for such an announcement. He looked perplexed; then he burst out, "They can squat in Macy's window as far as I'm concerned, but rules say latrines have to be used on a post. What if some brass was to see 'em? You'd better shape 'em up, Captain, or we'll never have another party!"

I answered noncommittally but managed to be looking the other way whenever one of our little guests made purposefully for the door. Despite this threat to the sanctity of the area the evening passed safely, with no irreparable damage done to our sanitation standards. The whole thing came off so well, in fact, that, after the squadron leader heard about it, he mentioned it one night in the officers' club.

Someone reminisced that the girls had been so pretty and clean, and then it was suggested that I ought to have them brought out to the field for an officers' party. The commander endorsed the idea—but I flatly refused. Couldn't I honestly assure the mayor and their parents that these girls would be as well protected at an officers' party as they had been with the enlisted men? I assured him that the officers *could* behave as well as the enlisted men, but I was afraid that not all of them would. Within the group were a few who were on the make for anything in skirts. They were living a free, loose life with few restrictions whatsoever upon their activities on the ground. Living under daily flying tensions, there was a bit of the "tomorrow we die" in their attitude toward natural pleasures. I was afraid that they might try to exercise with these French girls some privileges to which they thought they were entitled as officers and gentlemen by an act of Congress. Doc Baxter backed me up, and the CO let the matter pass.

One of the wildest of this wild bunch was a reckless young lieutenant—a short, dark, heavy-set Casanova. He was an able flyer, but his main interest on the ground seemed to be clandestine meetings with Frenchwomen and with some of the nurses. More than once Doc Baxter had confined him to quarters for venereal disease, but he would go out again and at the first opportunity nullify the treatment. He took particular delight in needling me with these exploits, obviously trying to shock "The Preacher." He would show me letters that he had received from girls in the States, where he had evidently been quite a lover, as well as recapitulate in considerable detail his activities with the women available here.

Once when I walked into the club, where he was sitting with a couple of nurses, he shouted across the room, asking where I had been—"Out to take a pro?" Immediately half the men present came down on him, and he shut up. But he aroused no antipathy in me. Obviously something was troubling him to make him bait anyone he associated with the ministry. He was a very disturbed boy, apparently specifically troubled in his relationship to God.

In our combat missions he undoubtedly realized something basic that he had forgotten for years: that life is a valuable possession not to be lightly frittered away. Yet his pattern of living was such that he felt unable to make up for some of the wild and irresponsible actions of his past even if he wanted to. Like the rest of us he was basically afraid, and this was his way of covering up his fears. Occasionally a telling remark would slip through his veneer. He'd stand at the bar and say in a loud voice to no one in particular, "They're not going to get *me*—not *me!*" And then he'd laugh. I was certain that there was no truly evil intent in him, and I longed to reach out and touch him in some way.

In the spring of '45 we were on a mission together over western Germany. Suddenly he called on his radio that he was hit—badly. I told him to bail out. He replied that he couldn't because the canopy of his plane was stuck. I told him to look for a place to put the plane down on its belly. As he glided down, heavy smoke spiraled up from behind his plane. I could see that he was going to overshoot the smooth area that he was heading for, that he was going to crash. When he was about fifty feet from the ground, he cried into his radio, "Preacher, say a prayer for me!"

As I answered, "I already have," he hit a high-power line, and the airplane went over on the side of the road, bouncing in a great flash of flame, and then rolled on, still burning. Circling above it, I could see no indication that he was still alive, and I returned to the base with that terrible dead feeling of multiple failure within me. I had failed to save this boy either spiritually or physically.

But I was wrong. Years later I heard that he had survived, and been taken prisoner of war. His reaching out in his awful moment of complete loss had been answered.

vi

In the field General Eisenhower was hammering at the Siegfried Line with six armies on an axis running from Holland to the Swiss frontier. Our operations from St. Dizier were stepped up as a part of the increasing air offensive. Weather permitting, we flew continuous fighter-bomber missions, hitting forts, gun emplacements, supply depots, rail lines, bridges. Sometimes we went behind enemy lines on interdiction missions or gave our own troops close support. A mission averaged from two and a half to three and a half hours, and we often flew two a day.

At night I often took walks on the bleak field and, looking at the frosty heavens, wondered if Mary was looking at those same stars. Frequently I made a point of walking out to talk to men on guard duty. Loneliness is apt to descend on a man at such an isolated post. Under vast sullen heavens he feels inordinately small. Yet as we chatted, he was often able to tell me his feelings on all kinds of subjects—from the fidelity of his wife to the existence of some Superior Being or Providence. As for the flyers, their nights were for the most part spent in noisy drinking, talking, and card playing at the little shack that served as our club. It was as if by the very volume of their laughter and the loudness of their voices they could chase away the specter of the next day's mission. I sat with them while they drank and lent my voice to the general din. Or at least I did at first.

Inevitably I felt that some of them had begun to look upon me as a chaplain, which I did not pretend nor presume to be—a suspicion given substance when Sam Weinberg brought me a crucifix and asked if I wanted it.

55

I thought that he might have looted it until he explained that he had found it lying near a bombed-out church. Pleased that he had come to me for something besides arranging another party, I thanked him for it and took it to the group chaplain. I don't know what he did with it, nor was it particularly important; what impressed me was that a Jewish boy should bring to me, a Protestant, a Catholic crucifix. As one whose personal beliefs were beginning to transcend sects or denominations, that crucifix became an important symbol of unity to me. Moreover, that cross, as a symbol of the Resurrection, embraced an idea in which men at war have a special stake.

Ground crews, with so many hours to spend waiting for planes to return, had much time to think. They would talk endlessly among themselves, like boys in bull sessions in a fraternity house, discussing everything from the female form (American and European styles) to the Deity. Partly because they had grown to love their planes (and sometimes the pilots in them) and partly because their waiting hours were often tense and melancholy, they discussed serious, even philosophical subjects. After one of these discussions an armament man and a couple of crew chiefs came down to my shack with a question they'd obviously been arguing about. Did I really believe there was a God, and if so, how could I prove His existence?

I have found that people who ask such questions are usually already half convinced. I answered that it was not up to me to prove it, that they must do it for themselves. No one else could prove it for them. But just as surely it was up to them to prove that there *wasn't* a God if they wanted to be certain in that belief. The chiefs promptly launched into an argument that it is impossible to prove that there is no God, and by this roundabout method ended by halfway convincing themselves of His existence.

During the winter months flying was difficult, and tensions built up heavily. I wasn't cognizant of the added strain at first; the only change of which I was aware was that I no longer wanted to be with the other pilots when we were off duty. I began to avoid them and gave up sitting around in the club during the evening. Right after dinner I would go to my shack, read a little, and sack in. All I cared about was to get on with the next mission —I had over thirty now—and then the next.

Doc Baxter kept asking me how I was eating. He started sitting next to me at meals, insisting that I at least take my daily vitamin tablets from the bottle on the table. These pills were one of his fetishes. If he felt we were slacking off on them, he would line us up like a bunch of schoolkids, dole out the dose, and then make us open our mouths to make sure that we had swallowed it.

Our outfit was blessed in having Doc. Not only was he a fine medic, but his humanitarian gifts made him the hub of our lives. He was father and brother to us. A pilot knew that, if he didn't return, there would be one man anyway who would miss him.

Doc came for a talk with me one evening and suggested that I had better go back to England for a rest tour. I objected, snapping that the only reason anybody ever went back to England was to get drunk. He shrugged. If such was the case, why didn't I do it here? If I would agree to do some drinking, for medicinal purposes, he wouldn't send me back to England. It would save the Air Force time and money. Smiling at this turn in the conversation, I agreed to take his medicine.

That night Doc quieted everybody in the mess tent by announcing that we were all going to the local tavern where "The Preacher" was going to hang one on! He invited the whole squadron to come and watch. About seven o'clock we went to the tavern, and a bottle of champagne was put in front of me. An assortment of grins was turned my way as I filled a glass and drank it off. Urged on by applause, I emptied the bottle within ten minutes and was the proud possessor of a happy jag. The other men had started on their bottles soon after I had, so their mood matched mine. There was much laughing, shouting, and singing. My inebriation lasted about an hour, and then I suddenly sobered up. The others were having such a good time that I went back to camp by myself. Falling onto my cot, I slept as I hadn't for weeks.

In the morning I awoke without a hang-over or any other of

the bad effects I had heard about. I just felt pleasantly relaxed. The weather was bad that day, so no combat missions took off. It was like being on a vacation. Doc Baxter came to check on me. Seeing how well I felt, he explained his treatment in medical terms: the alcohol evidently had produced the vascular relaxation necessary for people who are under the steady strain that combat produces. He added that in showing the boys that I wasn't averse to tying one on, I'd probably find myself even closer to them than before. Not bad for a single dose of pleasant medicine.

While the squadron was working over near the Saar Basin on December 16, 1944, Bill Myers was hit. Bill was our flight leader—a fine, aggressive pilot of the cowboy type. Hailing from Denver, Colorado, he called his plane "Poco Loco" (Spanish for "a little crazy"), always carried a hunting knife in his belt, and got a special kick out of calling our new pilots "dudes."

I was flying his wing when he crash-landed in the Saar Basin. Circling him as he went down, I saw him get out. He evidently was wounded, but it was an enormous relief to see that he was still alive. As acting flight leader I kept the squadron above him until an American weapons carrier came around the bend and picked him up. I had to tell one of our pilots who kept whining over his radio, "Let's go home, I'm running out of gas" to shut his mouth. It was the first and last time in over 300 missions in two wars that I ever had to speak in this way to a fellow pilot. Myers was to be hospitalized for several months for flak wounds, and I took his place permanently as flight leader.

No matter how rigorously we held ourselves against being affected, it was always a sickening blow when a familiar face disappeared from among us. This was particularly hard to bear in the case of a youngster named Charles Loesch, whom we called "Junior"—a favorite among us all. This blond, attractive twenty-year-old was always so pleasant, so willing, so eager to prove himself the equal of the older pilots that he would go out of his way to be assigned to extra missions.

I was leading a flight of four airplanes toward Luxembourg

58

when we got a call from the radio controller that two enemy aircraft were strafing a major command post. We responded to the request for an interception. As we approached the town from behind a hill and at a low altitude, our own antiaircraft opened up on us by mistake. I called for the flight to disperse. Junior was on my wing. He had been so well trained to stay with the leader that he now failed to break away from me. Ground guns, invariably shooting at the lead aircraft, hit behind it, and anybody flying there may get the fire intended for the leader. This happened to Junior. He went down and hit an embankment, and his plane blew up.

Being the responsible man on the mission, I was sickened by this accidental death of such a fine boy. When the flight landed back at our base, a little dog ran out to meet us. It was Junior's puppy, come to look for his master. We walked in silence from the field as it ran inquiringly among us.

All we could do was call upon Nineteenth Tactical Air Command headquarters to inquire of the Army about the incident. We received humble and heartfelt apologies. Actually, this kind of dreadful error was not a rare occurrence and most veteran pilots were wary of our own antiaircraft installations. We understood how mistakes were made. A plane swoops low over a hill at 300 miles per hour and the AA gunner, who has been waiting with gathering tension all day for some target, lets go. And once one gunner fires, the whole battery automatically follows suit.

In the spring the squadron was moved from St. Dizier up to Asch in Belgium and then to Bad Kitzengren in Germany. I became group-operations officer and was promoted to major. The war was slowing down to a halt. We no longer could find targets; enemy fields would be empty of aircraft, and whole units of enemy troops were surrendering to our advancing armies. Our pilots now were sent on morale flights over POW and concentration camps. We would fly low over these wretched establishments, circling and waving our wings at the prisoners still held there.

A rumor broke that the German High Command had surren-

59

dered. A previous similar tale had been proved untrue by the Battle of the Bulge, but this one had the enemy's evident dissolution to back it up. Yet it still was hard to believe, and I tried to hold my deep relief in check. Then the group commander called for a general assembly on the flight line to inform us that the armistice would be officially announced and that we soon could expect to be relieved. As he spoke, the drone of approaching aircraft was heard. Though we were lined up at attention, heads and eyes began to turn in the direction of the ominous sound. If it was enemy aircraft, we were lined up perfectly for their guns. . . .

It was the enemy all right—a flight of four Focke-Wulfes and three Stukas. The group commander must have been certain that it wasn't an attack, or else he feared that we might panic; for he calmly finished his talk. It was one of those split-second decisions required of command, and in this case it turned out to be a sound one.

The Germans circled the field and started landing right before our popping eyes. Three of them "ground-looped"—swerved off the runway with a wing dragging—obviously intending to damage their planes before surrendering. The others came down perfectly. Men climbed out with their hands up. Our commander dismissed us, and we surged toward them.

A young German came running forward, jabbering frantically. Astonishingly, he seemed to want a screw driver. Given one, he was accompanied back to his plane, where he started unscrewing the radio panel in his fuselage. He had brought his girl along. She was hauled out of the cramped space, somewhat bedraggled but still identifiable as a girl, and that was enough to provoke whistles and hoots from our ranks. It was a thoroughly bizarre scene.

Interrogation revealed that the group was from the Russian front. Rather than surrender there, they had peeled off in search of an American field at which to turn themselves in. Among them was Colonel Roedel, a leading Luftwaffe pilot who was still active though he had lost an eye and a leg earlier in the war.

60

The group commander appeared to feel that so famous an ace deserved special treatment. During their talk in his quarters he ordered some sandwiches for his "guest." But as they were brought in by an orderly, a Major Saunders, whom I remember mostly for the deep, jagged scar on his cheek, burst in. A big, dark-visaged man, he had been captured by the Germans after being shot down. His wound had not been given any treatment at all by their medics, and a deep, disfiguring scar had been the result. With his escape he brought back an abiding bitterness; he was not one to see these German pilots given extra courtesies.

Grabbing up the tray of sandwiches, he threw it out the window. The startled Roedel had to wait until regulation time to be fed. The group commander was furious but wisely did nothing, as Saunders had the sympathy of every man on the base.

With this queer incident I hoped—and prayed—that "The Preacher's" fighting days were finished and that my generation's war was now the stuff of which history books are made. Already plans were forming in my mind, plans involving a little country church somewhere in Ohio. . . .

Our next move, after the end of hostilities, was to Straubing, Germany. Here we saw at first hand what war can mean to a civilian population. The roads teemed with people driven from their homes by the hostilities which had raged around them. Numberless children were separated from their parents. They wandered along the roads in pairs or groups with little, ragged packs on their backs. At night they slept in the fields. They were dreadfully quiet, diffident, and frightened. At first it was difficult for us to get close to them or even to give them food. I had never seen a sadder sight, but it was only a prelude to the horrors I was eventually to face in another war.

Our group was broken up. The commander remained in Straubing with the ground echelon, while I was ordered to take the air echelon, planes and crews, down to Passau, near the Danube River, while the runway was being repaired at Straubing. At the new installation, in a lovely rural setting, we found a mixed group of

Hungarian cavalry and flying officers and their families. They had come up the Danube to get away from the Russians on the Eastern Front and had set up homes in the facilities located on the field.

We allowed them to remain in their present quarters, while we occupied the facilities on the other side of the field. We had no indication from our headquarters whether or not they were to be considered displaced persons or prisoners of war, but they proved so eager to cooperate with us, and even to work for us, that we felt obliged to give them every protection. Their commander was a distinguished old gentleman named Eros. Together he and I coordinated the maintenance of the field. They took care of the physical labor, while we provided them with subsistence. High-ranking Hungarian officers were perfectly willing to roll and stack gasoline drums and ammunition in return for our protection and friendship.

The two organizations began to fraternize. Eros appeared one day with a request which a few months before would have seemed most peculiar. His group wanted to put on an entertainment for the Americans—our own group and a number of ground-force troops in the area. It was a mélange of dancing and comedy acts, made more endearing by the pains the Hungarians had taken to learn English well enough to tell some otherwise pretty stale jokes. The high point of the evening was a performance by Colonel Eros's daughter Eva. Formerly the prima ballerina of the Budapest Opera Company, she staged an excellent ballet to Ravel's *Bolero*. She was beautiful as well as talented, and the next day I was besieged by calls from some of our officers who wanted to meet her. It wasn't too difficult to detect what else they wanted. I considered it best not to oblige.

Not long after, in the summer of 1945, I received word that I was to return to the States for subsequent duty in the Far East against the Japanese. I drove out to the farmhouse to say good-by to Colonel Eros. It was the last time I was ever to see the fine old man and his family, and it was my ardent hope that they would not fall into the hands of the Russians. Having seen what was going on across the Inn River in the Communist-held area, I was developing a violent dislike for everything they stood for. The Russians were employing ruthless occupation techniques, restricting the people's movements, ousting them from their houses, confiscating their possessions. And rumors, whether true or not, were drifting up from the south concerning far worse atrocities—murder, torture, rape. I advised Eros to take his people west to democratic occupation sectors as soon as he could.

Eva walked with me out to my jeep. It was parked near one of the roadside altars familiar to that part of the country. She went to it and knelt before the crucifix. I followed and knelt beside her. She did not speak English, but I knew enough German to gather that she was praying for my safe deliverance to the United States. I felt the tears in my eyes. I hope that my prayer for her and her people was similarly answered, but I shall probably never find out.

The next day I took leave of what remained of the 405th Fighter-bomber Group and started back to Marietta. So much destruction lay behind me that it was hard to believe there was to be an end to it. Perhaps I had done something to keep inviolate the land toward which I was flying. If it is true that in order to save we must at times destroy, I had done my part. With petitioning heart I repeated from Psalms, "Deliver me from blood-guiltiness, O God, thou God of my salvation; and my tongue shall sing aloud of thy righteousness."

vii

A return home from war is like no other. All during the overseas
hitch I had thought much of our old town and of those I held
dear—Mary and my son Larry, my folks, members of congregations to whom I had preached. All my hopes and expectations were
at first realized. My loved ones surrounded me with happiness and
attention, and the townspeople greeted me with the undeserved
praise of a returning hero.

We went to live with Mary's family on their place near Lowell.
To keep myself occupied I helped with the farm work; but though
I would exhaust myself physically, my mind became increasingly
restless. It struck me how little people in rural communities like
this were affected by the war, despite all their fathers and brothers
and sons who were in it. There was a curious insulation here
which made their absences, sometimes forever, no more than sad
farewells. Europe contained so many ruined farms and villages,
destitute refugees, and leveled cities that the tidy order in Lowell
seemed part of another world. The memory of those gutted
houses, forlorn on their abandoned acres, somehow rebuked this
somnolence. I did not feel at all critical of these people—only
puzzled how they could remain so undisturbed. I was not unhappy when my leave expired and I could take my restless soul
to Foster Field.

This time I was able to take Mary and Larry with me. I
bundled them into the old family Chevrolet, and we started for
Victoria, Texas—where, of all things, I was to undergo gunnery
training in a P-47.

After all I had been through it seemed a ridiculous activity, but I did not mind. Living in a court near the field, I had more time to become reacquainted with my wife and child. How soon I would be transferred to the Far East, where the war continued, we did not know, nor did we allow ourselves to think too much about it. Then came the news of Hiroshima and soon after the official end of World War II on the deck of the battleship *Missouri.*

As far back as St. Dizier I had often discussed wistfully and hopefully with other pilots what we would do after the war ended. Many were greatly concerned about their lack of training for postwar work and about how they would earn a livelihood. To those who had no special qualifications I usually commented on the advisability of going back to school as I intended doing. I recognized the gaps in my education.

Before fully embarking on the ministry, I felt that I should take graduate studies to further what abilities I might possess. Mary was uncertain that this was necessary. After these haphazard years to which I had subjected her, she wanted a stable life. But I did not think I could manage this with the tools I had. Perhaps I could find work as a teacher and carry out the functions of a minister on Sundays until a pastorate could be found that would support us. So, when I was placed on inactive status, we started back for Marietta. I had a little over 5,000 dollars—not much with which to begin a new life at twenty-eight—but we would manage.

I enrolled at Ohio University in Athens, a state-supported school of five thousand students, tall trees, and old buildings. The alumni magazine ran an embarrassing tale about how a minister had gone forth to combat, gloriously acquitted himself, and returned in one piece to go to graduate school before reembarking upon his career. I stayed indoors for a few days after that article was published but when I reappeared no one asked me for my autograph.

I had a comforting lack of difficulty in adjusting to civilian life.

The anticipation of studying once again and the subsequent occupation with schoolwork erased for me that trying period so many returning veterans were to undergo. At the university we lived in a hut consisting of one room about ten by twenty, which went by the name of living room, bedroom, and kitchen, depending on what we were doing at the time. Mary was pregnant again, and the confines of the little cabin were trying on temperaments. There were aggravating periods of incompatability.

Mary was interested in the tangible symbols of security—a house of our own, a living income, a car. To me security lay in ideas. Too often I had seen how a lifetime of acquiring material possessions can be wiped out by a flash of gunpowder. I had done the wiping out myself with hundreds of bombs. But war doesn't destroy ideas; it only delays their development. True wealth lies in the intangibles, I was convinced—love, family, friends, knowledge, education.

While I did not ignore Mary's concern over our dwindling bank account, I'm afraid I was curt when she questioned the merit of our struggle. Wages were good everywhere; she felt that, if I took a job, we could save enough to try again under better circumstances. But I was determined not to permit any more delays toward my ultimate goal. I immersed myself in the world of books. And finally, in June of 1947, I received my master's degree.

I concentrated my studying in the field of history. I had just returned from Europe, where I had been thrown into intermittent contact with Frenchmen, Germans, Hungarians, Englishmen, and even a few Russians. How pitifully meager was my store of knowledge about these people, their past, their national origins! If I was to devote my life to ministering to people, I needed the tools with which to work; one of these was a knowledge of history. I studied the German culture from medieval times to the present, with emphasis on the German urge to seek strong leadership and a symbol, such as Bismarck or Hitler, of absolute authority. Next, burying myself in English history, I sought some clear-cut relationship between the people of this island nation and their democratic institutions and parliamentary system. There was an element of self containedness, of quiet self-respect, in the Englishmen I had known that fascinated me. Somewhere in my studies of England and its institutions I happened upon the theory that monarchs who allow their people to retain their self-respect are the wisest and most successful rulers. If not a startlingly original idea, it was still a theory of leadership which I could heartily endorse, having watched it operate in two areas—that of religion, and that of war.

My thesis in my major field concerned parliamentary legislation in England from 1830 to 1840. It covered the period in British history when new laws were necessary to alleviate the conditions of women and children working in mines and factories as beasts of burden for from twelve to sixteen hours a day. The women were required to haul carts of coal with yokes around their necks and straps running between their legs. Little boys were required to crawl into narrow veins and dig coal, even though many of them had tuberculosis at the age of ten. The moral decadence matched the physical degradation.

Parents who cause or allow young children to work violate a basic law of nature. Even animals will protect and care for their young—a fundamental obligation not always met by human beings. The parental responsibility is the most basic there is; when it isn't honored, one sees the terrible helplessness of little ones in a world of big people.

Once, discussing this with some friends at a party, a couple of us decided to spend the rest of the evening on our knees to see what it is like to be small. Though it started out in part as a joke, it was actually a frightening experience down there, with large human shapes towering overhead, brushing by us, bumping into us, speaking down to us. To this day, partly as a result of that party stunt, I stoop when I talk to children to meet them at eye level.

67

But man likes to play God, even though it be necessary to make children the victims—when in reality it is the children who are the godly.

In the fall of 1947 we went to Columbus, where I entered Ohio State University to study for my doctorate. I retained my interest in history but managed also to do considerable work in psychology —educational psychology, industrial psychology, practical psychology—anything offered along those lines which I felt might help me understand people. If a minister needs a knowledge of history and of the pasts of whole groups of people to be effective in his profession, he needs a firm grounding in psychology and the inner workings of man's mind even more. I remember too many wrathful ministers from my youth who were entirely incapable of dealing with sick souls and upset personalities because they lacked an adequate knowledge of the inner workings of the mind. Many times, though perfectly well motivated, these elderly fundamentalists did more harm than good in treating each member of their congregations to the same big dose of the Good Book no matter what the specific problem might be. One minister of my boyhood, a stern evangelist type, spent many Sunday-morning hours haranguing against alcoholics. This white-haired, glowering man would point his long finger at us—and I'm sure that his audience each Sunday *did* include a few hung-over celebrants—and shout, "Sin, sin—repent, repent!" until it got to the point where I would hunch down in my seat and repeat over and over again to myself that wonderful piece of wisdom from Matthew 7:1, "Judge not, that ye be not judged." Christ, I always thought, must certainly have spoken in a low and gentle voice.

The minister's job is to understand, and any man of the cloth today who ignores the modern tools that psychology offers him can hardly be fulfilling his obligation to the best of his ability. I don't mean that a minister should confuse his function with that of a psychiatrist; far from it. This could lead to dangerous practices. But there is an important area where the two fields overlap,

68

and that is where the dedicated man of God, well versed in psychology, can perform with maximum effectiveness.

I did not engage in any kind of ministerial activity at Athens or in Columbus, but I did occasionally return to Marietta to conduct services as a guest minister. But each time I spoke I was reminded of how much there was still to be learned and accomplished before I was equipped to take up ministering as a full-time occupation.

The war years had made me more aware than ever of how much broader a background and deeper an understanding I needed in order to get across to people the compassion that I felt and that they needed. I was increasingly appalled by the sickening thought of speaking to people and not being able to supply the sympathy (not the answers—who has all the answers?) that they required, the spiritual renaissance that they needed when they came to church. I felt that I wasn't getting through to them—as I felt many other ministers were also failing to do.

In June of 1948, with only a few months to go before I would get my doctor's degree, I put in my application for teaching at a number of places. Once I got a college assignment, I could easily locate a pastorate somewhere in the area and work the two professions in conjunction.

But in the spring of 1948 I had received a card from the Air Force asking if I would accept active duty were I called. I answered that I would out of my sense of obligation to the Air Force. To justify my accepting a reserve commission, I had to respond in the affirmative. Mary had mixed emotions, but I actually doubted that I'd be called. In any event it would be but a temporary assignment and a short tour of duty. To my surprise, on July 5, 1948, a lengthy wire came from the headquarters of the Continental Air Command ordering me back into uniform. I had no idea what the job would be; but if the country wanted me again, I could only answer yes.

This time it was even harder to say good-by than before; now there was another little boy, Alan, to leave. Hastily assembling a uniform, I went to New York and reported in at Mitchell Air Base. There I learned that my assignment was to be on an officer-procurement program. I would travel around the country, visiting colleges and universities to meet with college presidents and executives, and examine young men for admission to and training in the Air Force. I did well enough on the procurement program to take over eventually the office of this liaison activity.

In April of 1950 my name came up for rotation overseas. I could have waived the assignment, but when I found it was to the Far East Air Force, I accepted. It was an area of the world I had never visited containing teeming millions of whom I knew nothing. At Ohio University I had studied the struggle of Korea for her independence and the heroic part played in that struggle by her president Syngman Rhee. But those Korean place names that I was to know so intimately—Seoul, Pusan, Taegu, Pyong-yang—conjured up only vague, romantic images now.

At La Guardia Field, parting from Mary and the boys, I had a peculiar presentiment of the onslaughts to come. Attempting to mask my heavy-heartedness, I told her that I expected they would soon be able to join me in Japan. It was cold comfort, for while dependents were allowed to travel to Japan, there usually was a six- to eight-months waiting period. Somehow I knew that they would never be able to come to me, but I had to give an indication of hope to them as well as to myself. Later Mary told me that she too intuitively sensed that she would never get there.

I kissed them and went inside the plane. Looking through the window, I could see them huddled against the fence, waving forlornly. Then the big engines revved up, and the plane taxied down the runway, shutting them from sight.

viii

Beneath the military air transport that carried me toward Japan that April day in 1950, the Pacific was an enormous floor of blue glass. As the big plane droned on, I had the same feeling of strangeness which had been mine crossing the Atlantic to World War II six years before. Again a crazy grinding in the world's cogs had put me in uniform, plucked me from Ohio, and spun me toward an alien land.

Before the name Korea sprang so dramatically into the headlines, my feelings about it were impersonal. As a graduate student in history I had become aware of its position in the galaxy of nations, its strategic importance to Japan, China, and Russia. But I little suspected that there were forces at work that would involve us in a major armed conflict in this faraway country known as "The Land of Morning Calm," or that I would be honored by a close association with the president of Korea.

On many maps I had noticed this clublike peninsula jutting down between the Yellow Sea and the Sea of Japan. What I learned of its background after many months of fighting and living there I shall set down now as concisely and unemotionally as possible. This will not be easy, for I have come to love both the land and its people.

By our standards Korea is a small country about half the size of California, very mountainous in the north and along the east coast. It is also a poor land, most of its inhabitants toiling long and wearisome days in the rice paddies and small fields. But, though poor in natural resources and backward in its standard of living,

71

Korea has been coveted for strategic reasons for many years by the Japanese, the Chinese, and the Russians (the Siberian port of Vladivostok lies only 80 miles northeast of the Korean border). From the turn of the century until the end of World War II not only was Korea occupied by Japan, but it seemed to be the Japanese intent to reorient and even absorb the country. But the Koreans do not really resemble any other people in Asia either in custom or in language, and the Japanese effort to impress their own language and religion (Shintoism) on them backfired. It resulted in the rise of Korean nationalism and, ultimately, in the election of Korea's foremost exile, Dr. Syngman Rhee, to the presidency of an independent Republic of Korea south of the thirty-eighth parallel.

How many Americans before that fateful day—June 25, 1950— ever paid much heed to the way in which the thirty-eighth parallel knifes across Korea, virtually cutting it in half? In 1945 Manchuria and North Korea were occupied by the Russian armies, and South Korea by American troops. The dividing line was established roughly along the thirty-eighth parallel merely as a practical measure: the Russians were responsible for rounding up and repatriating the Japanese north of the line, and the Americans to the south.

But as Russia ruthlessly sovietized the northern half of Korea and as the Korean Communists liquidated dissenters and organized a menacing army, the thirty-eighth parallel froze into an important line of demarcation as part of the Iron Curtain dividing the Communist from the Free World. This development further propelled Korea toward economic helplessness, as the industry was concentrated north of the line and the agriculture south. To give just one example, the fields in South Korea, farmed for over two thousand years, were totally dependent on the fertilizer produced in the north.

In 1947 the United States presented the issue of "two Koreas" to the United Nations, which resolved that all the Korean people were to hold free elections in 1948 to create a national assembly. Unfortunately only the South Koreans were free to participate, the North Koreans being entirely under the heel of the Communists. The newly elected national assembly formed a Korean government, drew up the first constitution in the land's 4,000-year history, and elected Dr. Syngman Rhee to serve for four years as the first president of the Republic of Korea. The American Army of Occupation, fifty thousand strong, withdrew in 1949, and General MacArthur, in Tokyo, by the summer of 1949 no longer had any defense responsibilities in the peninsula of Korea. The United States had left in Korea only a small military advisory group and its embassy personnel in Seoul, headed by Ambassador John J. Muccio.

Such were conditions in that unhappy country when I arrived in Japan. Like so many others there I soon came to have a feeling that at any moment an explosion might erupt in Korea, just a few miles across the cold Sea of Japan, where two ideologies were in seeming deadlock. The feeling of imminent danger was so strong that I could take no great satisfaction in being assigned to Yokota Air Force Base in Japan as an information and education officer.

During my fortnightly tour as duty officer in the radar filter center, where twenty-four-hour surveillance was maintained over all air activities, I followed the flights of Communist planes on the screen. These would frequently approach the thirty-eighth parallel. It was an ominous threat. Our commanders were resolved not to lose the initiative in a surprise and unwarranted attack. The appearance of these aircraft was the signal to alert ours and to dispatch them to strategic intercepting positions if that now historic line of demarcation should be crossed. As soon as our planes came up—and flashed on the Communist radar screens— the latter's planes would retreat northward. This happened so consistently that with the constant build-up of tension it was difficult for me to concentrate on supervising off-duty education programs for Air Force personnel and their dependents.

While I was busy setting up schools at the Yokota, Johnson, and Tachikawa bases in Japan and assigning civilian teachers from the States, sporadic border fighting was breaking out between North

73

and South Korea—skirmishes which deepened the apprehension that at any moment a full-scale engagement might be expected. Armed Forces Radio Service kept us apprised of the southward movement of Communist land forces. Seoul was being air-evacuated of American personnel, government officials, advisers, and businessmen. C-54s under fighter escort were used to get these people out of the danger zone.

Then on June 25 we got the electrifying news that the North Koreans had crossed the line in force. A few days later a Red YAK fighter fired on a loaded C-54 near Suwon. A U.S. F-82 promptly shot him down, and air war was on.

For a few days there was brisk action. Our Air Force moved fast and effectively. The area was full of Communist YAKs, which we soon cleaned out. The Russian-made planes stopped coming into South Korea, but the damage was done and full-scale activities had started.

When I had left Europe, I had felt that my time as a combatant had been served; now I was faced with the prospect of more violence. I loathed the very idea of dropping bombs and strafing personnel, but here again was the hour of decision. Could I, now more qualified than before, hold back from contributing my highly developed fighting skills to my country—to all of mankind in fact? I knew the answer before I even asked myself the question. I applied for hazardous duty.

Nothing happened. I persisted in bombarding my commanding officer Colonel Zoller with written requests, telephone calls, personal pleas. He must have wearied of the badgering, for at last word came that I was to be assigned as liaison officer and courier between Tokyo and Seoul—a disappointment, as I had hoped for combat status.

Then there occurred another of those coincidences, seemingly small at the time, which direct the path of a man's life to totally unexpected fields. The telephone of our bachelor-officers' quarters happened to be right outside my door. I happened to be in my room, when I heard Lt. Col. Clifton Tangburn, the wing exec, talking to someone in command headquarters. His side of the conversation revealed that the wing was to provide a major who would volunteer for a special assignment in Korea. I grabbed my pants, ran outside, and told him that I wanted it, whatever it was.

Cliff said that we would have to go to Colonel Zoller, who would make the selection. Another major who had applied for the assignment was waiting when we arrived. The Colonel, after interviewing us, decided to determine by lottery which of us was to get the assignment. He told us to take a number from one to ten; he would flip the pages of a book. Whichever one of us had the number closest to the last digit on the page at which he stopped would win. I took seven and watched the riffling pages with suspended breath. I had a deep feeling that something of great importance, not just another job, was at stake. My seven came up, right on the nose. I was so elated that the other major left with a laugh.

Colonel Zoller told me to get my gear together and go to Itazuke Air Base for further instructions. Returning to the BOQ, I did not take long to pack. I left my bicycle for Cliff Tangburn to use as a token of appreciation for the lucky eavesdropping. In a few minutes my room was stripped to await the next solitary transient. The houseboys had learned of my fondness for flowers; I left the vases which they had kindly filled every day and some potted vines and plants in case my successor might want to offset the bleakness of the room. A cage of birds I took across the hall to my friend Father Pohl, a quiet, red-haired, red-faced chaplain of whom I had grown quite fond.

I would miss Father Pohl and our many long talks on comparative religion. He got out a bottle of rock and rye, toasted the new mission—whatever it was to be—and sent me on my way with his enthusiastic blessing.

At Itazuke my excitement increased. The instructions called for command of a new project, a classified organization with the nebulous title "Bout I." I was to take ten American pilots, four ground officers, and a hundred enlisted men to Korea, where we would train a number of South Korean pilots in the F-51 (Mustang). Some of these Koreans were veteran flyers who, ironically, had flown for Japan in World War II—an indication of how during their forty-five-year occupation of Korea the Japanese had attempted to absorb these people. But now their country was independent once more after forty years of subjection, and these Koreans were waiting to be taught how to fight for their freedom with our modern weapons.

The Far East Command had donated ten F-51s which were to become the nucleus of a South Korean air force, at this time totally ineffective. Though it had around 5,000 personnel, most were being used as airfield maintenance crews to keep American pilots and planes in the air. Their only planes were ten advanced-training aircraft, called "Harvards," and perhaps fifteen more L-5s, light liaison planes. At the outbreak of hostilities they had lost some of these in suicidal attempts to defend their country—for these planes were not intended for combat. They had no armor plate and small firepower, and their gas tanks weren't bulletproof. To be a match for the speedy, hard-hitting YAK, the ROKs had to learn to use its equal—the F-51.

I was told that it was to be a training mission only. We would be located on a field near the town of Taegu and thus be the only friendly air power in Korea. But we Americans were to stay out of combat. The men we were to instruct would become the nucleus of what might prove to be a valuable addition to the United Nations forces. They in turn would teach more of their compatriots to fly the F-51s.

My team looked anything but suited to the role of instructor, which ordinarily requires men of patient temperament as well as finished skill. The men I had drawn, all volunteers, appeared to have stepped forward for many causes other than dedicated service. Among the officers the usual reason for wanting transfer showed on their "201" files: boredom, desire for adventure, personality difficulties. A few of the pilots had been flying top cover

76

for transports on the Seoul evacuation run; these at least knew the F-51 from Able to Zero. The rest were either nonflying officers (communications and engineering) or little better acquainted with the plane than the Koreans. A mixed lot, all right, but I would have been more kindly disposed toward them had I known that within a year seven of those first ten pilots would be dead.

Some of the enlisted men appeared to be fleeing from trouble. They were trying to avoid court-martial, to escape from marrying Japanese girls, to dodge irate husbands. In short, they were the roughest bunch of characters I had ever encountered. But let it be quickly said that they proved to be as solid as a teak log. I came to love every one of them.

Lt. Milton Bellovin, who was to act as adjutant, was already at Itazuke and had organized my men administratively. He was a stocky, hard-bitten West Point graduate, a professional soldier if one ever walked or flew, alert and inventive, a good organizer with an unbreakable, cheerful spirit and a love of action. Many times I was to give thanks that Mike put in for our expedition.

Mike was living at the BOQ, where he had reserved a bed for me. The men were billeted in a gymnasium, and I moved us all in there so as to be together from the outset. Calling them together, I told them that I was happy they had applied for the expedition and that, while I couldn't say exactly what it was to be, at least I could guarantee that it would prove interesting. This was probably the classic understatement of a commander to his men in all the annals of warfare.

Trying to get rolling was like running in a maze. Everyone assigned to the base appeared to have some responsibility for us, and yet no one really did. Finding out who was really in charge was so exasperating that we ended by taking orders from anyone who showed signs of being able to do anything for us. I kept getting words of assurance ("Don't worry, everything will be all right—everything is perfectly planned for you—"), but our progress far from bore out these brave words.

Our equipment was to come from other units on the base;

each was ordered to turn over specified items of equipment to us. This emerged as a horrible way to supply an outfit. Understandably enough, no organization likes to part with good and possibly irreplaceable material. Thus, if a group was assigned to give us a stove, one of its members would go to a salvage depot, dig up a discard, and present us with it. This became somewhat difficult for them as time passed, however; we usually had been to the dump first, to comb out anything that looked at all usable.

Occasionally something almost new would be added to our hoard. But I soon learned not to thank our reluctant benefactors; the item, if new, usually had been "appropriated" by the invaluable Mike Bellovin. In the time to come I often marveled at his unexcelled ability in "requisitioning." He must have come by it naturally, for he denied it when I suggested that there must have been a course in After-dark Pilfering at the Point.

Then all at once the pieces fell into a semblance of shape. We rounded up our dubious equipment and were ready to be airlifted to Taegu. It was typical of this venture that none of the C-47 pilots who were to take us there had ever seen the town. They knew its location only from flight maps and nothing of the condition of its landing strip. It was equally portentous that, at last airborne, bad weather forced us back.

As we retraced our path, I gloomily wondered if Bout I would ever get off the ground. "Perhaps," I thought, "I should ask Father Pohl to take back his blessing."

All that made the next two days endurable was that two or three eager boys from the base asked to be allowed to join the tour. I liked the glint in their eyes and at once got the base's personnel director to give them to me. Then the skies cleared, and once more the transports took off.

Now I was glad for the delay. Our work would begin tomorrow —on the Fourth of July. Perhaps it sounds presumptuous, but it seemed to link us to those who, centuries before, had made that day ring. We of 1950 were a long way from those signers, but in a sense we all were part of the same fight. Freedom isn't inviolate; its principles must be kept in repair if they are to continue in health. We were a mixed lot of doctors in a little cavalcade of flying ambulances on our way to a plague area. And if we died in trying to help stamp out the infection, it was no more than better men before us had done.

The plane in which I was riding, the lead ship, carried my jeep, a trailer, and a power unit. Crawling past them, I worked my way to the cockpit to visit the crew. We had been talking for a few minutes when both engines suddenly cut out and we started falling.

The pilot's hands flew over his instrument panel, pulling switches, turning valves, making adjustments in the sudden, frightful silence. The Sea of Japan started rising up to swallow us. "So I'm not going to get to Korea after all," I was thinking. "This is the ignominious end of Bout I." Then, with a reviving roar, the engines started up again.

The coastline of Korea showed up low on the horizon, as that of France had done on my first approach to come to grips with an armed enemy. An even more malignant one now was loose in the world—anti-Christ as well as antifreedom. The "Battle Hymn of the Republic," sung with such fervor in many of my little churches, welled up from within me and joined the great, purposeful roar of the engines.

ix

The field on which we landed at Taegu, about halfway between Seoul and Pusan, matched the rest of our operation. Bordering a rice paddy, it had no foundation. The stench of human dung, used for fertilizer in the fields nearby, was overpowering. The runway was a vague path in a bog with no rock ballast or hard surface upon which to operate aircraft. I jumped out of the transport in mud up to my ankles. The rest of the establishment consisted of a couple of ramshackle buildings. Clearly there was a monumental amount of work to be done before we could receive our planes from Itazuke.

We were to get our supplies from the Korean Military Advisory Group—we thought. Then an officer, a member of its detail stationed at Taegu, came to me and said, "How soon can we start drawing supplies from you?" A chill jumped down my spine. They believed that they were logistically dependent on us, and we believed the reverse; somebody was going to get awfully hungry.

The Koreans had little to give, and with everything we needed having to be flown in from Japan, it looked as though we would have to stretch the rations we had brought to the breaking point. I wondered if we soon would be forced to live off the land—an unpleasant possibility, for I had been warned to beware of local food. Human dung was used to fertilize the vegetables, a practice which supposedly could result in painful intestinal cysts. Because of primitive slaughtering methods the local meat was said to be equally hazardous for the American consumer, and the water was safe to drink only after heavy chlorination. The area was not a dietician's paradise.

Yet what incidence of sickness the group suffered was to come from carelessness; we kept in remarkably good health. KMAG soon had a supply line running to us, and again I learned how wasteful of energy it is to worry too soon.

First we had to set up housekeeping in sleeping bags and pup tents. We had some larger tents but no tent poles, these having been put on a ship that was to come over eventually. We had five gasoline field stoves which had been declared unfit by a unit in Japan, three of which would operate—a better ratio than for most of our equipment. Our C rations were suitable to our social position but so limited that it was apparent we would have to scrounge for fresh vegetables or starve. The human fertilizer decided us in favor of starving.

That we didn't starve until the supply situation got straightened out was largely due to Mike Bellovin. His prey were service depots he could reach in our limping jeep. When he couldn't talk provisions away from a quartermaster, he would confiscate them. Somehow he kept us fed.

For ground defense we had six-quad .50 caliber machine guns —four to each mount. They would have been sufficient except that only one gun in the lot would fire. Having been told that we were under surveillance by guerrillas and spies in the surrounding hills, and having seen their signal lights at night, we had to improvise a maneuver to conceal our weakness. We would take our workable gun to one side of the field and test-fire it from that position. Then we'd dismount it from its carriage, put it in a jeep, and carry it over to another battery. We'd mount it on that battery and fire it again. Then we'd take it to the third battery, do the same, and repeat the procedure on the fourth battery. We hoped to give the impression that all four batteries fired and that we were well defended, rough, and ready.

Another relic was a little mobile radar unit mounted on a trailer which had come from one of the islands in the South

Pacific, where it had been since World War II. As half its parts were missing, it wouldn't receive or send; only the antenna rotator functioned. Conspicuously we set it up in a tent on a hilltop overlooking the field. Guerrillas hidden about the field could see well-armed men going up for a shift and others coming down, while day and night that little antenna rotated as though searching for enemy aircraft. What these guerrillas did not know was that the would-be operators would go into the tent to sleep— before Lt. George Haines, our radar controller, finally got the necessary parts from Japan to make the set operational.

To keep the men dry and get them out of the water-soaked rice paddies, we cut shelves on the side of the mountain overlooking the field where we pitched our tents. There we first spotted a Korean burial ground, easily identified by its high and evenly spaced mounds of earth. As soon as we began to dig, trying carefully to stay off the mounds, a group of worried-looking but ever courteous Koreans crowded around to watch. Finally an old man stepped forward—a dignified gent, probably a landowner of some station in the community, dressed in the traditional black stovepipe hat made of mesh and the flowing white coat of muslin. He leaned on a crooked stick, and above his wispy white beard he was the picture of a patriarch. Through an interpreter he very politely requested that we not bother the sacred graves of his ancestors. When I gave him every assurance that we would not, he thanked me and quietly dispersed the crowd.

Two nights later I found a couple of my American ground-crew boys sitting on one of these mounds drinking a few cans of beer that a plane had brought in from Japan. In words of one syllable I tried to explain how they were desecrating a virtual shrine of our hosts and how much our future depended on the friendship of these natives. Only they could warn us about guerrilla activities in the hills as well as augment our meager food supply.

We also did our best not to destroy adjacent rice paddies. With them all around the field the water table was only a foot below the surface of the ground. A foxhole couldn't be dug without its immediately filling with water. At first we didn't disturb these paddies because of the earnest effort of the farmers to get in their rice crop; we knew how important it would be to them later on. But ultimately it did become necessary to drain them in order to make the runway suitable for heavier operations.

Our Korean trainees—all officers—arrived, and we at once began our training program, on the ground and in the air. They had been selected for the assignment by Gen. Kim Chung Yul, chief of staff of the ROK Air Force, a man who was to become my very good friend. Since their air force was virtually inoperative from lack of modern planes as well as personnel trained to fly and to maintain them, the Koreans realized this opportunity to the full. They were the cadre from which the country's future air-power might develop.

Just a few days after we set up shop at Taegu, General Kim flew in from Taejon in a limping, obsolete Harvard to check up on Korea's infant air academy. Our six Korean pilots lined up on the field and stood at attention on the muddy runway to greet their chief formally. It was a pathetic and at the same time a stirring scene. These Koreans always referred to Kim as "My General" in warm and admiring tones. I loved to hear them say it.

Until now the Korean pilots' few missions against the enemy had been in small, light, outmoded planes, dropping homemade bombs in World War I style and pecking away with .30-caliber machine guns. They would hold the bombs in their laps until over the target, then take the caps off, and drop them by hand while flying at an altitude of a couple of hundred feet. Despite the crudity of this operation they were amazingly accurate against stationary ground targets. They were in a frenzy to get into the war with the F-51. Each had had one brief flight in it in Japan, and they were enamored of its strength, speed, and equalizing firepower. It was hard to restrain them until they were prepared to fly it properly. They had a lot of spunk, but their feeling that they could handle anything that flew received a setback when one of their best pilots, Colonel Lee, made an attack on an enemy tank only four days after our arrival.

During World War II he had shot down over twenty American planes while flying for Japan. He was extremely confident of his abilities as a pilot and rather dubious about the prospect of learning anything new from us. This was a double mistake, for the Zero's maneuverability permitted it to make a letter S—a flipover onto its back during a dive for a quicker pullout—at altitudes as low as 1,400 feet. Heavier and slower, the F-51 needed to be at least at 2,000 feet to describe such a tight arc. Trying this tactic now, Colonel Lee dived into the ground and was killed.

It was a needless loss of both a plane and an expert pilot. I made it clear that it must not happen again. They seemed to accept my firmness in good part, and our relationship bettered in the little shack we called an operations building.

As there were no maps of the area in English, the ROKs helped us read the Korean maps and were most patient in explaining place names and locations. We in turn restrained ourselves when the chickens they had brought along to supply them with eggs would meander into the hut and when the powerful odor of their *kimchee* (sour rice) dominated our mess.

By this time Korean and American pilots, under my direction, were flying on the same missions. Theoretically the American pilots were not supposed to be fighting, but under our system it was hard to tell where the teaching stopped and the fighting began. We were fighting the North Koreans and teaching the South Koreans simultaneously, though the teaching operations were not made any the easier by the fact that most of our radios did not work. The Korean pilots followed our hand signals and played "follow the leader," diving down on our tails toward the target. My "on-the-job instruction" course was to have surprising results in the days to come.

One special tactic we employed in an effort to encourage them to be "hot pilots" was a unique landing pattern developed in World War II and then outlawed afterward as too dangerous. In formation we would approach the strip not more than fifty feet above the ground and then cut back on the throttle and zoom up and to the left in a 360-degree circle while lowering the wheels and flaps. Such a landing pattern gets the planes on the ground in a hurry and sometimes precludes running out of gas at mission's end.

Gen. Earle Partridge, commanding officer of the Fifth Air Force, witnessed this maneuver one afternoon and ordered me to raise the landing pattern to an approach of 1,000 feet with a normal spiral landing. I immediately complied and so ordered my pilots. A few days later Partridge was back, asking if I had complied with his order. No sooner had I answered in the affirmative than one of my pilots, Captain Hook, led three Korean "hot pilots" in a zooming dive down toward the field at an altitude of approximately ten feet and rolled into our spectacular landing pattern. The General eyed me with elaborate patience but allowed as how it had better not happen again. It didn't.

The war was getting hot on the front lines. The Korean Military Advisory Group, an American organization assigned to work with the Korean land forces, was already engaged in stopping the onslaught from the north. I began to get calls from KMAG to fly in close support of troops. This was simply because we were the only combat-ready flying group established in Korea. Our air force, based in Japan, was deployed against the enemy aircraft— the number-one priority of air operations. We readily complied with KMAG's urgent request. Although we Americans were not supposed to be in aircraft over enemy lines, the situation was urgent, and the Koreans weren't ready to fly by themselves in combat in the F-51. So in those first frantic days it was we Americans, breaking the rules, along with a few advanced Korean pilots, who flew those planes marked with the ROK symbols. However that may have troubled other authorities, it delighted the field commanders, whose men were under such enormous, mounting pressure.

Two heroic American generals who were to become famous under rather tragic circumstances—one in death and the other by capture—came often to our little field. Gen. William Dean, a strapping front-line soldier later captured and imprisoned by the Communists, took us out one day and indicated the exact whereabouts of the front lines, the disposition of troops, and the advantages and faults of our position. He often referred to the front-line troops as "my boys," and I was impressed by the way he seemed to carry the whole war around in his head. Gen. Walton Walker, later killed in a tragic jeep accident, was a short, heavy-set bulldog of a man who in reality was gentle and quiet by nature. Once, in the first chaotic and tumultuous days of the war, he suggested to me a unique way of spotting the enemy on the ground: "If they look organized, shoot at them. It couldn't be us."

General Dean and General Walker would personally conduct ground-air operations from our operations shack. From us they wanted air support for their front-line units. We American pilots gave it as best we could until definite word came again that no Americans were to fly combat missions in Korean aircraft. Once again this was to be a Korean responsibility entirely.

We were deeply disappointed with the order because our pupils were having enough trouble making take-offs and landings in the strange planes, let alone fight in them. We stayed on the ground for a few days, letting the Koreans fly all the missions. Then I received a message from Fifth Air Force headquarters authorizing me to utilize the aircraft any way I saw fit.

I interpreted this message as an indication that I again could engage the American pilots in combat operations. I went with this information to General Walker. Happily he promised that his front-line units would let us know where to hit. With a feeling of exhilaration I knew that we were in business again.

Looking down from the skies, we could see how hard pressed

86

Walker's men were. Our troops were being overwhelmed—from the air it looked like a rout. Outnumbered by Communist manpower, whole units were being forced to leave their guns and backpedal in full retreat.

Then General Dean reorganized the Twenty-fourth Division and attempted to stand. On a Sunday morning we were grounded by bad weather. An enlisted man was trying to get a radio in one of the F-51s to work when he heard an urgent call for air support from a ground-forces radio jeep near the front lines.

As it was impossible for aircraft from Japan to take off and come through the bad weather, I recognized the fact that ours were the only aircraft available. Our runway was still inundated from the rains, half of it actually covered with 6 inches of water. While I felt the obligation to try at least to answer the call, I didn't think it right to order any pilots to take off with me. I asked for volunteers, and Lieutenant Timberlake, one of my ten original pilots, offered to go. We taxied out on the runway through the mud, opened throttle, and barely made it off the ground with our loads of bombs, rockets, and .50-caliber ammunition.

On the way up to the front lines I called the radio jeep. His target was a Red armored division coming down the road north of Taejon. There was nothing in the way to stop it; the ground forces had no antitank guns or heavy ordnance capable of doing the job.

The weather cleared as we approached the designated area, so that we could see the armored division. It was an appalling sight. Tanks, trucks, vehicles of all kind wound like a disjointed snake somewhere from ten to fifteen miles along the dirt road—a threat of such magnitude that the excitement of the radio operator was in every way warranted.

The situation patently required more than our two aircraft. Since I had the only radio that worked, I hand-signaled to Timberlake what I wanted him to do: bomb the end of the column while I hit up ahead. We were lucky in that each of us found the target with our bombs. We neatly buttoned them up with bomb craters and knocked-out vehicles at either end; they couldn't go anywhere. Then I sent a "May Day"—a general signal for help. Repeating it at intervals for thirty or forty minutes while we waited for a response, we circled the column, keeping clear of its antiaircraft guns. We did not fire on it unless vehicles tried to pass those blocking them ahead or to disperse off the narrow road. As soon as one moved, we would go down and strafe it, leaving the rest alone to conserve ammunition.

Then my May Day finally raised a flyer over Japan—one going in to land at the Itazuke base in anticipation of the storm approaching Japan. When he answered, I described the situation and requested all available aircraft. I also called the radio jeep and told him to have Taegu get all our aircraft up front as soon as possible.

It was a little like one of those early western movies with the covered-wagon train, surrounded by Indians, waiting for the U.S. Cavalry. You knew for sure the mounted heroes would get there in time. I felt the same certainty now; the Communist armored column had no place to go.

Within another half hour they got there. I instructed them to circle the enemy and do exactly as we had until more help arrived. Timberlake and I had to go back and refuel, so they continued our holding tactics until the planes began arriving from Japan. In came F-82s, F-80s, B-26s—apparently everything flyable. They brought the big punch, and the greater destruction began.

I flew three separate missions attacking that armored column that day. By the last the road through the hills was outlined by burning vehicles. There was little wind, and the smoke rose vertically for miles. By nightfall the whole armored division was totally destroyed.

I went back to the airfield with mingled emotions. It clearly was a victory of great importance. General Partridge later described it, probably too generously, as one of the turning points of the war. If the Red armor had been able to break through to the south, it could have split the UN forces in two and perhaps driven us clear out of Korea. But now that armed might was a pile of smoking junk. I was weary yet exhilarated. Optimistically I told my men back at Taegu that we already were in the home-stretch: the Korean "police action" was about over.

No one was ever more wrong.

X

Our strange little outfit gradually shaped up. In the process no one was more valuable than Capt. Red Varner, who in years gone by had been a crew chief for Hap Arnold. Red was known to all the veterans in the Air Force and was on first-name terms with most of the general officers. Though we thought him a bit old— he was around fifty—for an operation like ours, we soon found that he could pay his way. Like all experienced service operators, he knew every rope and how to pull it. He thought straight as a ruler. But best, his unmilitary antics kept up the morale of the whole organization.

On gloomy days when we were grounded or when Communist troops came perilously close to the field, Red used to regale us with stories of his amorous exploits and dispel the tension. The way he told it, every Korean girl between the ages of six and sixty used to trail him around like his shadow, allowing him no peace at all whenever he stepped off the field. Our theory was that, if any chasing was being done, Red was the pursuer, not the pursued. This resulted in this salty old member of our outfit becoming known as "Birddog" Varner.

Red became our initial procurement and ground-maintenance officer, and did a marvelous job in keeping our aircraft flying under the worst possible conditions. He was as handy in other fields. We had side holsters for our pistols, quite inconvenient in an aircraft, and we had been wishing for shoulder holsters. Speaking lightly, Red volunteered one night to get us some. He disappeared and two hours later came back with shoulder holsters for all of us. I never asked where he had got them.

One night he invited me to the operations shack for some Korean beer. Wondering where he had got it, I followed him. Out on the porch of our dilapidated operations shack, in the weak light of one bare electric bulb, the Korean and American pilots sat around a small table downing a few bottles of Korean beer. One of our boys was using his hands in wild gestures, trying to make himself understood to a laughing Korean pilot. Another Korean pilot, always polite and respectful toward General Kim, who was with us that night, was formally pouring the General a beer. Red grabbed it out of his hand, grinned down at the General, and poured it himself. "I'll take care of the Old Man, Johnny," he roared—and if I ever worried much about the ice not breaking between Korean and American flyers, I stopped right then. Some people have a genius for this sort of thing, and Red was one of them. Though a number of these Korean boys had flown Japanese Zeros against our air force during World War II not so many years before, the subject was never brought up.

Red was at his most characteristic when a planeload of stars, conducted by General Vandenberg, chief of staff of the U.S. Air Force, and General Stratemeyer, commanding general of the Eastern Air Force, visited us. Everyone climbed into his best togs, but we still were a sorry-looking lot. The men were tired and bleary-eyed from lack of sleep, and needed shaves. Yet that was to be expected up here close to the lines, and I was not too concerned—until I saw Red. He was wearing a pair of rubber Korean boots, and on his head was a black Korean stovepipe hat with his captain's bars pinned to it. General Vandenberg saw him and looked startled. Then he recognized the old-timer and began to grin, finally laughing as he greeted Red warmly. I'm afraid it was one of the few laughs the Chief had in those grim days.

Try as I might, I never could steel myself for Red's harmless and cockeyed flaunting of military manners. Months later when General Stratemeyer dropped in again, Red, this time more or less in uniform, met him on the field and slapped him hard on the back. I saw the poor General wince. Then Red shouted, so loud everyone on the field could hear, as well as probably a few Communist guerrillas in the hills, "When are you going to promote me, you old s.o.b.?" I gritted my teeth and waited for the explosion, but it didn't come. There was laughter instead. Red had been a good friend of the General's when I was in high school. Besides, he had a way of calling you an s.o.b. that made it sound like a warm and affectionate compliment.

Our routine at the field, always changing with the fluctuations on the front lines, had us working around the clock. My night's sleep was usually a two- or three-hour catnap, and I was up before dawn. Our field was a stop for planes supplying UN ground units. When they arrived from Japan at daybreak, we had to handle their parking and fueling, and get them ready for daylight take-offs. The situation in the front line was so fluid that the latest information on troop dispositions and landing strips had to be passed on to the pilots flying the lift.

This function was in addition to the routine maintenance and organizational requirements of running a base—the "housekeeping." We were working hard on our living facilities, trying to make permanent quarters, when a heavy thunderstorm one afternoon sent torrents of rain flooding down the hillside where the sleeping tents had been dug in. Water cascaded over terrace after terrace, washing tents and personal possessions into a soggy, muddy mass at the edge of the field. Sorting them out, cleaning them up, and building again took a couple of wearisome days.

There were also the tricky personnel matters which come with command that have to do with sickness, discipline, or advice. Sometimes I thought that every man in the outfit had something special to take up with me come evening.

Most important—and time- and energy-consuming—were the close-support missions we were flying for the Army. These averaged two or three a day. Sometimes we would get as many as eight planes in the air to answer a call for a strike, but usually we were able to oblige with only three or four. I felt obligated to go on as many of these not precisely authorized flights as possible.

About three in the morning Major Britton of the Korean Military Advisory Group would arrive from his front-line units with information about where our troops were deployed and how we could help them on the next day's mission. Throughout the rest of the night and early morning people would come in with reports to brief me on the tactical situation and to help plan the next day's strikes.

One of the petty annoyances around the field were lights flashing in the mountains—obviously enemy guerrillas signaling. Although there wasn't much reason to believe they would attack the airfield immediately, they kept the men in a constant state of apprehension and jittery nerves. It's no fun when you know that the enemy is watching you from above as you work on an open field all day. We decided to organize a patrol and go see exactly what and where they were.

Few things can be more ridiculous than a bunch of airmen on night reconnaissance on the ground. Armed with carbines, ten of us left camp one night as darkness fell. We walked about fifteen miles up into the mountains, trying to move quietly in the pitch dark; but I suppose to any guerrillas who heard us we sounded like a herd of elephants. Somebody was always tripping, sliding, bumping, or falling.

One boy, an American airman, slipped off a ledge and went sliding down a 40-foot slope. We stood holding our breaths in the darkness, wondering if we'd seen the last of him. But apparently he'd landed on another ledge below. I heard a low call from the dark: "Major, where the hell are you?" and then a stream of eloquent, whispered profanity. After a moment's pause there came a plaintive, "Where the hell am *I*?" A brave UN reconnaissance party stood on a dark hill in South Korea and shook with barely controlled laughter.

A Negro enlisted man, a big, quiet fellow with an unusual

dignity about him and a matching amount of nerve, was with us. The normal procedure is for the man ahead to look back occasionally to count those behind, to check if anybody has been lost or knocked off. I kept missing one man and finally realized that it was the Negro, whom I couldn't see. I asked him to smile once in a while so I could know that he was there. I immediately thought it might sound as though I were mocking his color, but he understood my apprehension apparently, for later he assured me voluntarily that he knew that I was just looking out for him.

At last we saw some movement which might have been guerrillas, but it was away from our camp; so without bothering them we stumbled back down and told the men not to worry. One valuable piece of intelligence came from the expedition: we picked out the peak from which the enemy was observing our activities during the day. Shortly after when Army antiaircraft moved in in a company to protect us with 20- and 40-millimeter guns, we took care of this peak. The captain in charge, wanting to test his guns, asked me what he could use for a target. I pointed out this mountain, and they laid a dozen shells right on its top. No more lights ever flashed from it.

"Luxurious" is not the word I would use for our Taegu establishment. Beside having no large tents, we had very few sleeping bags and even fewer cots. Mine developed a split about three feet long down the middle. I gave up on it and slept on the ground in a bag. Standing on my sleeping bag, I would undress down to my T shirt and shorts, roll my clothes up, stick them down in the sleeping bag, climb into it myself, and pull the flap up over. Rain or shine this was my nocturnal routine.

One night, after climbing into the bag and zipping it up, I felt something cold and clammy move up my leg, hitting it in three different places. The next instant I was out of my bag, my heart banging against my teeth. A friendly frog had been my undoing. Then I looked again incredulously: the bag was still three-quarters

94

zipped up! It is impossible for a man to get out of so small a hole, but momentary panic had allowed me to do it easily.

Our first ground tragedy at Taegu was occasioned by our old field stoves. In attempting to light one in the early hours of the morning, a staff-sergeant cook exploded the gasoline it used for fuel. I had just lain down in a pup tent on the flight line when I saw the flash.

When I got to the mess tent, the medics already were tending him. It was one of our first close confrontations with violent tragedy, and the men stood around in silent groups. Wearing only a T shirt, he had been so badly burned that I could hardly recognize him. He was sitting in a chair, unable to lie down, his flesh hanging from him in strips. I spoke to him the empty assurance that he would be all right, that we would fly him to Japan the next day. His eyes rolled up in his blackened face to look at me, but he was in such shock that I doubt if I got through to him.

I couldn't show the emotion I felt; this was no time to have the men talking and brooding about death. I sent them away quickly. With nothing more to be done I went back to my tent, sure that he was to die. Alone, I gave a silent prayer: "Not my will but Thine be done—" and took up my Bible. I had little light to read by, but it was reassuring just to hold the worn book in my hand.

The sergeant died a few days later in a hospital in Japan. I never heard anyone in the outfit discuss it.

Cargo carriers now started using our field to bring in supplies, equipment, and personnel for the forward ground units. In addition to our combat operations we had to see that these aircraft were unloaded, parked, and serviced. But immediately another problem arose. These heavier planes began wearing deep ruts in the runway. Taking off in an F-51 became a teeth-rattling experience a little like taxiing across a recently plowed cornfield.

But there is always a way. Major Britton had told me that

95

there was a lot of pierced steel planking around in Taegu which we could use to make excellent runways if we could get our hands on it. After World War II a lot of this planking had been taken to Korea and then abandoned. The natives had picked it up and used it to fence in their compounds. I told our Koreans that we needed all of it they could find. The next day they began bringing it in truckloads, and in two days we had all we needed. Had we asked permission and then negotiated, it would have taken weeks. We laid some five hundred feet of the pierced steel across the rutted mud and stopped wincing every time a big cargo plane came in.

In the air, puny spearhead though we were, we managed to keep thrusting at the enemy with a fair amount of effectiveness. We were carrying the explosive especially dreaded by roadbound military movements—thermite bombs. We would find the enemy and go in low before making the drop. The 500-pounders exploded burning magnesium in all directions, proving equally damaging to personnel and vehicles.

We gave close support to infantry divisions, particularly the Twenty-fourth. It had a number of light liaison aircraft used for artillery-target spotting. The "Dragon Fly Squadron," as they called themselves, would pick targets for us and direct the strike. We especially admired these boys in their tiny, unarmed planes, and we never refused their calls. Flying at no more than eighty or ninety miles per hour, they would spot a target and radio back to their regiment, which would pass the target information along to us. Sometimes these pilots, hovering over an enemy position, would get so frustrated by having no bombs or armament that they would shoot .45s and drop hand grenades on the enemy. One pilot I knew swooped low and in a frenzy of rage and frustration threw his tools—wrench, screw drivers, hammer—at a Communist gun emplacement.

One afternoon I proved an accidental delight to one of them when we were trying to prevent an enemy river crossing. He called to say that an element of troops had gotten across and were crouched in a culvert where a creek went under a roadway leading to the river. Coming down across a hill on a low pass, as I had to that afternoon, there was no way to pin-point a bomb hit. I had to depend on dispersion of my bomb blast to hit the target. I made two releases, one at a time, stretching them over a 500-yard area. By accident the second bomb hit directly in the underpass where the North Koreans were hiding.

The "dragon fly" went into ecstasies; he thought I had done it deliberately. He was so excited that he started to loop and roll his little plane, shouting, "You got the sons-of-bitches!" over and over on his radio.

It was in this area that a number of enemy barges were crossing the river loaded with troops. We attempted in every way we could to stop them, making frequent strikes against them, firing rockets, and strafing. The wooden barges would not sink, but the soldiers would jump overboard as quickly as they could and swim to shore. Those not able to swim, however, had to stay with the barge, and they had no protection whatever from our guns. Few escaped. It was a gruesome business; soon the river would be reddened twenty to thirty yards downstream from each barge. But still they kept coming—relentless hordes of men pressing across the river and hurling themselves on the Twenty-fourth Division.

George Haines, formerly our radar operator, was with me one day when we caught three in midstream and made pass after pass at the helpless targets. He was deeply distressed, gray of face, and shaking by the time we returned to base. I spent a long time with him walking up and down the flight line, trying to wipe from his mind the picture of bloody slaughter. It was as if suddenly he realized what war was all about. I assured him that the killing we had done was our obligation, that we had no choice. We were here to destroy as many of the enemy as possible. We actually *sought* mass destruction of enemy military personnel; it was the only way to save what we believed in. Without that deeply rooted conviction in both our purpose and method, an American pilot might well go mad after such a mission as this one.

After our talk he seemed less shaken, firmer of mind again. I knew his convictions matched my own. Remorse was not justified —especially in his case, for he was an intelligent and humane pilot. Oddly enough George had gone to Korea with us as a radar controller. In the economy cut in 1948 he had been removed from flying status and given ground duty, thus saving on his flight pay, gasoline, and other flight expenses. When Bout I was being organized, he volunteered to go along to try to operate the little portable radar set. He got a radar station going at Taegu just as orders came authorizing his return to flight status. We let him get some transitional training in F-51s around the field before he began flying missions—usually with me.

Hit on one mission, he had to make an emergency landing at Taejon; he had bashed in the front end of his wing and was low on fuel. As he waited for gasoline and assistance, some crew chiefs pasted some material over the leading edge of the wing, making it safe for one flight. In George's attempt to take off to return to Taegu the plane hit a deep rut, went out of control, and cracked up. George climbed out of it unharmed, and immediately afterward it blew up.

George came back to the base by jeep in a depressed state of mind. As he reported in, he apologized profusely for having lost an airplane. I told him that it wasn't essentially his fault and that what counted was that he had got back safely. But he knew the worth of an airplane and felt so strongly about our cause that he was wretched over the mishap. Some men fight because they're told to, some because they believe. George Haines was one of those who fully grasped the importance of our work in training this cadre of men who later would head an ever expanding ROK Air Force. It was one of the many things I loved him for.

A few days later George and I were returning from a mission in which I had expended all my ammo. We saw a YAK-9 about fifteen hundred feet above the ground strafing some American forward units along the road. I knew that George had plenty of ammunition and signaled that we would attack. I presumed, evidently erroneously, that George knew the procedure for such an attack: going in, I would draw the enemy onto my tail and make a turn to the left, letting him stay on me; then Haines was to make a turn to the right, intercept the aircraft, and as he had the only ammunition, shoot him.

I made the bounce and let the YAK-9 start after me. I kept looking over my left shoulder, wondering when George was going to hit him. When he didn't, I looked out over my other shoulder —to see George close on my wing. It was one of those cases where a new pilot, constantly drilled to stick to the lead airplane, got a little buck fever. All I could do was make a quick turn at the YAK-9 to try to bluff him. It worked; he headed for home before he was aware that no one was firing at him.

Back at base Haines was contrite. Once again I had to assure him that he'd have better luck next time. Unfortunately he never did; he was shot down the next time out. His aircraft hit on the edge of a clearing that was under enemy fire. Our ground forces —in this case Korean troops—made a thrust to recover him. They were close enough to see that his plane had been riddled. They couldn't see anyone in the cockpit, so they assumed that he was slumped down, dead. His body was never recovered.

The procedure we followed when a pilot—a friend—went down was an official—and a heartbreaking—one. The pilot's personal possessions were left intact that night. It was our way of saying, "Please, God, have the ground patrol report in that they've picked him up alive." The next day, when the pilot was reported either dead in the wreckage or missing, I would call in Mike Bellovin as adjutant and tell him to turn in a "missing-in-action" report. Bellovin and the first sergeant would gather the flyer's personal effects for shipment to next of kin. Even when Bellovin was absent, I would never let a flying officer, though he might be the missing pilot's best friend, handle his belongings. Nor would I ever let a flyer go near the scene of the crash.

I had been a minister. I hoped to be one again. I continued to think of myself, even here, participating in all this slaughter, as a man of God. Yet I knew full well that we could hold no memorial service, speak no prayer aloud, for our dead or missing friend. Any such service would have had a devastating effect on the morale of the pilots; they would have stood around with heads bowed thinking a dozen variations of, "This time it was George Haines; next time—me." George's name wasn't even mentioned around the field for days. It was as if we had never known a boy by that name. Then, perhaps two or three weeks later after the danger period had passed, his name crept back into our talk, his person back into our minds.

But I prayed for George Haines. I prayed for him while he lived, and I prayed for him as I watched his powerless plane plunge to the earth. To me only his body had returned to dust. As long as an airplane flies, George Haines remains alive in spirit and accomplishment.

I felt a particular grief for him: he reminded me much of Junior Loesch, lost over Germany years before—another fine boy with every reason to live. Again I had that heavy feeling of guilt that follows the loss of a fellow combatant: he had expended himself all the way, given everything; I had held back in some way not to meet a like fate. That night I touched my worn Bible and counseled myself as Paul had to the Corinthians: "Watch ye, stand fast in the faith, quit you like men, be strong."

The death of George Haines increased my concern about a lack of religious services at the post. We weren't big enough to warrant chaplains on our table of organization, and I felt strongly that I could not formally engage in such duties. The commanding officer cannot also be the chaplain; the two identities are too different.

Thus, when a Protestant missionary named Reverend Campbell, who had been in Korea for many years, visited us, I invited him to conduct regular chapel services on Sundays.

Thereafter he would appear every week with a little choir of Koreans, and in a dilapidated hangar everyone—Protestants, Catholics, and Jews—would gather for services. The sermon was in English, and the hymns were sung in two languages simultaneously. Being of different tongues and of different faiths mattered not at all.

xi

Our last weeks at Taegu were turbulent ones. I had my first of many meetings with President Syngman Rhee. Then the Republic of Korea Air Force died—though it was resurrected soon after.

While our activities were a mere rattle in the thunder of the over-all campaign, we were attracting a degree of attention. Ambassador John Muccio and the first secretary of the embassy, Dr. John Noble, came to visit us. These two had been sent to Seoul when it was simply the capital of Korea only to see it become the hot spot of the world. They had remained in Seoul when the Communists made their initial attack to see that all Americans connected with their staff be airlifted out. They themselves barely escaped, for by the time they made a break for safety the Han River bridge had been blown up. They had to wade the river, leaving all their possessions behind.

Dr. Noble was frequently at the airfield. He wanted desperately to see the front lines from the air and begged me to take him up in an F-51, even suggesting that I could sit in his lap in the single seat and fly it from on top of him. I had to take him out on the line to my F-51 to prove that this would be impossible even for midgets. It was he who first suggested that I call on President Rhee. He explained that the President was under a great strain and that it might be some assurance to him if I were to tell him about our efforts to train his Korean air force.

Dr. Noble accompanied me to the house in which the President and Madame Rhee were living in Taegu after having escaped from the Communist invasion of Seoul. It was an unpretentious

European-type house with a pair of uniformed guards outside and one within—rather light security, I thought, for the head of a country under siege. At the door I was asked to leave my pistol, a Colt .45 in a shoulder holster, with the attendant. There were no other formalities before the interview.

We were shown into a modest living room, and in a few moments a small lady of middle years with a smiling, gracious manner entered from an inner room. Though Viennese, she wore an Oriental robe. Dr. Noble presented me to Madame Rhee.

She told us that the President was just rising from a nap and apologized for his not being on time to meet us. He had been deeply fatigued, but he was most anxious to hear about the progress of the ROK pilots. I was to find that this was typical of the way in which she assisted him and helped ease his burdens—with a glowing devotion that warmed everyone she encountered.

We chatted for a few minutes; then the door opened again, and through it came the subject of my term paper at Ohio University a million years ago.

Here surely was the greatest man I would ever know. Seventy-five years before he had been born into a medieval world, in a nation four thousand years old. Most of his life he had struggled to break Japan's death grip on the land of Korea. He had suffered six years in prison, seven months of which were spent in solitary confinement and torture. Here, in prison, his conversion to Christianity had become his strength, and he had established a lifelong pattern of opening and closing each day with a prayer.

He had suffered decades of exile in Europe, Hawaii, and the United States. At Princeton, whence he graduated in 1910, Woodrow Wilson used jokingly to introduce this dedicated and single-minded undergraduate as "the future redeemer of Korean independence." All over America for decades he had been vaguely known and even ridiculed as "the champion of that lost cause in Korea." He has dealt, in the name of Korean independence, with at least six Presidents of the United States, from Woodrow Wilson

103

to Dwight D. Eisenhower. He was in prison in Seoul with an established record of political action and idealism already behind him when Franklin Roosevelt was still a Harvard undergraduate. He has been persistently active for more than half a century in the name of a single cause. Only one other contemporary figure—Winston Churchill—has lived as long and figured as prominently in world affairs.

He was about five feet eight inches tall and thus a bit over the height of the average Korean, white-haired, and solidly built. My first impression was of a pervading kindness. His studious eyes seemed those of a visionary with great personal magnetism. While his voice was that of an old man, the eyes were those of a dignified young one.

When he spoke, his perfect English carried only a trace of inflection. He was glad to have me working with *his* boys, a designation expressed with endearing fondness, and only wished that I had gotten here sooner. How were they doing? Could they fly the plane yet?

I answered that they were progressing rapidly and would prove the equal of everyone's hopes. This appeared to please him considerably yet at the same time to add to the deep impatience locked within him, which occasionally was evidenced by a harried look and a deep frown.

"If only it had come more quickly," he said, almost distraught, "we might have been able to stop them." He mentioned that his own military intelligence had told him months before of the impending Communist attack, even predicting that it would come in June of 1950, but that no one would believe him. Whenever he referred to the Reds it was usually as "they" or "them," as though the enemy were so fixed in his consciousness that further identification wasn't needed.

The strained, harried look, the moments of distraction, the old-man's voice, all spoke of sleepless nights and fearful tensions. (Interestingly enough, during my many meetings with Rhee later on, when the war was going better for the ROK cause, I noticed that the cracked, "old-man" quality disappeared entirely from his voice.) But through his fatigue showed an amazing vitality and his inspiring spirit of dedication to a cause.

As for Madame Rhee, it was fascinating to hear this gentle Occidental speak of the Koreans as "*my* people" with such warmth. Originally from Vienna, she spoke perfect English, and every moment of our discussion manifested her concern for her husband's health and well-being. Later, during the winter, in another such interview as this one, I watched her put a shawl gently around Dr. Rhee's shoulders with the tenderest solicitude and lovingly pat it into place. That little scene will always remain in my mind to symbolize their marvelous relationship.

As we talked, I watched his hands. They seemed gnarled and appeared to bother him even now. I remembered that these were the hands—holding tenaciously onto Korean freedom—that the Japanese had tortured by placing split bamboo sticks between the fingers and then binding them tightly together.

When he asked if more planes were to come, Dr. Noble interjected that this was beyond my capability to answer. As an expression of beleaguerment once more crossed the remarkable eyes, Dr. Noble directed the course of conversation to less sensitive ground by asking him to have his photograph taken with me.

The President gave the short sigh of a strong but frustrated man and replied that he would be honored, and the conversation turned to the general war picture. When we parted twenty minutes later, I was sure that I had met a man upon whom history will confer many honors. In his integrity, dedication, moral fiber, and true humility he synthesized all that must be found worthy in the final summing up.

Then circumstances beyond my control began slowly to strangle the Korean air force to a premature death.

As the activities around the airfield built up, it was obvious that we needed more personnel and vehicles to take care of unloading supplies, handling transient aircraft, and keeping our own F-51s in the air. Ours was still the sole working airfield in Korea.

One day late in July Col. Curtis Lowe appeared. He had been sent by General Partridge to take over the increasing airbase responsibilities so that I could concentrate solely on training the Korean pilots. Outranking me, he also took over command of the whole operation. Distressed by the amount of work and the few people to handle it, he soon began to receive men under his command. He asked us to turn over all our vehicles (including my jeep) and supplies to him, letting him take care of all maintenance.

Then an American fighter-bomber wing from the Philippine Islands was moved onto the field to operate from Taegu. The flyers arrived aboard the aircraft carrier *Boxer*, but it would be a matter of days before their F-51s could be unloaded. Being combat-ready, they were given ours. This was a severe blow to our morale, for my Koreans were almost to the point of becoming proficient enough to fly truly effective missions.

The Philippine squadron also took over the hangar facilities we had been painstakingly assembling since we arrived. Then some of the American newcomers tried to take the tents away from my Korean enlisted men. That did it! I told them to go and get their tents back in whatever way they chose; if they didn't succeed, I would come and help them. They went to one of their tents in which the arrivals had ensconced themselves, picked up men, cots, and belongings, threw them out on the hillside, and moved back in.

To put in mildly, there was obviously going to be friction between the two groups. The recently arrived Americans persisted in the attitude that now that they were here, the war was in the bag. This was a matter of no small annoyance to men who had been flying and fighting up and down the peninsula for some months. Also, I remembered the day that big armored column north of Taejon had been destroyed, and how I foolishly had thought that the Korean War was over then. Had I known that this column was just one of many divisions pushing south all over the peninsula, I would not have been so cocky.

I was also worried about our Korean insignia on planes an American organization was now flying. I kept trying to persuade them to put on the correct identification, but to no avail. I was told they were only going to use our planes for several days. Sure enough, trouble developed for which my poor ROK pilots, sitting in their tents gnashing their teeth, were blamed.

Members of the incoming unit went out to strafe some front-line positions. Instead—through a wrong direction from a ground controller—they strafed our own troops.

I was called in to advanced headquarters of the Fifth Air Force in Taegu and asked why the Korean air force wasn't better instructed. Furious, I answered that those were American pilots in planes with Korean markings. In truth, theirs had been an understandable mistake, for troops were scattered all over and pressure was heavy for close air support. But to have my outfit blamed for another's error added to my frustration.

Before and after this particular incident the Oriental markings on our planes made for considerable confusion among the unwary or the trigger-happy, and at times we were fired upon by UN aircraft. It was discomfiting, to say the least, to sit there under fire and not even be able to take evasive action (evasive action is considered hostile action). We could only hope that, if they missed on their first pass, they would recognize our F-51s on second glance and realize that we were friendly—though it must be admitted that this isn't precisely the word to describe our feelings just then.

The reverse of the situation pleased us more. At times, through a like misunderstanding of our planes' Oriental markings by Chinese troops, we could get close enough to fire upon them.

Now another blow was dealt Bout I. Colonel Lowe was instructed to form a fighter-bomber wing—Number 6002—and to absorb all my Americans. My spirits hit a new low. Every day or so I had to move the Koreans out of this building and out of that building, away from this spot and away from that spot, until finally they were all huddled in a tent at the edge of the field. There they must sit, silent and morose, watching others fly out to do battle with their country's enemy. The fact that they weren't quite ready for effective combat operations made their resentment at being shunted aside all the sharper. My upset was mainly over losing my American pilots, crew chiefs, and airmen. Once broken, an organization, especially one of such strange components as Bout I, like Humpty Dumpty, can never be fully put back together again. Transfers for specialists like Red Varner and death for fine pilots like Captain Hook and Lieutenant Smith, both of whom were killed within the next few months, were a cause for major despair.

I finally got word that made my gloomiest predictions come true: Bout I had been dissolved. We now were part of the 6002d Fighter-Bomber Squadron, Colonel Lowe commanding. He said that he wanted me for his staff as his operations officer. Concerned over the Koreans, I asked what would happen to them. I was told that there would be no more Korean air force.

All the planes transferred to the Koreans during the first days of the war were taken back. My Korean pilots sat in their tent and waited for the word. They would look at me, and I would look away. I don't believe it's much use merely to say that you're sorry.

One night a good friend came to the field—Don Nichols, chief of our Office of Strategic Intelligence in Korea. He too had been working with the Koreans for a long time and was a close friend of General Kim Chung Yul's. He wanted to know about the future of the Korean air force. I responded dismally that it had none, unless something were done quickly.

Nichols suggested that we go and talk to General Kim, who by this time had been put clear off the field. We went into Taegu to see him one evening in the latter part of July. At dusk he met us at the door of the private home where he was staying. As always we took off our shoes and, inside, sat on the floor to talk. General Kim looked depressed, even distraught. Later I was to discover that his entire family had been trapped in Seoul by the Communists. He didn't know where they were or what had happened to them. Yet he didn't mention a word of his great sorrow to us that night. He spoke only of the Korean air force. When were they to get their planes back? I could only answer sadly that I did not know. This discouraged him the more. He had about five thousand men in his air force scattered around a number of fields, where they were principally engaged in maintenance and housekeeping for American installations. Only the pilots of our Bout I had combat planes to fly—and now even these had been taken away. Utterly downcast, he said that, if I would give the word, he would dissolve the Korean air force and turn its members over to the Korean army, letting them fight on the ground, where they were wanted.

It was a major decision that I wouldn't let him make until I'd exhausted all the possibilities of reviving the idea of a ROK Air Force. We talked late into the night, and it was finally decided that I would go to General Timberlake next day to ask for help. The General was now the deputy commander of the Fifth Air Force, having moved into Taegu to run a part of headquarters, now located there.

I went to see him the next morning with Don Nichols. He was working under a lot of pressure, but he received us with his customary patience. I skipped the preliminaries and launched right in. I pleaded with him to let me take what remained of the Korean aircraft and the pilots, and go someplace to start again. I was relieved at the outset that he didn't cut me off, that he seemed receptive. I stressed what a fine potential the ROK pilots had, how well they had performed considering their few hours in the air, how great was their dedication to the job and to Korean independence. All the time, in the quiet of my mind, I prayed that the General would understand what I considered to be the importance of this little group. It concerned not only the immediate fighting of the war itself but the pride and morale and future of the Korean people.

He listened patiently and without response to my oratory. When I had finished, there was a moment of silence in the room. Then he smiled slightly, nodded, and made one of those characteristically swift and incisive one-word decisions: yes!

I may have been foolish, but, exhilarated by success, I stayed for a moment and pressed my luck with another request. Could I lead the Korean pilots into combat? Could I, at least in part, train them in this way? I knew that my Korean outfit—that the whole idea of a ROK Air Force—would never gain a secure position and recognition in the over-all command setup unless they earned a combat record, and quickly.

Once again my request was granted. Clearly General Timberlake still held to his conviction of the importance of a Korean air force. He told me I could have the remaining six F-51s. The aircraft belonging to the Philippine squadron had arrived in so much better shape that they planned to abandon the Korean planes. I could have one other officer and a few enlisted men, and take my ROK flyers where we wouldn't be interfered with.

I returned to the base happier than I'd been in weeks, but my elation was as nothing compared with the excited shouts and broad grins of my no longer grounded Korean pilots. Then, somewhat dubiously, I called for volunteers among our American officers to go with me. None offered except Mike Bellovin—ingenious and faithful Mike, as eager as I to stay with the Koreans. On the strength of his volunteering I was able to muster thirty enlisted men to work under him. We weren't allowed any equipment because it had all been taken back by the 6002d. We had no tents, only one cookstove, and very meager supplies. But we had the six F-51s, and we were operational again. That night we had a drink to General Timberlake, our sponsor.

My instructions, received almost immediately, were to set up an airfield at Sachon, on the southeastern coast. My primary duty was to maintain the field as an emergency airstrip for the United States Air Force. As a secondary job I could train pilots for the Korean air force.

Mike and I got our group aboard some old trucks which in operation violated every principle of physics. I learned to respect the Koreans for their ability to keep this junk running as we rattled down to the new field. Parts of hoods were missing, the threads were showing on tires, and a number of old batteries were connected in series to supply power.

At "K-4"—our field's military designation—we all moved into some old buildings by the hard-surface runway, Americans and Koreans bunking near each other. I planned to ferry all six of the F-51s down myself, one at a time, to this excellent field built by the Japanese. By the time I arrived with the first one the men had made themselves comfortable and were cleaning up the strip.

But I was met on the runway by Mike Bellovin with terrible news. We would have to evacuate! The enemy had broken through in a serious attack to the west. The Twenty-fourth Division, sent down to the Sachon area for a rest, was being pulled back, and the field would soon fall. We had to get going again.

A moment later a couple of Army men drove up in a jeep and saw the F-51 on the runway. They asked if I would strafe one of our own trucks and a gun that had to be left behind. During the retreat the truck had broken down, and they weren't able to get the gun out. They didn't want either to become Red property. Sadly I took off, found the equipment, and shot it up. This was the one mission I flew from that particular strip, the finest our little outfit had ever had, if only for a day—and it was against a beautiful American truck we would have given our eyeteeth to possess.

I told Mike to pack up and get our group out as quickly as possible. They were to head east and locate where they could. Forced to leave quickly, they had to destroy many of their personal possessions—portable radios, clothing, souvenirs; but as I was to discover later, they saved the "Old Man's" books!

While we were still at Taegu, all my gear had been brought from Japan, including a foot locker full of history and religious books. Before leaving the States for Japan I had anticipated having a lot of spare time for reading, but most of the books had remained unopened. I had sent them down to Sachon with instructions for Mike not to worry if they were lost. But when the men evacuated, they took particular care to save the foot locker. Having seen the books, perhaps having thumbed through them, they gave them a significance which I didn't fully appreciate until later in the war: those books had become a symbol of the ideas for which they were fighting—peace, knowledge, a better way of life—and they did everything they could to bring them through, even though many of their own effects had to be abandoned.

This strange little incident of war will probably live longer in my mind than a hundred missions.

My F-51 had to be delivered to a safe field, but I was loath to start the trip that would separate us. I stayed on the ground until everything had been loaded up. As our trucks moved out, I could detect guerrilla activity in the hills. I went up and circled the convoy to discourage attack. Below, it stretched out like a line of children's toys on the road to Chinju. I thought of what each of those small blocks represented and of the men in them, each now as close to me as though I had always known him. Now I didn't know where they were going or if I would ever see them again. In my mind's eye I saw them sitting glumly in the trucks—especially the Koreans, frustrated once again in their desire to strike a blow for their country.

I thought of the redoubtable Mike, now the only American officer. I knew that, if anyone could keep them together and find another field, Mike would. But ahead lay difficulties enough to defeat even his resourceful spirit—no field, no food, few friends. Would my next word about our unit be that it was a bloody pile of smoking junk on some shot-up road? My eyes began to smart in the dying sunlight. The gauge showed that I was getting low on fuel. With a last look down at the crawling cavalcade, I swung off toward Taegu.

xii

For a few days I was like a hen without her chicks, a fretful mother separated from her brood. My affection for the infant ROK Air Force was exactly that of a parent—fierce, possessive, single-minded. And at this moment my boys were wandering I knew not where in the Korean hills.

I was just as concerned about the safety of our aircraft in Taegu, principally about the danger of some American commander with an acquisitive eye; but they were waiting when I got there. Perhaps they looked too beat up to attract much attention, but mechanics of the 6002d on the field were working on them to make them more flyable. As I was examining the planes, one of the men laughingly repeated that cliché of the old war movies: "Sir—you're not going to send that boy up in that old crate?"

Then two of my enlisted men, Sergeants Schuitt and Engel, arrived with depressing news. Our group had found the Twenty-fourth Division but had had to strike out on its own because the division was retreating. They added that the men were short of food and, despite Mike Bellovin's efforts to keep their spirits up, discouraged from not knowing what was to become of them. I saw that it was time to get back to them. I didn't like to leave the planes again, but there was nothing else to do but go look for my band of gypsies.

A number of transport aircraft were delivering radio jeeps to the field. Having no authorized equipment, I wasn't scheduled to get one. But if I was to join my men, I had to have a jeep; it was as simple as that. I went to a plane where a jeep was being unloaded

113

and asked the sergeant in charge if it was mine. He looked at a form, answering that he wasn't sure whom it was for; it was merely marked for the Fifth Air Force. I told him that it must be mine, jumped into it, and drove away. I then went to the motor pool and latched onto a quarter-ton trailer. The motor-pool officer came out and wanted to know what was going on. I told him I had a job that needed a trailer, and before he could object, I drove off with it. From there I went around to the mess hall and had the trailer loaded up with C rations. Picking up my sergeants, I left rapidly.

Ordinarily the drive to where Schuitt and Engel had left the others should have taken an afternoon. Driving at night, we were still on the road after fifteen hours. Going through the mountains, we got lost; we got stuck in the mud; we forded streams. While we were crossing one, the water came up over the engine and the jeep stalled. We had to jump into the water and push it out with the assistance of some Koreans.

It was interesting how at first the Koreans on the bank stood there staring blankly at our stalled and flooded jeep, not making a move in our direction until I jumped out into the stream. Then, without hesitation and without our asking, they waded out to help us push. I had learned earlier that this was the secret formula for getting Korean aid: do it yourself first, and they would quickly lend a hand.

Next we had trouble with the radiator. Luckily a young fellow connected with the local military constabulary in a small village directed us to the house of an old man who had soldering equipment—where he got it I don't know. For a couple of cigarettes he went to work. While he was heating his soldering iron and all the time he was working on the radiator, his wife sat behind him, fanning him. It was a nice example of the Oriental wife taking care of the comfort of her husband.

At other breakdowns in small villages the native children would invariably crowd around the jeep, jabbering, rubbernecking, and touching the mysterious machine. Their elders, quiet and dignified,

114

would shoo them away only to fall victim, no matter how hard they tried to control themselves, to their own curiosity. In no time at all they would be crowding around closer than had the children.

I was amazed at how little the people in some of the small mountain towns seemed to be affected by or even concerned with the war raging on their very doorstep. The big Communist armies were literally a few miles and several hills away, and yet these simple people went their daily rounds—working in the rice fields, gathering wood, patching up their thatched homes. It was as if they had not been informed of the war. Certainly the political ideologies involved meant nothing to them; they had little to lose in the way of tangible wealth under either system. Yet this apathy was oddly disturbing to me. Bumping over a dirt road in the Korean hills, I suddenly thought back to quiet, peaceful Marietta, Ohio, after World War II. There too I had felt uncomfortably out of tune with a community securely isolated from the war I had just experienced. A chilling thought gripped my mind: perhaps it was I—perhaps I was the one out of step! Right then and there, in the silence of my mind, I prayed to God that I wasn't getting so war-oriented, so accustomed to being destruction's instrument, that I would forever feel restless and misplaced in a quiet, isolated community at peace.

On we went, looking for our lost Korean air force. I was beginning to think we'd never find Mike and his mixed lot when suddenly there they were, moseying along the road with men and equipment piled high on the four forlorn trucks. In all the history of war there probably have been no such helpless- and hapless-looking combatants.

Their fatigue uniforms were muddy. A couple of men wore driver's goggles, picked up heaven knows where. Most of them lay inert, like so many rag dolls, on top of mountains of luggage. The four trucks were strung out over a 5-mile area. But to me they looked like West Pointers on parade, and they seemed heartened that the "Old Man" was there to sweat it out with them.

We were together, but the problem was where to go. One of the Koreans spoke of a former Japanese naval base at Chinhae which had some old quonset huts. As we had no tents, the main thing was to find shelter, and this sounded promising. We turned around and started along the southern coast.

At Chinhae we found the abandoned huts as advertised, plus a usable administration building. The only drawback to the quarters we did not discover until nightfall, and it was a problem we could only solve with some strong insecticide: the place was infested with fleas. The susceptible suffered agonies that first night; the next morning my body was covered by nearly three hundred welts the size of a dime. But I almost forgot that I itched, such was my joy at finding an Army contingent nearby from which we could draw food. Our housekeeping worries were over.

The only problem was that the runway was too short. At one end of it there was the sea wall, and at the other some rice paddies. And no matter how many times I paced off the field, it only measured 2,750 feet. According to all technical orders the F-51 shouldn't be operated off less than 3,200 feet of runway. But there was nothing to do but try it.

I hitchhiked back to Taegu, climbed into one of our F-51s, and came back to Chinhae. As I circled warily above the field, it looked much smaller than when I'd paced it off on the ground. It also narrowed at the end, and the skeleton of an enormous steel hangar never finished by the Japanese squatted menacingly on one side of the strip. From the air it looked as if that hangar had moved 10 yards out into the runway.

I took one last, long look.

Then I increased the rpm on the prop so that I could gun her and pull out if necessary, lowered the landing gear and flaps, and turned the plane in a long approach so as to have plenty of room to jockey about. I flew in very slowly—just above stalling speed. When the sea wall bordering the field was just ahead of me, I cut the throttle, and the plane, traveling so slowly, settled immediately in a three-point landing, the wheels touching just a few yards the other side of the wall. I began to tap my brakes immediately, but I still didn't know exactly where I was on the field because it is impossible to see over the engine of an F-51 when it is on the ground with the tail down. Slowing to a stop, I turned the plane slightly sideways to look for the end of the runway.

To my amazement I was hundreds of yards away from the end of the runway. In fact, in my extreme caution I had managed to stop the plane only a few feet past the middle of the airstrip. Some of the ground observers of my landing told me later that their worry had been on another account—that I would hang myself up on that sea wall!

Still, I knew that this short strip was no place for the Koreans to practice; we had so few planes, and none could be replaced. Even now something might be happening to our five other ships at Taegu—batteries going dead, tires flat, air leaking out of landing struts, coolant out of radiators. Back I went to Taegu to bring down another, planning to shuttle back for the remaining four as soon as I could. I did not plan to fly them operationally immediately—only to put them in the hands of the Koreans and let them maintain them and get them in shape again. Then, if I could dig up another American pilot somewhere, we could start our fighting-training operation once more.

Another pilot arrived out of the blue. Capt. Harold Wilson was a public-information officer going around from base to base with a photographer, getting stories about Air Force operations. Hearing about our treks from one field to another, he visited us in search of a story. But when he saw the two F-51s idle on the strip and learned how badly we needed additional pilots, he asked if he could lend a hand. If he could fly an F-51, he could start the very next day, helping me ferry down the four left at Taegu. Though at first his was to be a temporary helping hand, Hal Wilson never left us. Ultimately he requested a permanent transfer to our outfit, and over the months he and I flew over fifty missions together.

At this time our ground troops were in desperate need of support from the air. One morning an Army liaison aircraft saw our 51s on the field. Landing, the observer reported that the Twenty-fifth Division, stationed at Masan, 10 miles from Chinhae, was in need of close support. All our divisions were now retreating south, as we were going into that holding phase of the Korean War called the "Pusan Perimeter"—hanging on by our fingernails under the gigantic press of men and armor the Communists were pouring south in what they hoped would be a finishing blow.

"They're giving us a bad time, Major," the observer added. His casual phrase meant that we were taking heavy casualties on the ground. "Will you fly a strike? I've got some good targets."

I had some .50-caliber ammunition and a few rockets; I would do what I could. He gave me the directions and I took off.

Flying over the enemy lines to where the target was indicated, I came around the knoll of a hill. About thirty North Korean troops were walking in file along a wall separating two rice paddies. They were lined up perfectly in my gun sight, and my finger was poised over the button on the stick as I flew.

I pushed it, and my six .50-caliber guns roared in unison as I swept along the file. The Red soldiers toppled over like duckpins falling. At the end of the sweep I looked back and saw that nothing was left alive on that dike.

I looked back only that once to check the result of my attack. I didn't look back in the emotional sense, to consider what I had done. It was better left behind. Strafing allows no time to think, less to regret or philosophize. The pass is so quick and the attacker's whole being is locked in such a deadly moment of concentration that there is no time for thought. It is a type of hypnosis, and it leads the pilot immediately on in search of the next target, mind blank to the destruction tumbled in his wake.

The thinking—the full realization of the act committed—comes later. It is then that a man must be sustained by conviction. I had worked out to my satisfaction, lying awake nights and sweating it out, that I was doing the right thing. I believed that the North

118

Koreans had been completely and fervently indoctrinated with a brutal "means-to-an-end" philosophy during the five years since the Communists had moved in. All men are capable of brutality, but when a political system encourages it, particularly among the farming and peasant peoples, the animal comes to dominate the human being. People whose whole lives have been spent drudging on poor land for a marginal survival are easily stirred to hatred, especially against those whom they believe to be their oppressors. The Communists are past masters at setting up these oppressor symbols—in this case the "Western imperialists" and the "greedy American capitalists." Now their hate campaign had been so successful as to set brother against brother in a terrible civil war.

When hate and fear are the only bonds between people, eventually they must turn on and destroy one another, as history has proved and is still proving. But we cannot wait for this to happen; too much that is good will be killed before the frenzy ends.

Yet where there is a capacity for hate, there is an equal potential for love. It was our loss that hate dominated the North Koreans, our double loss that we had to kill them. I felt sorrow for them in my heart, and my prayer was that in another life they would be forgiven and find a better way.

But we had lost the opportunity that had existed earlier to preclude hate with love. That earlier opportunity, ironically for me, is symbolized in the role of a minister who propounds love, compassion, generosity, charity; hate wilts before these. But the chance had come and gone. Hate had flourished and was threatening all of us. My duty now was to kill to stamp it out.

I never hated the men I killed, nor can I honestly say that I loved them. I only pitied what they had become. For many circumstances, some beyond their control, dictated that they must march in file, shoot guns, kill other Koreans against whom they should have borne no malice. I would have made no attempt to judge the enemy soldiers, such as those I had killed, even if the very act of annihilating them had not disqualified me from judgment. In the final analysis I am no better or worse than they—

just luckier in that the love people gave me early in life caused my spirit to grow and stilled the hate.

Many men came back feeling guilty from missions like the one I had just made. They felt guilty because they had hated while killing, and hate is a shattering emotion. To me it was a job that had to be done. Having made the adjustment, I stuck doggedly to it, which in time gave me a reputation for coldness. I saw it only as an indication that I was not experiencing superficial qualms of conscience.

This philosophy might not work for someone else, but it was the product of what I am, the experience I've had, what I believe. I am still working on it, examining circumstances, rationalizing. But I always come to the same conclusion: that it was for me to do. . . .

I got back to the field. The Army liaison pilot asked, "Well, how'd you do?"

"Thirty troops taken care of."

"Good! Now I've got another target for you."

Another—always another. I took the ammunition out of our second plane and went after it.

I had planned for a small vessel to come into the harbor at Sachon with food, ammunition, and gasoline. After our move I requested that the supplies be rerouted over to Chinhae. They didn't arrive. We were running out of food and had little ammunition, and I was quickly expending what we did have on these ever increasing support missions.

I inquired at headquarters where our supplies were. The answer staggered me: Since we had no official function—weren't maintaining an emergency strip for the Fifth Air Force—they didn't think we needed any supplies! Some bright young officer of the Fifth Air Force had concluded that we were no longer eligible for logistic support. I yelled, cajoled, threatened, begged—and it was finally agreed a boat would bring us what we needed—C rations, ammunition, bombs, and fuel. It did, and promptly.

120

The Twenty-fifth's demands for close-support missions grew until I was answering a half dozen calls a day. We were only a few miles from the front lines. After taking off, by the time I went through the cockpit procedure—getting my landing gear up, getting my control settings, getting my gun switches and my bomb-release switches set, making a radio call to the liaison officer who controlled flights over the division area—we would be in enemy territory and ready to go to work.

I became quite familiar with Twenty-fifth Division's operations, and the coordination between ground and air became excellent. General Kean sent a radio van to give me direct communications with their headquarters. Then he laid two field telephones down to make sure that, if one went out, the other would keep us in contact. From his headquarters an air officer would call for a mission, and within seconds I would be off the ground and flying toward the target. It became a precisely timed operation.

On one occasion a patrol of fifteen men was cut off. Getting their exact location and predicament on the radio, I was able to strafe a path for them back to their own lines. They survived for the day at least. Another time I got a call from the 187th Regimental Combat Team, up near Haman. They were trapped in a valley. Flying over them, I could see them motioning and waving. Circling lower, I saw exactly how they were trapped and where the enemy troops were positioned. I made a few straight passes, dove low across the ridges, and managed to knock out enough of the enemy to let the team make it back.

On a similar close-support mission I ran out of ammunition to shoot. I tried to distract and scare the Reds by taking the plane down to treetop level over troops I could spot on the ridge. (I came back from this mission with leaves in my radiator scoop—cut up and thrown back by the propeller.) Finally I took off a shoe and threw it. In combat any object coming out of an airplane looks like a bomb from the ground; I hoped that the enemy would think the shoe explosive and keep their heads down for just a few seconds more. Those few seconds, in which our troops could shoot or move, might prove invaluable. Whether the shoe trick worked I cannot say. Perhaps it backfired: perhaps this was the odd weapon that gave the Communists a chance to claim that we were using chemical warfare.

During this phase I was described by war correspondents as a one-man air force flying for the Army. This did not go down so well with me, but, more important, it displeased some of our wheels; they felt properly that we should be identified as part of the Air Force and not as an arm of the infantry, no matter how much close support we flew. I didn't care one way or the other; what did our label matter as long as we were doing the job? But in military parlance we became known as "freewheelers"—a dubious distinction, it too often seemed.

Along with a measure of pride, I was somewhat disturbed when the Army awarded me the Silver Star. It was given, like most decorations, because a particular bit of action had been accidentally observed. In war there are so many meritorious deeds which go unreported that the recognized ones are the exceptions, and sometimes even flukes. I happened to catch the eye of the commander of the Twenty-fifth Division one afternoon when an enemy ground gunner shot up my plane—the day after it had been mended back into flying condition. With a wing crippled, I could have justified hightailing it, but, vexed that I should have been hit again so soon, I rolled over on a wing and fought back. I managed to knock out the gun position and then expended the rest of my ammo strafing adjacent ground troops. General Kean happened to be in the area, saw only that I had knocked out an important ground installation, and wrote up a commendation.

In actuality, I had lost my temper and run the risk of losing a plane. Because our few aircraft were committed primarily to training purposes, I had been insistent that we take no unnecessary chances with them. The irony of being decorated through a violation of my own rule shook a mocking finger at me.

xiii

Despite the abbreviated runway and the omnipresent problem of supplies, the early fall of 1950 spent at Chinhae was the making of the ROK Air Force. Also, Dr. Syngman Rhee had temporary quarters nearby, and I cemented my friendship with the gallant old man.

Hal Wilson, the former public-information officer who had never ceased trying to get into combat, was making the most of it now that he had the chance. Up until this time my code sign, "MacIntosh One," was the only one heard in the area. The boys in the front-line radio control were much surprised and pleased when "MacIntosh Two!" suddenly started ringing out.

Close air support was a tricky business. Air Force spotters in radio jeeps, working with Army battalions, would scout out information about targets and send it back to the commanders to be acted upon. Then the commander's headquarters would radio us the target positions. If aircraft were sent, the jeep continued to assist, particularly if the target was camouflaged. Coming up as close as possible, the jeep would direct the pilot to the target and assist in the attack by correcting the plane's fire ("—strafe 50 yards to the right—", "—second ship bomb 10 yards left of that burst—"). Because friendly troops may be only a few yards from the position, pilots must use extreme care in following the spotter's instructions.

The Koreans were not yet able to fly from the short runway. About seventy miles to the east at the city of Pusan was a lengthy macadam strip being used only by cargo aircraft. We sent a couple of planes over there for the Koreans to practice with. We marked off this longer strip to correspond to the length of the field at Chinhae, and they attempted take-offs and landings within these boundaries. To land on a short strip, a pilot must have a perfect "feel" of his aircraft as well as be an accurate judge of speed, distance, and altitude. There was no other way for my ROK pilots to learn but by daily practice.

The short runway caught up with us in another way, with the result that we had to take in our already tight belts a few more notches. A Fifth Air Force C-47 flying in with supplies came in too low over the sea wall, knocked up its wheels, and skidded on its belly across the runway. Though there were no casualties except the plane, Fifth Air Force headquarters forbade all its aircraft to land on our field, which cut us off from our most valuable source of supplies and forced us to depend on ship and truck transport. Our only solace was that we were allowed to keep the C-47 fuselage, minus its valuable instruments, in which to train a new group of Korean cadets General Kim had just sent us. But we grew ever shorter on supplies, even lacking replacement parts for our planes. We went back to prayers and baling wire, while Bellovin the Burglar rode again.

The training program clearly demanded additional personnel. Requesting it, I received Lt. Ernest Craigwell from a unit in Japan, an ex-crew chief in his middle twenties with whom I was to fly many missions and whom I came to love like a brother. Craigwell was a self-educated Negro with a fine knowledge of mechanics. Right off I made him aircraft-maintenance officer, and because he was for a time the junior man in our organization, he was buried under some fifteen additional duties, most of them trivial, which are to pilots like buzzing gnats about the face. But Craigwell stood up well under them until another unsuspecting junior officer came along.

Wilson, Craigwell, and I worked out a complicated shuttle system whereby the Koreans could fly combat missions. Two of them could go out with one of us accompanying them. We'd fly over enemy lines, perform our mission, and then the American would come back and land at Chinhae. The Koreans would proceed to their longer practice runway at Pusan. Then two of us would get into a light AT-6-type aircraft, fly it over to Pusan, pick up the F-51s landed there by the Koreans, and bring them back to Chinhae. The Koreans would get into the smaller AT-6, which they could land at Chinhae, and come back in it. This was the best we could devise to keep the maximum number of planes in the air.

But this took time—valuable time. We needed a longer runway at our base. General Kim appealed to President Rhee, and a civilian contractor was put on the job. It was quite an operation—the multitude of workers, the oxcarts, the baskets in which dirt was carried from the small hill on the edge of the airfield to the runway and out to the edge of the rice paddies. It takes a lot of dirt for a fill like that. General Kean made available a road company of engineers, and they contributed a scraper, a couple of shovels, and the dynamite to blast the rock for ballast. But mostly the large stones were carried by hand from the mountain to the runway by three hundred patient and tireless Koreans. Watching them admiringly, I could only think of a pharaoh building his pyramid. Slowly the strip was lengthened from 2,780 feet to 3,500 feet.

It was at Chinhae that I again saw President Rhee. Taegu was in danger, and he had come down to live in the former Japanese Navy yards. He was quite isolated from the war situation; no one, he said, would give him news about what was going on. Perhaps the embassy wished to spare the old man bad news—and it was mostly bad in the early autumn of 1950—on the theory that what he didn't know he couldn't worry about. In this they underestimated the strength and vitality of this man who, after all, had been carrying the hopes of Korean independence on his strong shoulders for half a century. Furthermore, our embassy undoubtedly considered the Korean president a zealot—which he most certainly was, and is—whose direct methods and outspoken ways might not coincide with United Nations policy at the time.

Finding that we were located at Chinhae, he asked me to come and visit him, and I complied as often as I could get away. Soon I got word from Dr. Noble to use utmost discretion in my talks with Dr. Rhee, and later I was advised through the embassy that I should not talk much to him at all. But the old man was becoming very nervous wondering about the United Nations forces. What kind of a stand were they going to make? Were we going to be shoved out of Korea entirely? He took to sending for me at all hours, day or night. Though the embassy still frowned, I continued to go. They were rightfully concerned about the subject of our conversations, but since I had no firm grasp of the over-all situation, there was little, either dangerous or valuable, that I could tell Dr. Rhee.

He felt that he was getting the runaround. At one time he became so distressed by the notion that he was being cut off from any responsibilities that I invited him to the airfield to witness a little firepower demonstration. Hal and I went to Taegu and scrounged ammunition, rockets, and napalm from an American unit. We then flew down to Chinhae and dropped the whole load on a small island in the bay to show what we were using on the enemy. The old warrior was delighted.

I would visit with him infrequently on those nights that he couldn't sleep. On one or two occasions late at night I would find him at his desk, concern etched deep into his face. "What is the front-line situation today?" he would ask.

"The line holds firm," I would answer, "at least where I saw it north of the field."

"And my Korean pilots, Major—how are they doing?"

"Fine, Mr. President. They flew a dozen missions today, and all came back."

Even this kind of simple good news seemed to relax him. And in his darkest hours he never failed to think of others. One evening the Korean commander of the Chinhae Naval Base was there when suddenly Dr. Rhee turned to me and asked, "Is there anything you need at the base, Major?"

Eying the naval commander, I suddenly thought of something.

126

Recently we had set up a rest area on the base for infantrymen. Two hundred of them at a time would come back from the front lines, and one of their favorite forms of relaxation was fishing. However, they didn't have much luck in the harbor, though the fishing was rumored to be excellent outside the harbor. I explained this situation to the President, going into details about the American male's passion for angling. He smiled and said something short and incisive to his naval commander.

The next day we got our boat.

Madame Rhee was a great source of strength to him. Once when I had breakfast with them, she read to us from a volume of wise sayings and aphorisms, The Golden Book of the Korean People, after which Dr. Rhee read from the Bible. Then, bowing their heads, each in turn said a little prayer. President Rhee prayed for strength and the moral integrity and fortitude to lead his people. I prayed with them on several occasions. Though suffering personally in many ways, not once did they pray for themselves.

Madame Rhee had lost all her wardrobe with the fall of Seoul. Now she wore a modest Korean robe, or full skirt, with a little jacket. I offered to send over to Japan for some new clothing, but she refused, saying that, while she appreciated the offer, she couldn't bring herself to be more comfortable or to have more conveniences than her countrymen. She carried this to the extreme of almost starving at times, because there were so many in Korea who were suffering from hunger.

At their house I horrified a secretary of the American Embassy by putting my arm around her and calling her my "Korean sweetheart." The embassy man's eyebrows shot up, and expressions of horror and incredulity chased each other across his face. I could easily read his thoughts: Who is this uncouth oaf perpetrating such a crude violation of diplomatic decorum? President Rhee saw the effect it had on him and shook with silent laughter.

xiv

At Chinhae we grew into a larger unit, and then our numbers
leveled off. We still had only three American pilots—Craigwell,
Wilson, and myself—and eight of the original ten Korean pilots
flying and being checked out in the F-51. On the ground we had
thirty American airmen under Capt. Mike Bellovin, about a hundred ROK airmen, and seventy-five ROK air cadets that General
Kim had recently sent us for basic training on the field.

This, then, for better or for worse, was the fighting arm of the
Republic of Korea Air Force—at least for the moment. Officially,
if less glamorously, we were designated the 6146th Air Base Unit,
with the code name "MacIntosh."

Training the ROK pilots in combat was probably our most
original contribution to the art of warfare. Our procedure from
the first had been a version of the "buddy system"—two Koreans
under the tutelage of two Americans. Most of the ROKs had
learned enough basic English to grasp what was being explained to
them. One of the words they knew best was "combat." We used
"training" in its stead, for the tendency was to tighten up upon
hearing the former word. While they knew that they were going
where there would be shooting, somehow they were more at ease
getting airborne and better able to concentrate on the techniques
of flying if we soft-pedaled the talk about combat. It lessened considerably the initial jeopardy of getting into the air.

Once the trainees were familiar with the F-51's operation and
habits, instruction in communication techniques was begun—
hand signals, wagging of the plane's wings for "Close formation,"

and moving the tail for "Line up in single file and prepare for attack."

The ROK pilots' planes carried no bombs during the initial stages of training. There was always the danger that they would crash on take-off, and furthermore bombs were too expensive and hard to come by to waste. Their guns were loaded, however, and they were expected to strafe ground targets on their very first mission.

Told that he was to follow the leader and to fly and shoot where he did, the student would stay on his wing about five hundred yards away. Here he would follow the instructor's procedure via radio calls for close support of ground forces, studying camouflage, and searching out and destroying targets. He had to learn to differentiate between friendly and enemy troops from the air. On his first runs he would follow the leader into the bomb run just as though he too were making a drop, to learn the proper angle of descent. He was taught to avoid target fixation (the curious hypnosis which will draw a pilot too far down for recovery) by observing exactly when to pull out of the dive. And he learned evasive tactics above antiaircraft fire.

The Korean who most often flew with me now was a Lieutenant who, it was said, had come down from North Korea in 1948. He had been accepted into the ROK Air Force only after convincing them of his dedication to the democratic cause. He had seen with his own eyes what happened where Communism reigned. While both General Kim and I believed him to be completely sincere and trustworthy, certain Americans were not of the same mind. Suspecting that he might be a Red saboteur, they advised me never to let him fly behind me or on my wing. This irritated me, for I liked him personally and knew of his excellent record since coming south. I took him on as my flying partner in the buddy system. Later he was to justify my faith in him magnificently.

Some of the younger American pilots *were* dangerous to be in the same sky with, however. One morning I was flying out of Chinhae over the Twenty-fifth Division sector searching for targets when four American aircraft bore in. Eager new pilots, they obviously had never seen the markings on a Korean plane. They only saw the Oriental symbol on the side of mine—and decided it must be the enemy.

Two of the pilots got on my wings while the other two stayed behind. One kept firing at my wing tip. They were trying to box me in, force me down, and take the airplane. I made several radio calls to try to identify myself as friendly, but though I could hear them talking back and forth, I couldn't get through. I called to the ground controller to advise them who I was. He replied that these were four airplanes working outside their regular sector and that he didn't have communication with them.

We circled for twenty or thirty minutes. When two of the airplanes were tight on my wing, I would adjust the throttle slightly and maneuver so that I would overlap one of them; that way they would have hit a teammate had they opened fire.

In desperation I took my helmet off, but I was so tanned from flying in the sun that they couldn't distinguish me from the darker Koreans. Then finally, exasperated, I looked down at the pilot I was hugging just as he glanced apprehensively over his shoulder at me, sitting on his back. I thumbed my nose at him, hoping this strictly American gesture might identify me. Shortly after they all decided to go back to Taegu, either because they had become uncertain about my identity or because they were getting low on fuel. I then broke away and sought my original target. I often wonder what they thought about the "North Korean" pilot who thumbed his nose at them.

At Chinhae we were given a close view of how war affects a civilian populace. The initial enemy thrust had come so quickly that there were very few refugees pushed ahead of the front lines. The Red tide had engulfed all the civilian populace as it swept south. But now, as the enemy was slowed on the Pusan Perimeter, many civilians had an opportunity to collect blankets, cooking pots, small bundles of clothing, and a few precious family relics together and to start walking the roads.

One evening a refugee column came by the field when the weather was bad and darkness about to fall. Discovering that they were going down the road about thirty miles to a camp, we hauled them there during the balance of the afternoon and the evening in our trucks. Our Korean flyers were frankly amazed that we, as Americans, should feel such concern for their people—more concern, in fact, than they themselves felt.

Flying out of Chinhae, I had a different kind of refugee experience—a terrible one. So many of a fighter pilot's experiences are terrible that it might be asked how one can be described as more terrible than the next.

It can, believe me.

I was flying alone one afternoon in close air support of the Twenty-fifth Division, taking directions from a liaison pilot. It was the kind of hazy day, with visibility 2 miles at the most, on which it was impossible to distinguish objects on the ground that were a mile away or even less. My general mission was to harass troop movements in an active enemy area opposite the Twenty-fifth. The liaison pilot spotted troops on the main highway between Chinju and Masan walking toward our lines. I saw them from a distance but, unable to make out their identity, checked again with the liaison pilot. He was sure they were enemy troops.

Masking my turn behind a hill to catch them by surprise on the road, I tore down on them at a speed greater than three hundred miles per hour. I had fired one short burst of my guns before I caught a quick close-up glimpse of my target: a column of refugees, now scrambling into the ditch. My finger leaped from the trigger as though shocked, and I turned quickly and looked again as I pulled away. A girl of ten or twelve lay on the road, obviously dead and mangled. I gasped into my radio to the liaison pilot, "Those were refugees!"

So many times I had missed my target with the first burst on a fast run; why not this time?

I carried around with me then, and still do today, a copy of a poem by Emily Dickinson that expresses her compassion for humanity. I felt that she was expressing my love for people too. That day, flying back to Chinhae, I repeated it over and over to myself, wondering if I could ever again claim it for my own:

> If I can stop one heart from breaking,
> I shall not live in vain;
> If I can ease one life the aching,
> Or cool one pain,
> Or help one fainting robin
> Unto his nest again,
> I shall not live in vain.

Man's inhumanity to man is developed into a fine science during wartime. The bay at the end of our short runway divulged further proof of this sad fact.

One end of our runway stopped at the sea wall by the bay, once used as a parking lot for seaplanes, and the other end terminated in a rice paddy. To warn landing aircraft that they were nearing the absolute end of the runway and still not panic them into braking too violently, we put up a big sign at the edge of the rice paddy which said simply, "Oops!"

But it was the bay end which gave us the most trouble. On a hot day with the wind not exactly right an aircraft would drop slightly as it went off the sea wall. We learned quickly not to take off with the tide in under bad wind conditions, for the water came right up to the top of the sea wall. Once, before I could get my landing gear retracted, my wheels skimmed the water just as I became airborne. After the flight we had to wash the plane off with fresh water because the salt would have deteriorated the aluminum.

Yet the presence of the bay did offer an opportunity for the men to swim in the evening, and in spite of all the difficulties of operating from the short strip, the men thoroughly enjoyed this compensation. That is, they enjoyed it until one afternoon some swimmers bumped into some bodies floating on the water. We got into boats and went out to haul them in. Several were in an advanced state of decomposition, and all had been tied together—apparently pushed in to drown.

Our inquiries disclosed that these had been Communist spies who had been captured by the South Korean forces. Ammunition was scarce; tried and convicted of being traitors, the spies had been taken out onto the water and, with hands bound behind their backs, shoved overboard. Our men lost their taste for swimming in the bay.

It is true that life was cheap in Korea and that bullets were expensive. Nor was it a question of their guilt, for that had been fairly established. Yet it revolted us that our allies the South Koreans would use this inhuman method of execution. Pushing a man off a dock to a struggling death with his hands and feet tied seemed unnecessarily cruel. There was a partial explanation: these bodies floating down the river were a warning to other spies and potential saboteurs, just as in the early days of the American West a rustler was occasionally left hanging from the branch of a tree for a few days.

This proved to be an isolated incident, I am happy to say, and not part of a policy of intentional cruelty. We reported it to the national police, and a vigorous investigation was begun. To my knowledge it never happened again.

Plagued by guerrilla infiltrations around the field, we set up double guard duty all night long. We took even more precautions after the cook's experience. Working one morning about two o'clock, he was pulling a big tray of biscuits out of his stove when he happened to look around. Standing in his doorway were two Communist soldiers. In ragged clothes, they obviously had sneaked onto the post in search of food. The cook, an American sergeant, tossed his biscuits skyward and went through one door while the

133

two guerrillas, twice as scared as he, scrambled through the other.

Though the guerrillas were a source of concern, we refrained from firing upon them to avoid their return fire, unless they got into critical areas like ammo dumps, or too near the planes. There was always the threat of sabotage. I am sure that this was responsible for the death of one of our Korean pilots.

One afternoon they were all lined up on the runway for a news photographer who wanted some pictures of the ROK Air Force preparing for a mission. General Kim and I were standing at the end of the runway watching. Hal Wilson led the flight off. As a Korean pilot followed, his aircraft went out of control, swerved sharply over the sea wall, and plunged into the bay with the canopy under water.

A dozen men immediately jumped into the water to shove the wing up and get the pilot out, but it was several minutes before Capt. Joe Weiner, who had recently joined us as maintenance officer, finally pulled him loose. The seat came with his body: the bolts holding it had been removed, and it was merely resting on the bottom of the aircraft. When the pilot opened throttle to take off, the seat moved, and the accident resulted. He had sustained a fractured skull. The necessity of using artificial respiration with his head down low, done under a Korean doctor's directions, drew the blood to his head, and he eventually died of a brain hemorrhage.

The American photographer had taken a full sequence of pictures of this tragic "accident." Their publication would have resulted in an unfavorable reaction to the Korean air force. It would have been impossible to explain that the plane had been sabotaged. Right there on the line, with the plane still upside down in the water, I asked the photographer what he was going to do with them. After a moment's thought he replied that, while it was the best pictorial story he had ever taken, he recognized what the Koreans were trying to do. He would not let it escape into print. It was one more instance of the understanding and assistance we had from war correspondents and photographers.

134

This plane we were able to save, but an earlier loss had reduced the number of our aircraft to five. We had been working on the assumption that we could keep going only as long as our aircraft lasted. Then, out of the blue, came word from General Timberlake that we would be maintained at a level of ten planes! It was the first indication that the Korean air force wouldn't end when the last handful of battered F-51s had been lost. It was the first assurance of strong official backing and approval. We fought on with the stimulating knowledge that, as long as we lived, we would have the equipment to be able to continue to fly.

The men, beginning to feel the initial stirrings of pride in the way the installation had shaped up, came to me for permission to erect our first identifying sign. A member of the group who was a fair freehand painter worked one up: "6146th Air Base Unit, Major Dean E. Hess, Commanding." It struck me right away that it was out of balance—not the inscription but its implication. We all were working together, everyone contributing an equal amount; for me to be singled out from the rest seemed singularly inappropriate. I tried to give the sign a suggestion of our basic characteristic by adding to it in larger letters: "EVERY MAN A GENERAL!"

Not long after, my Korean boys' pride received another shot in the arm. An F-80, belonging to the Forty-ninth Fighter-bomber Group, out of Japan, made an emergency landing at Chinhae. Lacking fuel, the pilot came in with his wheels retracted and made a belly landing on our grass strip. Then he got out, looked at his plane, and decided that it was damaged beyond repair. My men put him into a jeep and took him to Pusan for airlift back to his organization.

I came in from a mission to find American maintenance men about to snake the broken craft off the runway with pulleys and ropes. That would have torn the airplane apart, but they figured the pilot had washed it out. I noticed the Koreans examining it more carefully. Joining them, I saw that, while the metal of the wings was slightly warped, once the weight was off the plane's wing tanks, they would go back into proper position. They were only bent enough to make little buckles in the aluminum sheeting.

Any plane is a very expensive piece of equipment, well worth making every effort to save. As a bit of discipline I ordered the American crew chiefs off the strip, explaining that the Koreans would handle it.

Ordinarily, lifting an airplane is done with special heavy jacks. Lacking these, the Koreans dug holes in appropriate places under each wing in each of which they set two small vehicle jacks. Then they raised the jacks as far as they would go. As the airplane came up slightly, the patient Koreans would put blocks under it, remove the jacks, and place them higher, working the plane up by slow stages. Ultimately they successfully raised the plane without further damaging it. Then, lowering the landing gear, they pulled it off the runway.

The only damage was minor: the door, which encloses the nose wheel when it is retracted, was torn loose, and the pilot tube had been broken off. A supply depot sent new parts while the engine was being cleaned of the grass it had picked up. The American mechanics, now thoroughly chagrined to have been proved so wrong about discarding the ship, were eager to work on it.

These boys were experts in their field, their technical training far superior to that of the Koreans; but they had a certain youthful cockiness that rankled. They were sure that they knew more than anyone else about planes—certainly more than a group of uneducated Koreans. I had been wishing that they would be less condescending to the efforts of the Korean airmen and give them credit for being more than backward pupils. This F-80 taught them the necessary lesson. We had it ready to fly when a pair of men from the Forty-ninth Bomber Wing arrived to dismantle the instruments on what they believed to be a wrecked plane.

The Korean people, both civilian and military, often expressed, in one way or another, their appreciation of our efforts on their behalf. One day my Korean flyers decided to present me with an ox—a custom from the early days in Korea, when a victor in a duel or wrestling match was awarded one. They secured a mangy old beast from a farmer, and General Kim conducted the ceremonies—to an obbligato of moans from the farmer, who had had a last-minute change of mind about parting with it. I gave it back to him later, but its fleas stayed in my clothes for a week.

They managed a more practical gift on the occasion of my 100th mission. Returning in the afternoon, Hal Wilson and I found the Korean cadets, pilots, and enlisted men lined up on the sea wall along the runway waving as I touched down. As soon as I rolled to a halt, the enlisted men came out, picked me up out of the cockpit, and carried me over to a Korean colonel known as "Brush" Chang.

Chang, whose nickname derived from a bristly, black mustache, had a gold medal for me—not a formal military award, but a decoration in the form of an Oriental symbol for "100." I was both deeply touched and taken by surprise, having entirely forgotten that this was my 100th mission. I stood there on the field, with my little knot of Korean and American friends about me, looking at my shoes and trying to think of the right words. But I knew the limitations of words, especially when real emotion is involved. I could only say that I did not consider a hundred missions the completion of a tour; I intended to fly as long as I could. There always seemed to be another hill beyond this one.

A Navy doctor who worked closely with General Partridge's office was another who became deeply interested in the amount of flying I was doing. He came over to the base to check the general health of the outfit. When he found out about my one hundred missions, his concentration focused on me. In fact, he seemed downright fascinated by my "case." One morning we had quite a dialogue over my desk:

"Major, how are you feeling these days?"

"Fine, Doctor."

"Tired, aren't you?"

"No."

"How's your appetite?"

"Fine."

"Can you get to sleep at night?"

"Sure can."

"Do you find you're short-tempered?"

"No more than usual."

He left, a disappointed fellow. During the interview the conviction had grown on me that he had a couple of stretcher bearers waiting outside the door. He was later quoted in a national magazine as saying that I had some kind of psychological armor plate which protected me from all mental trauma. That might have been his way of putting it, but I had another version. It was written on the fuselage of my plane: "By Faith I Fly."

Another man who left our outfit thinking I was badly in need of a rest was an Army major, a biologist who came to look for insects that might be harmful to the United Nations forces. He was trying to track down the source of encephalitis, which was proving a problem with some of our troops. A professorial-looking fellow, small and with horn-rimmed spectacles, he looked as if he'd be more at home in a laboratory; but he was most active and eager to carry out his job.

He would often come in at night to describe how he had located a little-known mosquito in some swamp. He would become so excited, so lost in his insect world, that he seemed completely oblivious to the fact that a war was going on around him.

One night he was sitting in the room in which Hal Wilson, Mike, and I had our beds. It was infested with rats. We could hear them running all night long on the rafters overhead—boy rats chasing girl rats, Mike theorized. When we weren't throwing shoes at the ceiling, we often wished that the girl rats wouldn't be so heavy on their feet.

The Major's chair was under a place where a board was missing from the ceiling. I sat on the other side of the room fondling a Colt .45 loaded with birdshot from a survival kit in case a rat showed up. As we sat listening to his insect chatter, a rat came through the hole in the ceiling and looked down. I fired over the

Major's head and missed. When I turned to explain, he was gone. We could hear him running down the hall crying that Hess had gone off his rocker and was shooting his pistol all over the place! He never came back.

By this time the enemy, thoroughly annoyed, had put a levy on the head of my good friend, Don Nichols of the Office of Special Investigation. In dollars and cents it amounted to $7.50. One night we laughed at him for being worth such a trifling sum, only to have him answer in all seriousness that there was also a bounty on my head: $5.00 to anybody who captured me. I considered myself worth $7.50 too, and told him indignantly to get word behind enemy lines that I would pay the difference to whomever made the capture. Happily they never were able to collect on either of us.

We were similarly amused by tuning in on Red propaganda broadcasts that featured a woman called "Seoul City Sue." We particularly enjoyed her harangues about the American capitalistic warmongers. It bucked us up to hear ourselves described in such extravagant terms as attacking with an "armada" of aircraft when the foray had been perpetrated by two or at most four aircraft.

Yet the amount of damage attributed to our little outfit indicated that our activities were being felt. It was nice to know that we were finding targets with such accuracy—though I did get a chill at times when I heard Sue describe them invariably as nonmilitary. According to her we specialized in destroying school buildings, hospitals, and refugee columns. Across the years echoed the voice of the Nazi propagandist broadcasting about such an instance which had been true: Kaiserslautern.

XV

My little air force of F-51s could only be truly effective based near the front lines. So, when our ground forces advanced, we had to pack up our things and advance too.

In September the Marines landed at Inchon and began fighting inland toward Seoul. As soon as we learned that the landing had been successful, General Kim Chung Yul and I hatched the idea of transferring our group back to the national capital, nearer the new front lines. I went to General Timberlake for permission, and he authorized our move to Kimpo Air Base, once the international airport near Seoul. Though we were not yet fully equipped, we had picked up a few additional jeeps, a couple of trucks, and some carbines. We now were living in tents and had laid happy hands on a gasoline truck which held 5,000 gallons. At least we no longer looked as though a heavy wind would blow us away.

General Kim and I flew up to Kimpo only a few days after it had been taken. The Marine divisional head with whom I was to coordinate was cooperative, but the Air Force colonel at Kimpo had an indifferent attitude toward General Kim, refusing to recognize his rank. I took the liberty of reminding him that he was talking to a Korean general. His treatment of General Kim improved, though he obviously didn't enjoy being so addressed by a major.

He grew even more disdainful on learning that we were to use his field. He welcomed us aboard and then put us over in a place called "Mud Haven," appropriately named, where we couldn't even have taxied our planes in wet weather. The men would have been sleeping in mud puddles. The colonel explained that he wanted us where we couldn't cause any trouble.

"The first of your planes that gets in our way, I'll ground the whole lot," he said pleasantly.

While I was getting used to what we called the "short end of the stick," our misfortunes were usually caused by circumstances which arose after we had been established. Here I could see that we were being downgraded and classified as "nuisance" from the beginning. I told him that we were not about to settle in Mud Haven and left with Kim.

It appeared there was only one thing to do: make a base of our own. The area map showed an abandoned airfield near Seoul at Yongdungpo, a village on the south side of the Han River. There, beside some burned and flattened buildings, Kim and I found two ancient hangars and a liaison strip—a couple of runners of blacktop scarcely long enough to taxi on and even less suitable for take-offs and landings. The field itself was covered with weeds and brush.

But an old Japanese aerial map gave us hope. It disclosed that once there had been a landing strip here other than the bits of macadam. Following the map, we drove the jeep out into brush so high it would stall the engine every few feet. Kim stood up and directed me as we plowed along through the wilderness.

Finally we saw traces of a white, chalky substance. My heart leaped; we had found the boundaries of what once had been a sizable airstrip.

Clearly it would be a tremendous job to rehabilitate this field. Yet if we could do it, we would be beholden to no one. I flew back with misgivings to inform General Timberlake of our discovery and plans. It was not easy under his steady scrutiny, for I didn't wish to tell him of the inhospitable colonel who had necessitated our change in plans. It was not that I was reluctant to expose his marked lack of cooperation, but I didn't want to dishearten our sponsor by complaints and tales of the troubles we were encountering. I was braced for a chewing out and a curt "no." Yet he must have suspected that I wasn't just being ornery. A fine pilot himself, he thought like a pilot and commanded like one. He merely offered his opinion that I was out of my head to take on such a job and said, "Go ahead, you must know what you're doing." However, he could give us no logistic support.

We'd scrounged before; we could scrounge again. Excitedly I answered that we could manage by ourselves. Thoroughly convinced that I was unbalanced, he sighed, issued the order, and let me go.

Kim and I wasted no time. From the Korean navy we procured an LST to load us at Chinhae and bring us to Inchon. From there we would go overland to Yongdungpo—or, as we now called it, "K-16."

That LST smelled as though it had been used for years to haul venerable fishheads. "Shipshape" would have been a queer word in the log of this battered item of World War II surplus. The Captain wryly pointed to some .50-caliber holes in the bridge and mentioned offhandedly that an American F-80 had "made a mistake" in the early days of the war. I sincerely hoped that such a mistake would not be repeated with all our bombs, ammo, and gasoline aboard.

It wasn't, but we almost blew ourselves up. The second day out a guard chased an amazed native (we had a few on board) nearly off the ship when he found him sitting on our gas truck smoking a cigarette above 5,000 gallons of high octane.

We were a peculiar-looking air force, plowing up the west coast of Korea in that rusty can, but we had a thirty days' supply of food, willing personnel, an unquenchable spirit, and a field (as yet to be carved out of the bush) of our own. What commander could ask for anything more?

The trip took two and a half days. The two Korean doctors aboard to look after our people were both taken with monumental cases of seasickness when the first screws turned. Fortunately there was no illness except their own—perhaps because we politely declined our host's rice, fish, and *kimchee* and relied solely on cold C rations.

As we approached Inchon, the sun was coming up in the east. Its light touched the hills behind which the ground fighting was going on. I was impressed by how red the hills became; how symbolic of all the blood that was being shed there! That such beauty and serenity could exist here despite the conflict filled me with awe for the magnitude of our universe. And how petty and vicious our little war seemed, seen against the beauty of this dawn sky!

I was reminded of my favorite psalm. Almost every time I picked up my worn Bible at night, it automatically opened to these same strength-giving words. They seemed particularly appropriate at this moment:

> I will lift up mine eyes unto the hills;
> from whence cometh my help?
> My help cometh even from the Lord. . . .

The battleship *Missouri* was standing offshore at Inchon, its rails lined with seamen watching the slow passage of our dubious old LST flying a Korean flag. Inevitably one yelled, "Where'd you get that old tub?" The others grinned, hooted, whistled. They were stopped short by an answering voice, not in Korean but in accents of purest Brooklynese, recalling the "Mo's" recent mishap in Chesapeake Bay: "When did you get her out of the mud?"

The Inchon harbor has a unique 28-foot tide. A craft has to ride in with it to get into the tidal basin. If it isn't docked by the time the tide goes out, the ship will be stranded on mud flats. With many supply ships already using the port facilities, there was no space for us, and our Korean captain decided to unload us on the bank. Not wanting to be stranded by the outgoing tide, we urged him to hit the bank as hard as he could. He politely declined. Americans had designed and built the LST, we insisted, and we knew what it would do. He remained adamant. Instead he gently nudged his ship into the bank. Within twenty minutes the tide had gone out, and the LST was high and dry. But when I saw the rusted

143

and scarred bottom of our boat, I was glad he hadn't listened to us. If he had banged the bank just once, his decrepit craft would have folded up like an accordion.

The ramps were 5 feet short of the bank, and there was nothing with which to build a bridge. But if we couldn't get to shore, obviously we had to bring the shore to us. Right off I spotted an Army engineer running a bulldozer. Taking along a bottle of our precious whisky, I waded, then walked, over to him with an invitation to shove the bank out to us. Easily persuaded, he agreeably began pushing dirt out to make a runway to the ramp.

The port engineer, an American captain, saw him and came bristling down, quite upset that we were remodeling his harbor. But by then there was enough dirt in place for us to unload, and he could only stamp off, fuming. It was our unofficial—and apparently characteristic—welcome.

My main worry now concerned our most treasured possessions— the F-51s we had left behind. Not wishing to leave them unguarded on the Chinhae field, I assigned an American pilot, one of the two who had recently joined us in Chinhae, to ferry them to Taegu. He was to stand by until we were set up at Yongdungpo ready to receive aircraft. Several Korean pilots were with him, similarly instructed not to fly missions but to wait until we sent for them.

Instead, once in Taegu, they began to fly combat missions without benefit of crew chiefs or armorers to care for the planes. On one such flight antiaircraft fire near the city of Pyongyang drove the American off his target. Returning to Taegu, he vowed that he was going back "to get the ape" who had shot at him.

This was not an unusual reaction. Flyers frequently develop a grudge against a ground battery and hotly declare their intention to wipe it out. The attempt to do so often ends with the pilot becoming the casualty—as it did with this one. In anger and therefore not using his better judgment, he went looking for that bothersome gunner, and this time the gunner killed him and destroyed his plane.

We reached Yongdungpo in September of 1950. The field looked even worse than when Kim and I had seen it before. In addition we had not a single piece of equipment suitable for runway construction. Members of other organizations would stop by, ask our business, and then laugh aloud at the very idea of putting down an airstrip there. The more sporting would offer long odds against our ever becoming operational.

And then happened one of those incidents which made us realize the character of the people we were fighting for.

Without even hand tools to prepare the ground, much less heavy grading equipment, we had no alternative but to call on civilian help. Despite the fact that fighting was still raging in the hills north of Seoul 2 miles away, we managed to round up some native volunteers.

I said "some" native volunteers. Almost a thousand of them appeared on the field—including old men, women, and children—with any tools they could lay their hands on—wooden implements, crude picks and shovels, scissors, knives, baskets. A few of the wealthier ones brought scythes; many had only their bare hands. Lining up elbow to elbow, they started the tedious process of leveling the earth. Slowly they moved like a thin tide toward their objective 5,000 feet away—cutting, filling, packing, patting. They would pull clumps of grass and trample them into ruts and holes. Scooping up dirt and gravel, they spread it and rolled it with old oil drums. Cut weeds and hay were carried on their backs. The runway smoothed out; treacherous ditches disappeared. Within a week the strip was ready to fly planes.

Their efforts were given added impetus by the Communist atrocities turned up in combing the field. Bodies were found scattered in many places. One ditch held what appeared to be a family of five: an elderly man and woman, another younger woman with a baby strapped to her back, and a little girl of six or seven. All, including the infant, had been shot through the head.

What manner of human being—no, inhuman being—would deliberately put a revolver to the head of an infant and pull the

145

trigger? As each day passed and more such atrocities were uncovered, my Korean flyers itched to get back into the air against the enemy. At the same time it made them worry more than ever about the fate of their families. As soon as we became operational, I encouraged them to go into Seoul to try to locate them.

General Kim learned that his wife and children had been living in a cave in the mountains. As his family they were high on the Reds' "wanted" list, and had they been captured, they surely would have been murdered. He found them in miserable shape yet still alive, though his smallest child was very sick. Major Kay Won, a Korean doctor who had been assigned us by General Kim at K-16, reported that the boy needed an intravenous injection of saline in order to live and that this was obtainable only in Japan. Hal Wilson flew an F-51 to Itazuke to buy some, and the boy recovered.

Many of the Korean cadets found their entire families wiped out—the Red penalty for men serving in the armed forces of South Korea. Others, luckier, lost only a wife or a brother. One found his sister so maltreated that she required immediate medication. She had been unable to get any kind of assistance or relief while the invaders occupied Seoul, though her predicament was the direct result of their animalism. We put her in our infirmary, where Dr. Kay treated her for a month, utilizing what facilities we had. She regained a measure of physical health, though little could be done for her spirit.

The Communists had occupied Seoul so rapidly that few civilians had had an opportunity to run southward. The city had been a giant trap. Those who had been friendly to United Nations troops or who were adherents of Dr. Rhee's republican form of government were indiscriminately slaughtered. The Reds killed not only by families but by professional and social groups. In one churchyard 270 bodies were found; later these unfortunate souls were identified as professors, doctors, lawyers, and other professional men.

It sickened us, but it also strengthened our resolve. The Christian tenet of turning the other cheek, beautiful in theory and often

effective in practice, would make no dent in this kind of savage-
ness. Resolute in my desire to remain a good Christian, I also
wanted to get back into the air—to kill. The enemy was no longer
unknown; all around was the terrible evidence of what he was.
Now we knew his face.

Though a man undoubtedly changes in a war, I believe he remains essentially the same person. Therefore I was amazed to
learn that I had undergone a complete metamorphosis—become
part Korean, in fact.

Being so close to Seoul, we were handy for VIPs. One afternoon
Major Perkins, General Partridge's exec, brought over a past president of the American Medical Association. Calling me aside, the
visitor wanted to discuss the war situation. I doubted if my worm's-
eye view would prove very informative, but because of Perkins I
talked with him for a few minutes. He kept eying me intently
while listening closely, particularly when I talked about the ROK
Air Force. Later I learned why.

That night at dinner in Seoul the good doctor told his traveling companions that he had met this fellow Hess. He had been
interested because he had heard all about me from someone in
Tokyo. He told them how I had flown with the Japanese during
World War II; how I had given up my American citizenship; that
I was part Korean and thus uniquely equipped to work with them
under these unusual circumstances.

As soon as Perkins was able to stop laughing, he scuttled the
story as complete fiction. Where such a wild conglomeration of
rumors originated we never found out. The visitor was taken
aback—and so was I, listening to Perkins's account. Afterward, looking in my shaving mirror, it seemed like the same old Ohio face,
despite a certain thinness, a heavy tan, and the short cut of my
black hair.

Yet if an intelligent American could take me for an Oriental,
there must be something deeper. Perhaps it was because I had come
to feel such a strong bond of brotherhood with my Korean flyers.
Perhaps it actually showed in my face when I talked about them.

xvi

At Yongdungpo we began to accumulate our first orphans. Being so close to Seoul, we saw vast numbers of them, cast loose by the shattering of their homes. They were wandering about everywhere in the city streets and out into the countryside too. Suffering from general malnutrition, most were surviving only because it was summertime and they were able to dig and eat the herbs along the riverbanks and in the fields.

The orphans would cluster like flies around our garbage cans, into which the men scraped their trays three times a day. It was both heartbreaking and nauseating to see these ragged children lean over and dip into the swill with tin cans, trying to scoop up choice morsels from our garbage. Most of them had scabs and skin infections on their faces, and inflamed and running eyes. They were very dirty, though one hardly noticed that, and dressed in ragged, oversized adults' clothes. They were all over the field during the day, but at night they disappeared, probably back to the ruins of Seoul.

For me these children became the greatest horror of war, the most damaging blow man can strike against the future, against himself, against God. They were so pitiful that there was only one thing to do—care for them as best we could. All the men, moved by their plight, helped. It was a common practice at mealtime for a man to load his plate, eat part of it, and take the rest to the hungry mouths outside the mess tent. This became a considerable drain on our store of food—all that we could count on in the immediate future—but I made no effort to prevent it. The possibility of future hunger was nothing beside the immediate wants of those staring children.

In Seoul one day shortly after our arrival at Yongdungpo I was walking through the market section with a Korean pilot, Captain Lee, fingering a couple of Korean won (low denomination notes), intent on buying some little souvenir of the country to send Mary. It was the only Korean money I had with me. One of these grimy urchins kept plucking at my coattails, asking for alms. I shook him off two or three times, hardly noticing that he had a game leg of some kind. I was still fingering that Korean money and peering into the little shops for knickknacks. Finally Captain Lee removed the persistent boy from my coattails and gently sent him on his way. I bought my memento—I've forgotten what it was.

That evening something awoke in me that had been asleep, or even dead—some tremor of conscience, some remembrance of the old values and ethics I used to propound from the pulpit. A terrible image was stamped sharply on my mind—that of a young American flyer walking through the battered streets of Seoul, fingering his money and looking greedily for souvenirs, all the while shaking off the beseeching hands of a ragged boy with a limp.

I sat on my cot for a while, head in hands, not even trying to clear my mind of the scene. Then I went to Captain Lee and exchanged some air-force script for a pocketful of Korean wons. It was still early, so I climbed into the jeep and drove back to Seoul. There I spent a couple of hours in a hopeless search for the little boy with the limp. Of course I didn't find him; in the end I distributed the Korean money amongst a number of his dirty brethren and drove back to the field.

I forgot a long time ago exactly what trinket I bought that afternoon, but I'll never forget the little boy I didn't help.

About ten days later I was out on the field when word came from the radio jeep that General Timberlake was landing in General Partridge's B-17. My stomach quaked. Up to now I had been confident that our newly laid field would hold up under all conditions. The sandy soil grown with river grass seemed solid enough under our light planes; but would it hold up under a four-engine bomber? I would have preferred other means of finding out than with a B-17 carrying General Timberlake. If he were to crash, we would lose our best friend, and our field would be reverting to a weed patch before the smoke settled.

But he made a perfect landing, and taxied around to a parking position. He was getting out of the plane before I could move my feet forward to meet him, grinning like a baboon in my relief. I stopped when I saw the serious expression on his square face. What now?

"You're out of uniform, Hess," he said curtly.

It was more than true. I wore no hat or necktie. The sleeves of a soiled khaki shirt were rolled up, as were the legs of my pink trousers. I wore combat boots. One of the insignia on my collar was missing. I had a brief flash of gratitude that no members of the command were around to hear the impending chew-out.

Then he said, "We'll fix that right now." Reaching out his hand (was he going to box my ears?), he removed my major's insignia and, smiling broadly, pinned on that of a lieutenant colonel. "It'll take a full colonel to outrank you now," he said.

This I had not expected, and I was shaken. I thanked him, weakly, I'm afraid, and then promised that my eager Korean pilots would be back in the air in a few days' time.

He had one request to ask before he left. Might he bring over the administrative aircraft of Fifth Air Force headquarters? I readily agreed, grinning (inside, this time) at all the scoffers who had said we were crazy to try to rehabilitate this little field.

It was a cheering but also a Pyrrhic victory. To achieve it we had put in killing hours. The enlisted men had sometimes gone twenty-four to forty-eight hours with only two- and three-hour catnaps to keep them on their feet. We had built and fenced in a gasoline-and-ammo dump, cleaned debris from the field, scraped the roads, put up our quarters (we were back in tents), and built

150

a proud, permanent six-hole latrine. Every time we built a permanent latrine, it seemed, we moved out almost the next day; this time we had our fingers crossed.

We had no specialists for any particular aspect of the construction job; everyone pitched in, simply doing what there was to be done. There was no rank differential; crew chiefs served as laborers. No one beefed or dogged it, but the hours of heavy work had taken a toll. We were all bone-tired, and the morale of the enlisted men had sunk pretty low.

One of them, Sergeant Daffon, asked and promptly received permission to make a club out of a little shack still standing in a corner of the field. After cleaning up the rickety building, they located some chairs from sources into which I thought it best not to inquire. Old parachutes provided window curtains and drapes. They built a bar from scrap lumber and even had some whisky flown in from Japan for a grand opening. Finally they issued proud invitations to the officers inviting them to attend the big event.

We had a drink or two with them, and then I indicated we should leave. One officer thought he would stay to make sure that they behaved themselves. That was exactly what I didn't want; the men had earned a tear. I hustled this would-be chaperon out of there after passing the word that tonight I would be oblivious to the blowing off of lids.

The men took me up. Their tensions began to disappear with the whisky, helped along by a happy scrap with an Army-liaison bunch who tried to steal it. Things quieted down for a while after that, and I thought they might finish their therapeutic binge in peace. Then a free-for-all broke out that sounded like a full-scale bombardment.

I lay in my cot, laughing aloud and thoroughly enjoying the roughhouse in a safe, vicarious way. Grunts followed the thumps of blows; smothered expletives mingled with heavy breathing. Bodies crashed as tent ropes tripped luckless feet. I knew that I should stop it, but I didn't want to spoil their fun. Besides, a lieutenant colonel looks like anyone else in the dark; there was a good chance the Old Man might get on the receiving end of a Sunday punch before he could be identified!

The battle eddied about close to my tent. Then there was the sound of a really solid blow right at my door. A voice I recognized—that of Sergeant Savage—immediately wailed, "My teeth! My teeth! Look out or you'll step on 'em! Got no more!"

I knew what he meant. The teeth of Sergeant Savage were a perpetual problem. The front row of them, lost long ago, had been replaced by a removable bridge. He had a knack for getting into trouble, which usually resulted in their being violently removed and lost. I had sent him to Tokyo, where a dentist had made him a set that screwed in permanently and had given him a supply of spares. Now, alas, it seemed that the last of these had disappeared in the dirt.

Then a sergeant stuck his head in the tent and called for me to come out. Thus officially notified, I had to take cognizance of the mayhem. In the orderly's tent I found out how it had started. One private had decided that a friend needed to go to bed. The friend had resisted the idea, finding it utterly preposterous, and the private had sought to put him to sleep with his fist. They had fought around in the tent area for a while and then braced each other up and gone off to their tents, pals again.

The others, hearing the commotion, had run out to stop it, alarmed lest the noise should rouse the "Old Man" and they should lose their club privilege. They had started groping around for the culprits and, encountering someone, immediately hit him. In a few seconds the whole group had been blindly whaling one another. This anonymous battle had continued while the original pair were already soundly snoring in their tents.

Lacking better methods, this "Golden Gloves tournament," as it was referred to the next day, was in effect a boost to morale. Fatigue was forgotten. Three men who had put in for transfer came to ask that the request be canceled. They explained that they did not wish to leave until they had found who had smacked them the night before. It may sound odd, but I was secretly pleased that they should be thinking of themselves as a fighting unit. If we stuck together solidly, our little vanguard of the future Korean air force would ultimately prove its worth.

Once again we were ready to fly and fight. Our identity had crystallized, and the field's location was a special advantage—so close to the main source of supplies that we could obtain plenty of fuel, bombs, .50-caliber ammunition, and rockets.

I asked Hal Wilson, newly appointed executive officer, to notify the Fifth Air Force that we could accept missions again. He wired, "By the grace of God and a dark night we are ready to proceed. Praise the Lord and pass the missions." He signed my name and sent it to General Partridge.

While it wasn't the kind of message ordinarily received by a commander, it brought results: we began to get regular dive-bombing and close-air-support assignments directly from headquarters rather than from front-line units. It was recognition of sorts. More significant recognition was forthcoming from a representative of the Far Eastern Air Force, Gen. Lawrence Craegie, who dropped by to say that our complement of F-51s would be raised from ten to twenty and maintained at that level!

But while our combat record was growing impressive, we began to lose pilots—some in useless accidents. One we lost because of a characteristic of the F-51 supposedly well known to its pilots. When flown with the fuselage tank full of gasoline, the center of gravity is so altered that in a sharp pull out of a dive the aircraft is likely to snap quickly over on its back. If close to the ground, it will crash upside down.

Craigwell and I and two Korean pilots were on a mission to hit a target north of Seoul where enemy supplies were hidden among some trees on a hillside. One of the team was the same Captain Lee who had taken the beggar boy off my coattails in Seoul—a fine, intelligent Korean who spoke English perfectly

153

and was a top flyer. But like others before him in the heat of combat he apparently forgot to empty or use the gasoline in his fuselage tank before his dive. His plane crashed into the target, exploded, and started to burn.

Though obviously he must be dead, it was a problem for us to decide whether to continue hitting the target or turn away. It was a moment full of torment and revulsion. To fly down through the smoke of Captain Lee's burning plane to strafe and destroy the rest of the objective was a gruesome task; but I felt we had to do it. It was only his lifeless body which we may have further riddled; surely his spirit was with God. And Lee himself, an eager pilot if I ever knew one, would have wanted us to continue the attack.

At Yongdungpo we had no formal worship of God—no church services at all. It was impossible for an outfit as small as ours to secure a chaplain, and the Korean Christian ministers in battered Seoul were few and far between. At Chinhae, farther away from the front lines, we had had Korean ministers and priests visit us every Sunday. Now we had none, and our Sundays seemed barren and empty.

How my conscience hurt me on those Sunday mornings! Not only was I a man in need of spiritual help; I was a Christian minister supposedly capable of giving it. But I was also a fighter pilot and a commanding officer. It was impossible for me to make the switch no matter how sorely I might be tempted. Assuming the role of chaplain would have cut the ground out from under me as commanding officer. The two positions simply could not be held by one man. Besides, we flew missions on Sunday mornings. How could I come back from over enemy lines, my hands red with enemy blood, and get up before my men to preach of love and mercy?

When we were in Chinhae, the men had been forbidden to go off base at night or to fraternize with local girls because of the high rate of venereal disease in the town. But I saw no need of imposing such rigid orders here at K-16. One night a delegation asked if they could go into Seoul to "look around." I said they could if the necessary guards remained to watch the camp. An hour after dinner I couldn't find a vehicle on the base except my jeep. Then two enlisted men came and asked if they could borrow it— they wanted to go into town too.

Realizing that something special was up, I volunteered to go with them. I wanted to look around too. They began to hedge, but when I climbed into the jeep and waved them in, they decided to come clean. Word had gotten around about a district where prostitutes were available. They looked taken aback when I suggested we go look the place over.

When we reached the district, it appeared as if a squadron meeting were being held. The street was lined with our trucks and jeeps. The two men with me disappeared to pass the word that the Old Man, younger than most of these lovers, was outside. Men began appearing through doors, through windows, out of alleys. The street quickly emptied of vehicles.

I didn't leave until they were all gone. I had no wish to moralize to them, nor did I offer any disparaging remarks on their conduct when we got back to the field. The rebuke of silence sufficed; but to play it safe I issued an order placing the street out of bounds.

Every commanding officer faces the problem sooner or later of keeping his men away from prostitutes. Some consider it only a matter of health; their responsibility is merely to keep down the venereal-disease rate in their outfits. I felt my responsibilities included the men's minds and souls as well as their bodies.

Lying alone in a cot at night far from home, a man yearns for love, reaches out for his wife's nearness and warmth and vitality. He has drawn on his own for so long, alone these many months, that he has overdrawn. He's drained; there's none left. Desperately he seeks to replenish that warmth and vitality with the first girl he can lay his hands on, only to come away surly, disillusioned, and even emptier than before. The tenderness and compassion

155

and honest needs of love get all mixed up in his mind with a quick roll in the hay and hasty gratification of a mere physical desire. The pure image of love that once lived in his mind can die in twisted confusion.

For that reason, and not merely to keep the men clean, I flushed them out of that brothel and kept them out.

During all this period we were gathering stray children. For the sick and obviously homeless kids we had set up a big tent with cots in it—entirely against regulations, of course. They infested the camp like ants, becoming so numerous that at last we had to pack them up and take them to Seoul to deposit them in a central orphanage. This was to become the Fifth Air Force Orphanage, and the whole organization contributed toward maintaining it. By this time CARE packages from the United States and other outside help were relieving the situation a little.

Though these children had different racial characteristics from ours, it never occurred to us that that should prove a barrier. That's why it seemed particularly ironic to me that at Yongdungpo we had our one unpleasant "racial" experience involving Craigwell. Hundreds of Air Force officers and enlisted men had treated Craigwell like a brother, loved him as a man, and admired him as a fighter pilot. One crotchety colonel, a staff officer from Tokyo who deplaned at Yongdungpo one afternoon on his way to the front lines, marred that record. He asked for a place to stay the night, and I assigned him an empty cot in the officers' tent—a cot that happened to be next to Craigwell's. When Craigwell came in, dog-tired after a mission, and stretched out beside him, the colonel jumped up and sought me out in the operations shack, angrily demanding to be billeted elsewhere; he wasn't going to sleep beside a Negro.

We responded to his command.

We set up a cot 50 yards out in an open field and lugged his belongings there, in full sight of any Communist guerrillas that might be in the neighborhood—and there were always a few around the field. When he saw his segregated quarters, the colonel screamed in anguish and, staggering under the load of his belongings, walked across the field to another outfit to spend the night with them. I never saw him again.

Inevitably the old problem of encroachment began to plague us. We had been too successful in hacking an airfield out of the brush. One outfit after another began to move in, use our field, share our supplies, monopolize our facilities. If we prized our elbowroom, it looked as though it was time to move again.

A Mosquito organization—the T-6s that serve as target spotters for fighter-bombers from Japan—had begun to come to us for gasoline. They were from Kimpo, whence we had been shoved out, but the Marine aircraft there used a different fuel. The T-6 and the F-51 burn the same type, so they notified us that they would be unable to perform their reconnaissance missions unless we could supply them. We did.

Other units had been dropping in on us from the very beginning, usually in need of something. As practically everyone outranked us, our stores were dwindling even before we became operational. Sometimes I thought our three flags—United Nations, United States, and Korean—were lures that drew planes as flies draw trout.

General Timberlake had assured me that, since this base was our idea and creation, no other unit would interfere with our operation in any way. But in the mounting activity I could see pressures that we might not be able to withstand. Everything pointed to it—even the radio station which our Koreans set up to keep in touch with their headquarters in Taegu: as the Americans had no radio equipment or means of communication, our facilities were soon being used to relay messages to Fifth Air Force headquarters.

Now Troop Carrier Command brought in thirty C-46s with supplies and troops for the front lines. The miscellany and the congestion increased. Once again our field was the nearest to the

157

front. Though I remained in command, my outfit was being smothered. The established operational outfits were taking precedence over what was still essentially a training program. We were soon moving in less and less space, while our airborne activities were curtailed by the swelling traffic on the runways.

The same situation; the same solution. We would move again.

Scouting around to the north, I learned of an airstrip about eight miles east of Pyongyang, the former Communist capital. Built by the Japanese and long abandoned, it was declared unusable. I flew over to take a look. A battle was being fought over it, but an airborne division made a drop and the enemy lines collapsed. I blessed those boys dangling from their parachutes; they were getting me an airfield.

When our troops had made it secure, I went down and landed. It was a beautiful strip—all sod, well drained, and with good facilities. An infantry company commander told me that he had hoped to use it as a camp area, but I persuaded him to keep it clear for us, pointing out that it would be convenient for him to have air support so close.

Actually, he seemed more interested in coffee than he did in the airstrip. We had no sooner said hello than he began talking about hot coffee. His outfit had been without it for weeks. When I promised to bring him some, he said the field was ours. I flew back and returned with a 5-gallon tin. Those infantrymen acted as though it were pure gold. It was the last we had, but they needed it more than we did.

With my claim staked, I traveled the well-known road back to General Timberlake. With some trepidation I told him about the new site and described it. This time he thought I was surely off my trolley, for according to his information there was no field there at all. When I told him that I had been there and that the field was an excellent one, he not only told me to proceed but offered to provide an airlift.

This was more than just a reward for "discovering " an airfield; for us to get transport aircraft was an indication that headquarters felt we merited operational assistance. We were no longer the bastard offspring of an uneasy American-Korean alliance.

"K-24," the new field's designation, proved an ideal spot for combat operations. Natives in the vicinity welcomed us gladly. Numbers of them would come to the field and offer to work for no reimbursement of any kind, so happy were they to be free again. An old school building made comfortable headquarters, and seven unusually clean and well-educated Korean girls, aged fourteen to sixteen, were employed to work in the dining room. The men could now sit at tables and be waited upon like honored warriors of old. Nor did they run the risk of dishpan hands, for the girls cleaned up afterwards.

I called the outfit together one night in the mess hall shortly after the girls arrived and put it to them straight. No one was to lay a finger on these girls. The first one who did would get a court-martial. The men understood my seriousness; we didn't have a single unpleasant incident in this regard. Moreover, in time they developed an affectionate and protective attitude toward these gay, giggling youngsters that somehow mellowed our harsh, cold male world.

The girls were another revelation of life under Communist domination. They told of the curtailment of their lives; the fear, the denial of religious expression. One of them, still only sixteen, had been forced to marry a Red soldier, and had borne him a son. Unable to protest, she had submitted with the fatalism of Oriental women under a conqueror's rule, even now telling the story with no trace of emotion.

Their tales especially troubled Maj. Kay Won, our medical officer—and for a good reason. In 1948, in medical practice in Seoul, he had met and married a girl from Pyongyang. While she was home visiting her parents, the Iron Curtain had descended, cutting her off from her new husband. During the years following, Kay had lived for the day when they might be reunited. And now the hour was near.

After he had set up an infirmary, he asked for some free time to go in search of her. I volunteered to go with him. He had the Pyongyang address of his in-laws, whom he'd never met, and driving into the city in a jeep, we had no trouble finding the house.

I waited in the jeep. Several minutes later he came back. From the look on his face I knew that something dreadful had occurred. There was nothing I could say. I put my arm across his shoulder for a moment and then started the jeep back toward the base.

After a few miles he told me. His wife had been killed just a month before. She had been working as a nurse in a hospital. On her way home a flight of our B-26s had dropped bombs on the Communist capital. One of them had killed her.

We rode in silence for some minutes. I didn't try to console him in his grief— Not now. For a time he would wish to live with it alone. The voice and wisdom of a young minister of the past—Bob Updegraff—came back to me over the years from Marietta, Ohio: "I'll be back when it won't be such an intrusion on their grief."

xvii

Fall in Korea is beautiful. The days are brisk but dry, the nights cold, the blue skies so clear that visibility is good for miles. At this time of year the "Land of the Morning Calm" was an apt description. Just after sunrise, flying low behind enemy lines, I could easily spot their now-dead fires of the night before: the air was so calm that it still held traces of the smoke.

Our missions were now carrying us deep within enemy territory. We were doing very little close support because the front lines were moving so rapidly that the infantry didn't need it. Targets of opportunity behind enemy lines were plentiful—Communist vehicles, tanks, and troops.

Then the Far Eastern commander delimited a 20-mile area extending from the Yalu River southward in which aircraft could not operate for fear of violating the boundary between Manchuria and North Korea. Any likelihood of this violation was small because our attacks were made in daylight hours. Though champing at the bit, we abided by this decision—until suddenly an order came through one morning to operate on the highway to Sinuiju—in the privileged sanctuary!

I ordered a flight at once for fear that it was a mistake that would be corrected before we could take off. I took three different maps to make sure that, no matter what the targets might be, we would not fire at anything next to the Yalu River.

With me were Craigwell and Captain Jackson, who had joined the unit at Seoul. When I think of Jackson, I particularly re-

161

member his endearing habit of always folding his hands and bowing his head in a moment of silent prayer before a meal, no matter where we were or what the circumstances.

This particular morning on the highway to Sinuiju we found numerous Communist vehicles, bumper to bumper. We struck them so abruptly that we did not even take time to get altitude to dive-bomb. Within thirty minutes we destroyed around forty vehicles.

The map showed an airfield with two runways on the south side of the Yalu River. I wanted to see if there were any aircraft still there. At 2,500 feet I came over the border of what should have been an airstrip and saw suddenly that it was now merely a grass field. Realizing that I was in a critical position if there were enemy guns about, I banked and started down—only to look into the muzzle of the biggest flak gun I'd ever seen. Then the field defenses opened up with antiaircraft guns from all sides.

Being number-one man, I called, "MacIntosh flight—flak!" The number-two man, Jackson, asked, "What'll we do?" Craigwell spoke up with the only profane word I ever heard him utter in describing what he was doing right then.

Jackson was laughing on the intercom as we zoomed down to grass-top level, where the flak guns couldn't get at us. We went scooting out of there fast. Still flying a few feet above the ground, I overtook a truck going down a perimeter road alongside the field. As I passed him, the driver was hunched over the steering wheel of the truck, looking up at me with his eyes as big as saucers, expecting to be killed. It was one of those rare times when an airman comes face to face at close quarters with a victim—the kind of personal encounter that can be shattering. Still, I would have pressed the button of my machine gun except that my angle of flight wouldn't allow me to get the truck in my sights.

Flying northward in the darkness of a predawn flight a few days later, Craigwell, Jackson, and I crossed the enemy's lines, which could be identified by sporadic flashes of gunfire. (Though the

Korean pilots flew with us daily, we weren't as yet taking them on night flights because of their lack of experience.) Noticing the headlights of a truck coming down the roadway, I called to Craigwell that I was going down after a target. It was a mountainous area, and in the dark it was difficult to distinguish valleys. All I could see was the outline of the mountains in the distance and underneath the white line of a road. But I knew that at a lower altitude I at least wouldn't suddenly run out of a cloud and into a mountain.

The truck was coming toward us. I turned out all my lights, whirled around, and approached from its rear, firing upon it. It proved to be a gasoline truck, for its explosion lit up the entire countryside. I called to Craigwell, "There's one that won't get up to the front lines tonight."

"And what of the driver," something in my mind answered, "blown to bits. He won't be going anywhere tonight either." It was hard to feel any jubilance over my strike.

But Jackson was glad to hear my voice. He had not seen the truck or anything else in the darkness after we had fled from the ack-ack over the front lines. He had thought the flash of exploding gasoline was my plane crashing into a mountain.

Just after daybreak as we were nearing the lines on our way home, Jackson was hit by flak. He made a 180-degree turn for a glide down toward our lines. I covered him closely, waiting to draw fire, if necessary, from his plane to mine—standard procedure in cases of wounded pilots and damaged aircraft. As Craigwell and I anxiously watched, he lost altitude rapidly but managed to get a couple of hundred yards safe within our territory before making a crash landing. Though his plane did not ignite, he did not get out of it, indicating that he was either dead or badly hurt. Then an ambulance came plunging up, and we knew that, if alive, he still had a chance.

Back at base there was no word on him. I began calling various medical agencies; none had him on record. We eventually found him in a hospital in Pyongyang, severely injured. Unconscious

163

when picked up and so unable to identify himself, he had been turned over to the Koreans; since he had been flying an aircraft with Korean markings, the ambulance driver had thought him a Korean!

As Jackson had bright red hair, I couldn't for the life of me understand this mistake, until I remembered that Korean and American pilots in our outfit now wore exactly the same uniform without any distinguishing insignia. Later I learned that Jackson had received a wide gash across his face, and this too had tended to obscure his identity.

That one's friends and associates might die at any time was to be accepted with the equanimity with which one had to face one's own possible death. To those who were afraid of death I was able at times to bring consolation by explaining that there was nothing to fear. After Jackson went down and before we knew that he was still alive, I found one of his close friends sitting on his cot silently smoking one cigarette after another and staring morosely at the floor between his feet. I sat beside him, and we talked for a long time. I could not assure him that Jackson was alive or, for that matter, that he himself would be alive twenty-four hours hence; I could only try to introduce the idea that death is not something to be feared. I made a simple analogy. Life is like a shadowy room, crowded with people we can't see quite clearly. Beyond is a door to a lighted room. Occasionally the door opens, and someone from the room of shadows passes into the lighted one. That's all there is to it—just a step, a change, from darkness to light.

Christ showed us so clearly by example that death and the here-after are not to be feared. In His last moments on earth in His mortal form He was in a torment of doubt and agony, and He asked from the Cross, "My God, why hast Thou forsaken me?" But resurrected and returned to earth after seeing the light of Heaven, He was tranquil and pure in spirit. This glimpse of the Hereafter has proved gloriously reassuring to His followers for centuries.

164

Jackson lived, I am happy to say, and returned to us before being reassigned elsewhere to ground duty. It was seldom wise to encourage a pilot to fly combat again after such a violent crash as his.

Another afternoon I received a call to an area along the Yalu River. The privileged sanctuary had been countermanded, and aerial reconnaissance had discovered a number of vehicles up there. Craigwell and I went on the search. Coming up a valley, we saw a flight of American F-51s, apparently hunting the same target. Diving and circling but unable to turn it up, they presently moved on. Just to make sure, Craigwell and I decided to scout quickly over the area they had been working. Breaking out of the valley, we examined the flatlands and suddenly picked out fifty camouflaged vehicles.

We began strafing—straw stacks, bogus huts, everything. Having lived with the Koreans, we knew exactly how they stacked straw, and could detect it as camouflage. Craigwell was particularly good with green camouflage, and I could pick up brown. It was quite a day for the Korean air force when we turned in our report for that two-plane mission: we had been able to destroy forty-two vehicles.

For a time the general optimism around the base increased. Sometimes it seemed almost as if we were now engaged in a mopping-up operation. The phrase "It'll all be over by Christmas" crept into our talk. We were further buoyed up by the arrival one day of General Partridge, now in command of the Far Eastern Air Force, with the news that he was assigning us a C-47 to be used as an administrative aircraft. Since I was a C-47 pilot, I could check out our own flyers in it. Immediately upon delivery we painted our proud Korean insignia on the plane, and Hal Wilson took over as "administrative pilot." As another sign that we had come of age the big C-47 sitting on our runway made our hearts palpitate with pride.

On that same visit General Partridge, after a lunch of C rations (variations of which almost exclusively comprised our diet), asked how long it had been since we had had any fresh food.

I remembered easily. "We had some lettuce on the Fourth of July," I told him.

He made no comment, but soon after returning to headquarters he dispatched us a C-47 filled with fruit and vegetables, eggs, and —hallelujah!—fresh meat. For a while we lived mighty high on the hog.

Another general, Glenn Barcus of the Fifth Air Force, came to visit us. An able jet pilot, Barcus also had a reputation for being a stickler for correct military deportment and appearance. He believed that they reflected a necessary discipline. But warmth and humor pervaded his strictness, and when he remarked, bumping along in my miserable jeep, that he had never seen a vehicle in worse shape than mine, I interpreted it as sympathy rather than criticism.

Though my jeep was developing a miscellany of ailments, we successfully made it to Pyongyang, where the General and his aide wanted to look over the situation. General Barcus's appearance was impressive, and even the children in the streets promptly recognized him as a figure of importance. They waved to us, their dirty faces beaming. The aide-de-camp and I waved back, and I glanced around to see how their friendliness was affecting the General. He was sitting as erect as ever, staring straight ahead, apparently unmoved. I felt a flash of disappointment that he could be so unaffected by these eager salutations. Then the corner of my eye caught the surreptitious movement of his hand, hanging over the side of the jeep. Secretly this very correct military man was waving back!

That particular jeep kept getting more undependable every day. Finally its radiator began to leak like a sieve. It would have been a waste of parts to replace any one in particular even had replacements been available; but the radiator was its complete undoing.

166

Two views of pilot and plane just before taking off from Yongdungpo (Seoul) for a mission. I flew more than sixty missions in this F-51, Number 18.

This is where most of our orphans came from—bombed and battered Seoul.

Two glimpses of some of our orphans after a few months on Cheju Island. The Korean woman below is Mrs. Whang, director of the orphanage, and the airman trying to coax a smile from the child on the right is Cpl. Thomas D. Cabaniss of Union, South Carolina.

ABOVE: *I discuss the next day's mission with Gen. Kim Chung Yul of the Korean Air Force.* BELOW: *Four pilots of the ROK Air Force receive a briefing from Capt. George Metcalf as I listen in.*

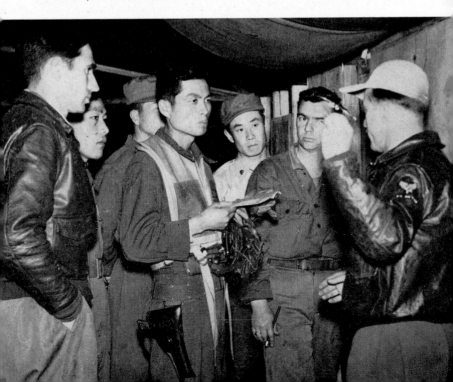

ABOVE: *Gen. Earle Partridge alights from our C-47 on Cheju Island after inspecting how we had fixed up the plane for President Rhee.* TOP RIGHT: *In front of the 6146th mess hall at Seoul. The House of Lamb indicated that Sergeant Lamb was Mess Sergeant.* BOTTOM RIGHT: *One of my crew members, Jim Mullins, gives me a hand before I take off on another bombing and strafing run over North Korea.*

President and Madame Syngman Rhee stand with me in the garden of their residence in Pusan the afternoon I was awarded the Korean Order of Military Merit.

Two views of my farewell visit at the orphanage on Cheju Island. ABOVE: *Before the orphans with Captain Erickson, our C-47 pilot, Mrs. Whang, and a Korean congresswoman.* BELOW: *Mrs. Whang.*

On that final visit to the Korean orphanage on Cheju Island in May of 1951, I was photographed with Mrs. Whang and one of the original children, all decked out in her American castoffs, whom we had evacuated from Seoul in Operation Kiddy Car.

I was plowing along a bumpy dirt road one day when a vindictive hiss heralded another opening seam. The little water remaining boiled happily out. I climbed out only to find that a headlight had also fallen off. I was examining this final damage when another jeep pulled alongside and a couple of GIs offered to give me a lift. "Shove that crate in the ditch—it's had it," one of them said.

I'm afraid I have very little patience with mechanical contrivances that let me down, and that patience was exhausted now. I pulled out my .45 and administered the *coup de grâce*, adding five more holes to the radiator's collection. I could only hope that General Barcus, had he been there, would have approved of my proper military dispatching of this crippled vehicle.

At Pyongyang we found more evidence of the tragedy the fleeing Communists had left behind. In a river bed about a mile from the field we discovered the bodies of forty civilians, most of them men, with a handful of women and even a child or two, strewn along a sand bar—all shot. Their hands had not been tied together, however, and I wondered whether in that last agonizing moment they had struggled desperately or fled for life, or whether meaning and sanity and beauty had long since disappeared from their lives, leaving them to face death apathetically. The Communist system of intelligence sought to include the neighbors and erstwhile friends of a suspected democratic sympathizer. Anyone could inform on anyone else. In Pyongyang I was told of a case in which brother had denounced brother, causing him to be killed.

There was also evidence of guerrilla activity around the airfield at night. Investigation by Korean air police showed that it was directed from a post in the vicinity. A search of houses revealed a woman who was keeping a detailed map of all the movements on the field. By moving quickly, they saw to it that she received a proper trial.

But our main problem on the ground remained supplies, particularly of rice and millet with which to pay our laborers. Some Koreans came in with a report that they had found a warehouse full of rice, locked, with a sign on the door. But they failed to inform me that the sign was written in English. Immediately I sent trucks to get some of the rice and Korean guards to keep looters away.

A Colonel Price, who had been sent to coordinate all Air Force activities in the sector, also needed rice to pay his workers. But when his men went to what he thought was *his* warehouse to get it, they were resisted by our armed Korean guards. Thus I was put in the interesting position of commandeering supplies from the area commander. Price might have caused me trouble if it had not happened that he was an old friend. Our interview ended amiably. "The next time I need anything," he said, "I'll come to you; you always have a way."

Then Pyongyang (K-24), like other fields before it, began to get overcrowded.

Coming in from a night flight, Craigwell, tossed sideways by a freak gust of wind, swerved into a gun abutment and banged up his plane. He was particularly chagrined because it was his first accident. Yet it was a wonder we were not having more. With the increasing load of operations, K-24 was getting so crowded that it was even becoming hazardous to take off and land. This congestion was heavily intensified when another airstrip nearer Pyongyang began to be overrun by transport, troop carriers, and supply aircraft. A diversion was thus made to our field.

On top of that, Colonel Lowe brought an advance fighter unit to stage out of K-24. His aircraft were to fly missions from our field during the day and return to a rear area for the night. This meant that they had to maintain a unit at our advance base for ammunition, gasoline, and bombs. As Lowe was senior officer, he assumed command of the field—and rightly so, for his operations were the most important there.

With him was Col. Milton Glessner, whom I hadn't seen since World War II. When I was a cadet at Napier Field, Ala-

168

bama, he had been my flying instructor. Now he was Colonel Lowe's executive officer. Despite my friendship with both men, there immediately was friction. Without interfering with the operations of others, I yet fought to maintain the growing identity and necessary independence of our group.

First a small unit used for parking aircraft was assigned to living space occupied by us. Next they needed our maintenance buildings. Old as they were, this was the first time we had been able to use buildings for equipment and supplies—a great source of encouragement to the men. It also gave them a more comfortable place than our cold and drafty tents to work in bad weather. But we had to yield again, for I was outranked.

I recognized that our buffetings from pillar to post were nothing new or strange in fluid, violent campaigns. Every combat CO in military history has probably felt the prime importance and unique contribution of his own organization and used his seniority to further it. Certainly this was true of myself, and of Lowe and Milt also. They were only acting for what they were convinced was the greater good. But being human, this kind of rationale did not reconcile me to the fact that every facility they appropriated on the field was at the expense of my group.

When they announced that they needed our last warehouse as well as the school in which we were living, I exploded. With my heels dug in I declared that we had been shoved around enough! Under no circumstances would I move out of those two remaining buildings! As my superior Colonel Lowe could have insisted; but he understood my feelings and let the matter drop. We remained in possession. After cooling off I apologized to him for my strong remarks. His attitude toward my uncalled-for popping off was magnanimous and even amiable. Sadly I never had an opportunity to tell Milt Glessner that I was sorry; he was killed too soon on a combat mission.

In the air we continued to push on as far north from base as fuel and light conditions would permit. One morning we saw a large company of enemy troops moving through the ground mists. This was unusual in that heretofore we had encountered only small bands, often in retreat, and this was a company of around six hundred, marching steadily southward. We went down, dive-bombed them, and returned to report on the estimated number we had destroyed.

That night I got a call from Air Force intelligence wanting more information—confirmation of the number of troops involved, the exact spot where we had found them, the direction in which they had been marching, their general appearance. Apparently ours was among many early reports indicating a massive troop movement from north of the Yalu River. We weren't particularly disturbed by the interrogation, though, as it turned out, we should have been: it was our first hint that the Chinese were coming in.

The gathering and piecing together of the intelligence by which you try to predict the enemy's next move is a tricky business. Another bit of information we passed on to headquarters wasn't taken very seriously, I'm afraid. When in the latter part of September Gen. Kim Chung Yul came to see us from Taegu, he brought a picture of some Korean pilots who had been in his class at Japanese flight-training and officer's school. A number of them subsequent to repatriation had gone to North Korea and were flying for the Communist air force. He had learned through sources unavailable to us that several had been taken to Manchuria, where they were being trained in jets. I thought that this might be an indication that the Reds were planning to use jet aircraft over Korea and took the information to Fifth Air Force headquarters. But since it had come from a native source, I am sorry to say that it was not considered reliable.

In November, 1950, those same North Koreans, some of them ex-classmates of General Kim's, came back into the war with MIGs. Then the Chinese Communists attacked across the Yalu River, committing their forces to a drive southward through the center of the peninsula. They split the UN forces and necessitated

170

immediate evacuation of the Marine units on the south bank of the Yalu. It was the beginning of what General MacArthur called "a new war." There was no more optimism.

This new war in the air and on the ground intensified the sad lot of noncombatants even more than it did ours. Maj. Kay Won administered to passing casualties in many ways. One afternoon a little boy was brought in who had found a Russian hand grenade of the potato-masher type and had been wounded playing catch with it. The Korean children, having no toys, were extraordinarily resourceful. They could fashion playthings out of old cans, empty cartridges, K-ration boxes. This poor little tyke had picked up the wrong discarded item. Though it was against regulations to take care of him, Major Kay and our enlisted medic, Sergeant Crowder, patched up his wounds and kept him in the infirmary with a chance for survival until he might be able to rejoin his parents.

Soon after, a war correspondent from the London *Times* arrived in a jeep with a Korean driver and the latter's pregnant wife. She was having labor pains. Kay Won performed the delivery, while the correspondent went on to Taegu. After a week the new parents set out on foot to look for him in order to regain the husband's job. In Korea even the most menial job was one a native would travel miles to keep.

But most distressing to me was the case of a woman who showed up one day with a sick boy of three or four. The child must have been conceived by a member of our occupation forces prior to the Korean War, for he was half Negro. The mother had no money, and when she had wandered back north to her home, her people had refused the child medical treatment—because he was a different color.

We took care of the little boy until he had regained a semblance of health. When she came to take him away, she offered me a little crocheted picture in a frame. It was the one possession she had left in the world, but refusing to accept something for

171

nothing, she wanted to give all that she had. It was a gift of such a heartbreaking nature that I could not refuse. I wish I could have showed it to her own people, to those who had forced her to come begging for aid among fearsome strangers. And I wished the more fervently that bigotry were not so powerful that it could visit even a battlefield.

xviii

The Red drive was by the beginning of December getting closer to the field every day. Pyongyang was midway between the front lines and the area to which our forces were retreating. It was beginning to look like a rout: tides of refugees parted to let UN troops stream down the highway past our installation. We kept it operational, but whenever we returned from a mission it was with some misgiving that we might not have a field to land on.

One night we were awakened by thunderous explosions from Pyongyang. We thought that the Chinese had declared all-out war and were attacking the city with heavy bombers. Later we found out that it wasn't an attack. An ammo truck had backed into the marshaling yard, caught on fire, and set off a series of explosions. The result was the complete devastation of the Pyongyang railroad yard and the American supply dump—a serious blow when coupled with the threat of the Chinese armies pushing down upon us.

The following night Sergeant Crowder came to report that in the infirmary was an American soldier who would have to be airlifted to a big hospital. He was bleeding internally from ulcers and required immediate attention beyond our medical scope. Our C-47 had just returned from an airlift to Japan. Major Wilson was extremely tired, and Colonel Chang, who had been the copilot, was worried almost to distraction about his family, near Taejon. Anxious to get them evacuated, he asked for leave. That left me.

The weather was bad—snow and rain, ice forming on our

173

planes' wings. Some of the fighter-pilots volunteered to serve as copilot, but their presence was too valuable at the field in the event that the aircraft didn't make it back that night. Instead I took Sgt. Ray Engel along to serve as copilot; he was crew chief on the C-47 and knew it well. With Dr. Kay and Sergeant Crowder we put aboard the American GI, semiconscious and in intense pain, and started for Japan.

The airways controller on radio gave us a minimum altitude of 5,000 feet along the route out of Korea. This information left me a little jittery, as I knew that some of the mountain peaks were considerably higher. Yet I would have to remain at 5,000 feet all during the flight anyway: the doctor had told me that the boy was in critical shape and probably could not stay alive at a high altitude. Normally I would have preferred flying 2,500 feet higher.

We stayed in the bad weather for several hours. Just as we came out of it, approaching Pusan, I momentarily looked over my right shoulder. My scalp lifted. A mountain range loomed alongside the aircraft, and we were considerably below the ridge line. I looked out on the other side—another range. Not knowing for certain that the radio beam was directing me down this valley, it was a nerve-wracking ride, made no easier by the constant forming of ice on the wings. But continuing at this low altitude, we made it to Itazuke Air Base and saw our passenger taken into the general hospital.

One morning, starting out with Craigwell and a pair of Korean flyers, my engine sounded rough and then cut out on the take-off. Not wishing to hold up the flight, I told Craigwell to take over. We were still tinkering with the engines when the trio returned.

Craigwell, who was an excellent flyer, made a bumpy landing for no discernible reason. One look told us that his plane had not been hit. Taxiing in, he cut his engines; but as the crew chiefs came toward his plane, he motioned them away. They

174

drew off, sensing that something had happened. By the time I reached him, he had gotten out of the cockpit and was standing motionless beside the fuselage, a kind of paralyzed expression on his face. I stood beside him, asking if he wanted to talk. Slowly the story came out—one that for me had a dreadfully familiar ring.

During the flight a ground control officer had called for a strike against barges of enemy troops crossing the river at Sinuiju. Finding the target, Craigwell had led the Korean pilots in to bomb and strafe it. Too late he saw that the barges held not troops but refugees being transported across the river. Under the hail of fire mothers were piteously holding up babies for identification; men, women, children, were tumbling in heaps, hanging over the gunwales, diving into the water bleeding. Craigwell saw all that in the flash of the strafing pass and, roaring on, knew that the control officer had made a mistake.

It was a tragic accident of war—not his fault; but what good would it do to tell him that? The scene was forever imprinted on his mind. I did my best to console him, even telling him how I too had fired on just such a target, undergone just such a shock. Sitting beside the battered plane, watching the waves of agony lessen on his face, I gave thanks that it should be I of like guilt who was with him now.

The Communist armies were upon us.

Orders came to evacuate the field. In two days we would receive airlift assistance out. Quickly and quietly we set about preparing for the move. But only a few minutes after we had received the news, a Korean pilot, practicing a landing, forgot to put his landing gear down. With its propeller, engine, and radiator folded underneath, the plane looked as though it would have to be left behind. The ground crew spiritedly volunteered to try to repair it, though I thought it impossible that they could have it flyable by the time we must leave. But on the morning of the third day, when we were clearing the field for the final time, they proudly came to me to report it ready. They had worked day and night without rest, without stopping, to install a new engine and to make the other repairs—a major task which ordinarily would have taken at least a week.

Colonel Lowe's organization had number-one priority for the airlift out of the field, and the Mosquito squadron was next. I asked headquarters what airfield we would retreat to; would it be possible for us to go back to Chinhae? By Korean efforts the strip there had been lengthened and made usable and I felt it belonged to the Korean air force. I received word that Colonel Lowe was to move his fighter wing there. We were to go to Taejon, about halfway between Seoul and Taegu.

This was discouraging news. I knew the airstrip at Taejon was suitable only for light operations. But far more upsetting news was announced at a meeting at Fifth Air Force headquarters. These moves south were a possible prelude to a complete withdrawal from Korea! I thought at once of Dr. Rhee and of the agonies of doubt and uncertainty he must be feeling at that moment.

When the North Korean laborers who had been working around the field learned about the approach of the Chinese, most of them simply disappeared. They left either to evacuate their families or to go home to await the enemy and then serve him.

The seven young girls who had worked so faithfully in our mess hall were alarmed because their association with us had been so close. The night before we were to leave I called them together in the mess tent. In the emptied, now gloomy tent they huddled together, inspecting me solemnly. Looking at their faces, I knew that they foresaw terrible trouble. For some time they had been referring to me in giggling whispers as "papa-san"— the GI-Oriental creation for "dear old man." Now this "dear old man" obviously had bad news for them.

I began, speaking through the interpreter, by giving them a choice. They could, if they wanted, go with us to Taejon. When circumstances permitted, I would see that they were brought back here to their homes. They were to go home, consult their families, and make their decisions. Those who wished to accompany us should come the next morning, fully packed and ready to leave.

For those who preferred to remain in Pyongyang I had another plan. They would tear their clothes, scratch their faces, and tell their neighbors that we had badly maltreated them when they refused to come along to the distant encampment. Such tales might protect them from informers only too eager to win favor with the advancing Reds by pointing out which people in town had "collaborated" with the Americans.

I knew that in the latter suggestion was some danger of adding fuel to the fires of Red propaganda; but I highly valued the lives of these merry, industrious youngsters and felt a considerable degree of responsibility for them. In weighing their lives against what meager help I might be giving the Communist propagandists, there was no doubt which way the scales must tip. Too, I was aware that the Reds didn't need such examples of our "brutality" for their claptrap purposes; they were expert at inventing "atrocities" out of thin air, and there were thousands who would gladly lie for them just for a little food and protection.

When I had finished, I could detect no reactions on their stolid little faces other than sadness. It seemed that they already had made up their minds to stay here and take their chances. They bowed and left. I was certain that I would never see them again.

The next morning all seven showed up, each with a little bag of possessions. Solemnly they packed the pots and pans, and without a single tear shed climbed into the C-47 and left for the unknown future that lay ahead. It was quite a testimonial if any of us had been curious about the attractions of life under Communist rule.

While these girls were with us, the attitude of the men was the same as that toward kid sisters. Their youth and fineness were respected throughout the unit. Finding themselves treated with this guardian kindliness, they worked like beavers, while their gay chatter rose above the kitchen noises. They soon exchanged their Korean names for American ones. Susans or Gerrys at home might have been surprised to learn that they had namesakes among Korean teen-agers thousands of miles away.

I was never able to make good my promise to send them back home; United Nations forces never again got as far north as Pyongyang. But time and God's help took care of that for me. Each one of them eventually married a young South Korean.

Our plan was for our vehicles to go overland to the new field with men, equipment, and stores, while pilots would fly the planes out. While the convoy was being loaded, some of us went over to Pyongyang. The city was seized by the terrible agony of a mass evacuation. Confusion and terror reigned everywhere. The enemy had wrecked the fixed bridges, and the pontoon bridges, put across the river by UN engineers, were occupied by our retreating forces. No civilians were allowed on them because of the problem of saboteurs, who might plant explosives. Again the Korean civilians had to suffer cruelly for the actions of their Communist neighbors to the north.

Enough of one bridge remained for passage across by the more agile of the forlorn refugees. Its girders swarmed with people crawling desperately toward the south bank. Those who couldn't perform this feat had to ford the freezing water. It was so cold that during the night ice would form a short distance from each bank. Women, older men, and children sought to wade across, some holding infants above their heads. Perhaps half would manage the excruciating passage. Others would reach the middle of the river and then slip or collapse from the chill. Swept from their feet, they would come up struggling, often losing hold of their children. Sometimes an entire family would drown together. Those who reached the other side would have their clothes frozen to their bodies by the biting wind. The chances of smaller children surviving this final trial were slight. No one will ever know how many died that night in the river; but yet they continued to come, driven by the fear of the Communist armies at their heels.

This scene will always remain one of my most miserable memories of war. Refugee civilians are many times more pathetic than combatants because they are so vulnerable, so defenseless. And we could do little for them. We carried some gas drums which we wouldn't be able to evacuate down to the riverbank, knocked the tops off them, and set them afire. At least these cold and miserable people could warm themselves when they came out of the water.

It was like a nightmare. Standing on the bank, I wished, even pretended like a child, that it wasn't true, that I could turn my back and the whole inhuman scene would disappear. That night I vowed never again to pray for myself—for my own well-being or happiness. I knew so well that I had had much more than my share of the fine things in life.

I thought of a group of Communist prisoners in an American POW compound near Pyongyang. While these refugees were struggling to get out, many dying on the way, children being separated from their parents or suddenly becoming orphans—all being forced to leave a lifetime's possessions behind—as this agony was being endured, those Communist soldiers, sharers of responsibility for it, were being treated like respected prisoners of war. They were being given new clothes and new shoes, put aboard aircraft, and flown out. The rules of war make for ironic contrasts at times.

Back at the field we continued to watch with growing bitterness the endless cavalcade of displaced people trudging to nowhere. We had a large store of rice, only part of which we could take with us. A Korean was posted in the road to tell the refugees that they could have what they could carry. Dazed men went staggering down the road under 50-pound sacks but with a new glimmer of hope.

Infantry units were already taking up defense positions on the far edge of the field, digging in and returning occasional small-arms fire. Our convoy was almost ready. The Mosquito squadron left the field, and then the Eighteenth Bomber Wing. Equipment was so scarce with us that we determined not to leave any behind. The men worked methodically on through the night until all the trucks were loaded. Once they were on the road, our aircraft also pulled out. Beyond lay the wretched city of Pyongyang, and then it was gone—tragic and broken.

At Taejon, designated "K-5," the field was short, narrow, and terribly muddy. It had no parking area, and had never been planned for use as a fighter strip. Still, these conditions which made no one else want it were why we were able to obtain it. It was our own, and it posed another challenge.

As soon as our trucks started arriving overland from Pyongyang, we set about making it operational. The weather was foul; it either rained or snowed throughout much of the day. We tore up some old quonset huts to rehabilitate those we were to live in and to build a mess hall. Our precious gasoline stoves soon made us relatively comfortable on the ground.

Flying proved to be almost impossible. The runway conditions made operations especially difficult for the Koreans who were not yet checked out in the F-51s. Nor did we wish to risk the more experienced ROK pilots. They were the nucleus of the dream which meant so much to their countrymen: a fighting air force. Once more it seemed more advisable to locate someplace else where we could accomplish our training mission, and to maintain this Taejon field as a fighter strip only.

It was in discussing with Gen. Kim Chung Yul the possibilities of other fields that I first heard about the island of Cheju, which was later to become the "promised land" for a thousand homeless children. Sixty miles south of the west coast of Korea, it is a volcanic island about twenty miles in diameter. Kim, who had earlier sent a few of his men there to maintain a stand-by base, said that it was particularly suitable for training. Considering the possibility that we might have to get out of Korea entirely, it sounded promising. I suggested that we keep an element at Taejon and send the more experienced pilots to Cheju to conduct an intensive training program. We would use it as a main supply area, and aircraft needing maintenance could be sent there, conditioned, and then returned to the mainland. We could "train and maintain" on Cheju and fight from Taejon.

Cheju, as I first saw it, seemed essentially one great volcanic peak rising gently, and then more steeply, 6,000 feet out of the sea. It is a bleak place with few trees and volcanic rock and ash everywhere. In 1948 bandits still lived in caves high on the mountain, from which they would periodically raid the little villages on the coast. Around these villages, inhabited mostly by fishermen, oyster divers, and farmers, are clustered small fields of grain separated by rock fences. Flying over Cheju the first time, I was sharply reminded by its bleak beauty of Scotland.

Korean legend has it that Cheju is the "Land of Three Manys" —many winds, many women, and many rocks. The "many women" is explained by the fact that most of the young men of Cheju leave for the mainland in search of work and often do not return until they are old men. This leaves women to do most of the heavy work.

Our planes were flown over, and a program was started for the additional Korean pilots being sent us. Our experienced Korean pilots could act as instructors under the supervision of American pilots. This cut down our combatant strength, leaving only a few Americans to keep the group's record up. However, that record was not only maintained but embellished by notable strikes, though in the weeks to come few knew that these were solely Americans flying those Korean-marked F-51s.

While we were setting up at Taejon and getting organized at Cheju, the front-line situation became even more acute. Our ground forces once more had to withdraw southward a considerable distance. This meant that the enemy, traveling rapidly, was overrunning the long columns of refugees looking for the protection of the United Nations. To the Communists the simple fact that they were refugees trying to get away meant that they were friendly to us. The Communists made capital of this supposition.

When refugee columns approached the United Nations front lines, our men would let them through. A great number of Red guerrillas would also come through, often dressed as women. A Communist would kill a mother, disrobe her, put on her clothes, take her children by the hand, and head for our lines. Other Communist women posed as refugees and smuggled in dynamite and ammunitions under their clothes. Several yards of primer cord (for fuses) was found wrapped around one woman's waist. Another carrying a very heavy pack aroused the suspicion of UN guards by running down the road and then veering into a field. Refusing to stop when hailed, she had to be fired on. One bullet hit her pack, apparently full of dynamite, and she exploded.

Because these saboteurs were slipping through with the refugees, it became necessary to plug our lines. This threw the refugees back toward the enemy. Seeing them caught in no man's land, he would open fire to drive them back toward our lines again, where kindness might open another gap for his spies to enter.

Battered from all sides, the poor creatures in the middle floundered in a mire of despair. Those who did manage to pass into the comparative safety of our lines clogged the roads in pitiful hopelessness, leaning against the vicious weather, bent under the load of what they had managed to salvage from their lost homes.

Now the fall of Seoul appeared imminent. A number of orphanages had been evacuated before the invader, throwing bands of children into flight. Most were trying to make their way south. We fed as many as we could. To replenish our supplies, such as those of powdered milk and stale bread, Mike Bellovin and I would make nightly forays on any dumps we could reach and still be back in time to fly in the morning. What we could not obtain by a brazen attitude with busy quartermasters we secured by abject pleading.

These expeditions gave us a closer picture of what the unhappy natives were undergoing in Communist-held territory. The stories told by the refugees were terrifying. But harsh as was the fate of the adults, that of the children shook the soul. Separated from their parents by panic or death, they were suffering from starvation, malnutrition, and disease. Bereft and with no place to go, many lay down in ditches or frozen roads for a sleep from which they never awakened. To most death was a benediction.

It was a sick world in which we fought. Descending from our daily duties in the sky, we would hear of fresh evidences of brutality that would send us on the next morning's mission more than ever determined to stamp it out: a pathetic prostitute, killed for having associated with an American . . . a boy slain for having a bit of GI boot polish in his little box . . . soldiers found with raw, ripped shoulders and arms, their eyes pierced with sticks, and some subjected to other tortures so revolting that the mind rebelled at the thought of them.

Was there to be any end to it? Had there ever been a place called Marietta, Ohio?

xix

What came to be known by the somewhat precious name of "Operation Kiddy Car" was born of the plight of the children wandering homeless among us. Like other combat units, we had to befriend those who came by. Misery resulting from the Communist onslaught touched upon millions all along the peninsula, but upon the little ones most harshly. Everywhere men were trying to give them succor, and this brought more. As with us at Taejon and at Seoul and at Pyongyang, they had swarmed around every encampment, until a concerted effort had been necessary to move them to a central orphanage in Seoul.

By voluntary contributions of money and by scrounging supplies, we managed to keep the pack who overran our field in a degree of health or at least alive, continuing to send a steady stream of them along to the orphanage at Seoul. We would come back from our daily missions to find their numbers increased like the Lord's loaves and fishes. But what we were able to do for them was obviously only a stopgap; something in larger measure must be undertaken if there was to be a future generation of Koreans. We hoped to win this war; but what good is winning a war if you lose the children?

Then Seoul began to fall.

A friend showed up with alarming news. Lt. Col. Russell Blaisdell, an Air Force chaplain, informed me that we should not send any more children to the central orphanage. It was being abandoned because no facilities were available for evacuating the children if the city again fell to the Communists. The kids were to be given the few CARE packages remaining, and a handful of faithful Korean women had promised to stay with them. But once the city fell, the doors of the orphanage would probably be opened and the children pushed into the streets to fend for themselves.

It seemed such a cruel prospect—for the hundreds of little girls and boys in the orphanage, for the loose mobs of children already roaming the streets, for all those strays like the ones we were looking after here.

Sitting there in depressed silence with Russ, I suddenly thought of Cheju. We had been flying the families of our Korean officers and airmen out there to live. Bleak though the island was, it could make a safe haven for these lost children. There was an old agricultural school out there with only a few students. A run-down building to be sure, but far away and safe from the Communists. It was a wild idea—but this was the moment for wild ideas. There was no time to clear it with Fifth Air Force headquarters, the United Nations Civil Affairs Commission, or anyone else; it was now or never for these kids.

The emerging plan filled me with an almost unbearable excitement and impatience to put it into operation. I told Russ that I would try to get an LST from the Korean navy. Would he go back to Seoul to procure trucks to transport the kids to Inchon, the port of Seoul? I explained that from there we could ferry them out to Cheju, where in the meantime I would make arrangements for our detachment to receive them. At first amazed, Russ quickly caught fire from the plan, sketchy as it was. He knew a United Nations civil-affairs representative who he thought could obtain the trucks. While he hastened back to Seoul to work on the trucks, I started pulling strings to get the LST, at the same time sending Craigwell flying down to Cheju to secure the old agricultural school for the orphans and round up native volunteers to receive them.

Meanwhile Seoul was falling all around us. The roads and rails leading south were jammed with refugees, troops, and military vehicles. The Fifth Air Force headquarters was moving out, as was the Eighth Army headquarters. Syngman Rhee, determined and courageous to the last, had finally been persuaded that his government must once again abandon the capital city. Front-line United Nations troops were even now staging a holding operation on the north edge of town.

After dozens of phone calls and radio messages I secured the promise of an LST. Blaisdell picked up the children at the orphanage and took them in trucks to the docks. For hours a thousand shivering children waited in the freezing cold, but the LST I had been promised did not appear. It was so cold and these thinly clad children were so weak already that seven of them either died right there on the docks or shortly thereafter. Then word came that the LST had been commandeered to evacuate the hard-pressed Marines from the Hungnam Reservoir area. It was awful news. Everything was in readiness at Cheju, and now the gate to safety for a thousand pitiful orphans was banging shut.

Our only choice was to start flying them over in our own C-47. We might take fifty or sixty a trip—the sick, crippled, and smallest first. Looking at their exhausted but hopeful faces, Blaisdell found it almost unbearable to tell them they must walk 10 miles back toward Seoul to the airfield at Kimpo and the bombardment dangers there. Even then lack of time would make it impossible to fly all of them out. It would take over twenty trips. Only a portion could reach the island before the Red attack overran Seoul and swallowed up the rest. The larger or more ambulatory would have to walk on south of the Seoul area toward another airstrip where we might pick them up later, if they were still alive. The chances of this were slight, though, once they were pushed back on the road again.

In desperation I set about getting more planes. I laid siege to Fifth Air Force headquarters. I made telephone contact with General Kim in Taegu. We readied our own C-47 to fly as many out as possible if worst came to worst. Coming back from a mission south of Seoul on which we flew cover for our retreating forces, I dropped into the Kimpo airport to try to corral some planes with my own two hands and my wagging tongue. Meanwhile Craigwell was reporting back from Cheju that the island was ready and waiting for the little refugees, and Chaplain Blaisdell was camping at Fifth Air Force headquarters, adding his powerful persuasion.

And still we had no planes, and the Communists were entering the northern sectors of the city.

The orphans made it to the airport at Kimpo by foot and in trucks, now colder, sicker, and more tired and bewildered than ever. Behind this mass of children, huddled together for warmth and security, the field was a fever of activity. Radios, generators, and other pieces of military equipment were being loaded into C-46s. On the edge of the field, drums of gas and oil were being burned to prevent their falling into Communist hands, spreading a pall of smoke over the whole field.

The answer to our prayers came like a miracle. A flight of fifteen C-54s from the Fifth Air Force appeared in the sky over the Kimpo airport and circled for a landing. The electric thrill that shot through those watching from the field, the emotions that welled up, would be impossible to describe. Out clambered flight nurses and doctors with ample supplies of blankets and medicines. General Partridge, though weighed down by the enormous responsibilities of his command at this turbulent moment, had sent all available cargo aircraft for an evacuation of the whole group!

These C-54s had doors far above the ground, so the children were loaded into trucks, which were then backed up to the high plane doors and the little ones herded inside. In all my life I shall experience no greater thrill of gratitude or relief than when I saw the last ragged little figure disappear inside the last plane—our own C-47.

Then I climbed back into my F-51 and with a light heart flew south for the day's work.

Every other day, or as often as weather and missions permitted, I would find time to fly over to the island, ostensibly to check on progress at our training field. Craigwell and Capt. George Metcalfe, an excellent pilot who had been sent us, knew that I had no doubts about their ability to handle the new classes of students. I would spend a few minutes with them on organizational matters and then hurry the mile over to the orphanage.

Its appearance never ceased to depress me. Since having been abandoned as a school, the building had fallen into neglect. A one-story frame structure on a mud and stone flat, it was drearily weathered. Many of its windows had been broken and patched with bits of tin or cardboard. At first we had nothing with which to make repairs, so it had to retain its dismal aspect. But at least it was a shelter for our charges.

Dr. Kay Won came over to minister to the children until a civilian doctor could be secured. He worked day and night, trying with scanty facilities and medicines to treat wounds and diseases of many kinds. Most of his small patients were in a half-starved state that left them a pitiful margin of resistance.

I made collections from my unit and from anyone else I met and bought a load of supplies. These were to be handled and distributed by two Korean welfare workers who had been given administrative responsibility for the project. But through Sergeant Hong, one of the Korean airmen, I learned that this precious pair were literally taking candy from babies. Many items of foodstuff which could only have come from the small larder at the orphanage were showing up on the market in Cheju. The two Korean administrators were promptly booted out.

Clearly an able and sympathetic person was needed to take charge. Madame Rhee, whose intense interest in the orphanage grew daily, suggested an old friend of hers, Mrs. On Soon Whang, who had been studying social-welfare procedures in England. She proved to be a wonderful choice. From a wealthy, educated family, she had returned to Korea to find her home leveled and her son gone—apparently killed by the Reds. She gave our orphans the mothering and the warm love which they had been so sadly lacking. She was a woman in her early fifties whose lovely face reflected her strong, patient character and great warmth.

From the first she threw herself into the work with whole-souled intensity. She had to. A number of the children were extremely ill; most were suffering from malnutrition; many were wounded. The luckiest suffered only from skin diseases and colds. The list of requirements just to keep them alive was staggering—food, clothing, medicine, equipment of all kinds.

The evacuation from Seoul had received much space in the local *Stars and Stripes*, as well as some coverage in stateside papers. People at home began to send small amounts of money, and around seven hundred dollars was contributed within a few weeks. Yet it was a drop in the bucket compared with our actual needs, and my own organization tried to make up the deficit. My tough samaritans gave every cent they could. But without official backing or continued assistance from some central organization, the threat persisted that the children had exchanged starvation in Seoul for the same on Cheju Island.

Then an epidemic of whooping cough broke out. Mrs. Whang was deeply distressed because she had no money to buy serum and vaccine. In the United States whooping cough is a light childhood ailment; in Korea it is deadly. Little children would contract it and slowly, violently, cough themselves into unconsciousness and finally die. In some cases I could not help but think that death was merciful, because some of the children had been so inadequately treated that they would never have regained their normal faculties.

It seemed to bother some people that Mrs. Whang was a Buddhist. It certainly didn't bother me. She had a goodness which transcended any particular sect or religious faith. "The main thing right now is to get these kids healthy," I told a chaplain who asked why I hadn't selected a Christian supervisor. "We can worry about their souls later." While Christians in South Korea equal or outnumber Buddhists, to attempt a change in belief in any of these tykes at their age and in their condition might have resulted in terrific emotional upheavals. The sense of security we wanted to give them would not have been accomplished by changing their faith. When Christ said, "Suffer the little children to come unto me," He meant *all* children.

Needless to say, Mrs. Whang made no distinction between the Christian and Buddhist children. All received the same love and care; there was no attempt at proselytizing for either faith.

My men continued to contribute generously articles they could obtain at the PX and donations they could extract from other outfits. They gave all the money they could spare and made it my responsibility at least to match that amount. I had already given what I had, so the $600 they now added was their donation alone. Craigwell took it to Japan in our C-47, where he and Dr. Kay Won obtained sufficient medicines to stem the epidemic. Other valuable supplies came through the chaplain's office at Fifth Air Force headquarters, but nothing was forthcoming immediately from the United Nations; they just didn't have anything to give.

In order to get heat Mrs. Whang got some old gasoline drums, knocked part of one end out, and put a stovepipe in the other. In them, horizontally propped above the floor, firewood could be burned. But wood was scarce on the island, so one of the first "contributions" my outfit made was a number of stoves and a little oil. I never asked where they got them.

Naturally fresh water was also in poor supply. What there was had to be made from sea water. This was done at a distillery which manufactured commercial alcohol from the local millet crop. It was a mile from the orphanage—a long way for children to have to haul all the water needed for drinking and bathing. They could only carry small amounts, and the walk alone was overtaxing to many in their weakened condition.

We solved that problem with an old weapons carrier. It had been abandoned by another American organization, and we had put it back together again. Even in its wretched shape, though, we had to account for it, so we submitted a "survey" report. With straight faces and good consciences, we reported that, parked on the dock to unload a small vessel, the vehicle's brakes had let go and it had run off the end of the dock and submerged in 50 feet of water. Not a very likely story, but no one was about to go to the trouble of disproving it.

A small boy learned to operate it, and the kids used the old machine for two years. When at last the engine wouldn't run, they pulled it with a rope—childpower—over to the distillery and then back with a load of water.

Other conditions in the orphanage were as bad. There was very little to eat. Mrs. Whang filled them up as best she could with rice soup (rice and hot water) three times a day, with occasionally a "treat" of powdered milk or powdered eggs which we flew over. Because of the war the usual charity channels were disrupted, and others had their foul-ups. On one visit Mrs. Whang showed me the food shipment she had received for the month from the UN. It was obviously a mistake: six bags of rock salt.

Within the first three months two hundred of the children died for lack of proper diet and medical facilities, many of them from whooping cough. They were buried in a flat, unenclosed plot adjacent to the Cheju cemetery—two hundred little mounds without stones or markers of any kind, the final resting place of children without parents, without homes, almost without identity of any kind. Some day perhaps we'll build a monument there; and if I have my way, the stone will be simply inscribed:

—1950—
Orphan's Home of Korea
Dedicated to the Memory of
Those Whom We Could Not Save

In most cases death was merciful. One tiny thing three or four years old, had so suffered from malnutrition that he was about the size of a newborn baby. He had returned to the prenatal state: with his knees highly inclined, he rested with his head thrust forward on them like an embryonic child. He finally caught the whooping cough. The other children would take care of him when he would start coughing, though they had not the strength to move. Though many were as wracked as he, they would prop him up until the spasm was over. Then they would lay him down gently on his side and cover him up.

I was holding him when he finally coughed his last. The look of peace that came over his wizened little face as life passed made me understand in an instant. Such a one as he could hardly have sinned during his brief stay in the world. On the contrary, the world had sinned, and sinned terribly, against him. Looking at the suddenly peaceful face, I knew that Christ in His mercy had opened the door of light and that the child had walked through into Heaven.

XX

Taejon in December means mud—mud over the hubcaps of trucks, over the wheels of planes, over the tops of boots. But we had to hold on. Seoul had fallen, and with it the fields at Yongdungpo and Kimpo. Suwon was overrun, and ours, at Taejon, became the foremost airstrip within that particular area.

In a fluid tactical situation like this one it was extremely important that an airbase be kept open as close to the front lines as possible. General Partridge instructed me to keep ours in operation until the enemy came over the edge of the field. I agreed; I wanted to be there to see them come over the edge of the field— and fall flat on their ugly faces in the mud.

But that was only one of our problems—though the stickiest, I admit. Guerrilla activities had grown into a formidable menace. A convoy of four Fifth Air Force headquarters trucks was ambushed between Seoul and Taegu, all personnel were killed and a few were partially skinned alive. We doubled our guard around the field only to find to our dismay and embarrassment that the South Korean police were stealing our ammunition.

But our old nemesis, the traffic problem, plagued us the most. An important rail line between Taejon and Taegu was sabotaged, and all the supplies for the front-line troops in our sector began flowing through our field. A very small field to begin with, the Taejon strip now had to handle our own F-51s, an advance echelon of the T-6 reconnaissance outfit, a constant stream of troop carriers, and finally, because the front-line supply problem was growing desperate, a fleet of large four-engined C-54s hardly able to land on the field at all.

Something had to give.

In order to sustain operations during the night, we would keep barrels of sand and gasoline burning on each end of the runway to outline the landing area. But when the wind was high, these flare pots would blow out despite all efforts to keep them lighted. To complicate matters our electric-light system was constantly breaking down.

One night when the wind was blowing and the field lights were disabled, a C-54 transport came in with fifty 50-gallon drums of gasoline to be unloaded. As the aircraft made an approach, the pilot evidently saw that he was not lined up properly with the runway. He had already extended his gears and flaps when he decided to go around again rather than try to land, and gave it full throttle. Something happened. The aircraft settled in, hitting the knob of a hill half a mile off the end of the runway. The fuselage remained pretty much intact, although the front end of the plane was badly broken up and caught fire.

Awakened by shouts, I saw the red glow in the sky. I didn't have to be told what had happened. I jumped in my jeep and sped to the wreckage.

Our ambulance driver Sergeant Crowder and a few enlisted men were trying to work their way to the cockpit to see if there were any survivors. Drums of gasoline were exploding in sheets of flame and bits of metal. Two or three times whole drums of gasoline were blown into the air, one such explosion bringing flames dangerously near the men. Ordering them back, I got as close to the cockpit as I could and lay down to look into it. I couldn't see a thing.

Though the gasoline was still blowing up, the men kept crawling up to me. Crowder said he'd be damned if he would go back unless I did. I knew he meant it. I didn't see how anyone in that cockpit could have survived the crash. I went back with them. Free of the flames, I told them they could only go up again when the gasoline drums had stopped blowing up.

Returning to the base, I made a report on the accident to headquarters. As I was finishing the call, Crowder came in to say that the flames had finally died down. They had gotten to the cockpit and under the wreckage had found two men thrown out of the aircraft and down into the mud. They were unconscious, badly burned, but still alive. He had rushed them to the Army field hospital in Taejon, where they both died.

To this day I wonder about it. If I had gone all the way to the cockpit, or had I let the men go, would we have seen those pilots and been able to dig them out from under the flames? Might they have lived? It is one of those decisions that a commander has to make quickly on the spot. After it is over, he has plenty of time to wonder what the other course would have proved. But he will never know and must only square himself with his own conscience. In this instance the jeopardy to the lives of a dozen men had seemed too great against the slim chance of saving two.

Tragedy continued to dog us. In order to get heat in their quarters, we had to let the men set up stoves equipped with gasoline-burning carburetors. Ordinarily we used automotive gasoline, but when short of it we would use 100-octane gasoline and mix in oil to cut the vapor point. Worried about these stoves in the men's sleeping quarters, I put out an order that no stove could burn all night unless somebody stayed awake to check it.

But the temperature was getting down toward zero, and sleeping bags alone weren't enough protection against the cold. Many of the men kept their stoves burning, assigning one of their group to watch each. Despite this precaution, the stove in one of the huts exploded. Had the watcher been awake, he might have prevented it, but all were asleep. One man failed to get out in time. Caught in his sleeping bag, he was burned to death. The quonset burned to ashes with all their possessions.

A report on the man at fault, if any individual could be described as solely responsible, would not bring the dead man back. The young officer in charge was deeply affected by the tragedy; he would never forget his share of the responsibility. Like him many of the officers were young and had been in the service for so short a time that sometimes they seemed to be boys playing a game. I was only thirty-three, but command being an aging business, I often felt three times that. Still, the "Old Man" was a good deal younger than some of his weathered crew chiefs.

There were two more fires in quick succession. We had a small control tower from which our radio operator directed aircraft landings. One day I was coming back in alone. Ten minutes out I called the tower, and getting no answer, presumed that it was off the air. It was: while I was gone, the tower had burned down, with all equipment destroyed. We had to cannibalize a radio jeep and set up control facilities in a little tent along the edge of the runway.

In the third fire we lost our base-operations and weather station. This was a particularly significant loss because the operations building is the nerve center of any airfield. In our case it also was the only spot not in the mud. About thirty feet square, built of plywood and backed by a quonset hut, it was the fanciest building we had ever had. Here also were our parachutes and flight records. In its back end our weatherman had been setting up his station. He had done several weeks research to get his standard pressure tables established. These were lost, along with everything else, when gasoline leaked from a rubber hose, giving off fumes that were ignited by a hot stove. The whole structure was consumed within a few minutes.

After the fire was out, all the officers came to my hut to discuss a course of action. Captain Muhlenburg, the weatherman, was particularly downcast over the loss of his work. In addition, headquarters representatives were due tomorrow to inspect his weather facilities, and he had just painted the inside of his office. It would have been a feather in his cap if they had found a shipshape weather station in a forward area with few facilities and no resources through normal supply. He bemoaned the loss of his weather station, but no more so than the pilots did their parachutes.

The burning of the parachutes was truly a body blow. With

the weather so cold and damp, we couldn't leave them in the planes for fear of mildew and rot. Every parachute that belonged to our fighter-type aircraft had been in the burned building, and we were not allowed to fly combat until we had received another supply. Furthermore a pilot needed to sit up high on top of his packed parachute in an F-51 in order to see through the windshield. I flew anyway, sitting on top of folded blankets, but I wouldn't let the other boys emulate my bad example.

To be grounded when the battle was still raging was acutely depressing to our already generally sagging morale. During the evening I was pondering what to do when I noticed one of the walls of my hut moving as though a strong wind was blowing against it. Going outside, I found the unhappy Muhlenburg with his burly shoulder against the wall, shoving manfully if somewhat drunkenly.

I persuaded him to stop and explain. He wanted to get started right away on a new weather station, he answered. My quonset would make a fine one, so he had decided to move it down to the flight line and get busy. With his broad shoulders and his tenacity I'm sure he would have managed it, but I convinced him to go along to bed and said we'd talk about it in the morning.

Then at nine o'clock, the hour when our weather report had to go in, our communications man appeared. Captain Schmidt was also loaded, and just as lugubrious as Muhlenburg. How, he wanted to know, could he radio in our weather when there was no report from Muhlenburg? It was evident that some of the group were poulticing their feelings with applications of alcohol. With clumsy facetiousness I wrote on a slip of paper, "Base-operations and weather station burned down. Whisky front moving in."

Calling for an enlisted man, I gave him the message with (I thought) an implication that it was not to be put on the wire. However, that's what he did—to the dismay of poor Schmidt, who visualized the apoplectic reactions of commanders in the area when they received the curious teletype.

With morale on all levels depressed by these mishaps and days on end of cold rain depressing it further, I was very pleased to hear that we were to be visited by a USO unit—the only one I ever saw in Korea. The troupe proved to be "Grandpa Jones and his Granddaughters," a country-music quartet of two men and two girls. An audience of nearly four hundred from the field and neighboring units gathered for the show.

Unfortunately for Grandpa Jones, etc., an unplanned incident brought down the house before the show even started.

The crowd of four hundred was larger than we had expected, and to make additional room a crew chief had to move a plane parked near our flimsily constructed latrine. As he gunned the engines, the exhaust blast hit the temporary structure and wrenched off one of the corrugated-tin sides from its two-by-four frame. Two shrieks were heard even over the engine's roar: Grandpa Jones's Granddaughters were inside.

A few minutes later they appeared to better advantage. But though this country quartet sang, played, and told jokes for an hour, they never did get such a big laugh as that one spontaneous roar that went up even before the curtain.

We began to lose airplanes. George Metcalf's engine cut out in a take-off and was demolished; he ended up in a hospital with a wrenched back. Then Jimmy Gillespie, a boy recently arrived in the outfit, had to bail out, and Hal Wilson glided back to the field for a crash landing. Neither were hurt, but two more planes were total losses.

Examining the wreckage of Hal's plane, Sergeant Wheeler, the line chief, located the trouble: rubber diaphragms in the carburetor had cracked, evidently from being in storage. We forwarded a report to a supply depot only to receive in return a letter of reprimand for having torn a carburetor apart in the field; we should have sent it to the depot for checking.

Then a loss occurred which brought to me in all clarity the value of St. Francis of Assisi's counsel about substituting faith for doubt. One morning a flight of four of us was crossing a wooded sector which we believed to be free of enemy installations. Suddenly a heavy burst of ack-ack opened up on us from a circle of guns which evidently had been moved in during the night.

In an instant the lethal little bursts—looking like harmless bits of orange cloud—were surrounding us. "Hit the deck!" I yelled into the radio, and veered right in a rapid descent only to have another gun pick me up immediately. I banked to the left again and, since fire is usually concentrated on the lead plane, told the others to turn away from me.

As I made my turn, I looked around. Craigwell and one of the Koreans had obeyed and were taking the proper evasive action. But the other Korean, the one who reportedly had come from the north in 1948 and whom some warned me never to trust, was diving straight at the gun that was giving us the most trouble. Down he thundered, straight at the barrel, making himself an easy target. His intent was to draw their fire away from us— there is no other explanation. I saw his plane and the enemy gun explode in two almost simultaneous bursts.

On the other side of the hill the rest of us regrouped and flew on without looking back at his smoking grave.

To compensate for these losses we were sent replacement aircraft in order to maintain a complement of twenty planes, half of which were being used at Cheju to train new ROK pilots. With the ten at Taejon we kept grinding out missions until our over-all operational record began to take on a little luster. After one FEAF briefing an officer present told me that because of inclement weather only twelve sorties had been flown that day, all by the Korean air force. (What we had done was to fly four planes on three missions apiece in different areas.) General Stratemeyer was reported to have smiled broadly and said, "Those are my boys!"

Winter was hardening. The runway was usually under mud or covered with snow. This was a particular annoyance to Hal Wilson, who despised getting his feet dirty. Instead of sloshing through puddles on the way to the flight line, he preferred to use a vehicle. If one wasn't available he wore rubber boots, which he would remove before getting into his plane. We teased him about his fastidiousness, but he was right for one reason. A fighter-bomber in combat is frequently upside down or over on one side. If there is dirt on the bottom, it cascades down and can temporarily blind the pilot. Close to the ground this may prove disastrous.

As usual, mud was a constant trial. With all the traffic on the field the runway would become cut up during the day. When darkness fell crews would drag it with planks to smooth it. If no planes came in after dark to chew it up again, the night's freeze would enable an F-51 to take off smoothly in the morning. But if big ships landed, the consequent ruts were a hazard, particularly for the Korean pilots.

Being the forward unit, we were able to fly when others could not. Mountaintops often would be buried in a murky overcast as though holding up the sky, preventing aircraft from rear areas from getting up front. But our particular location allowed us to fly close to the ground northward, staying under the clouds and following highways, tracks, and passes. The commander of another air unit once accused us of going through railway tunnels.

Because of my impatience with the deplorable runway conditions during the day I would occasionally fly night missions. One night in January I went out earlier than usual because the weather forecast was for a storm moving in on the field around four in the morning. In the area north and northwest it was already snowing, but I could operate over the enemy lines, using the moon and snow on the ground to help me detect targets. If I could find a vehicle and set it on fire, it would light up the countryside and help me find others. I only had to get back to K-5 before a low ceiling set in, because we had no radio aids with which to find the field.

About fifty miles north of Seoul is a valley containing a railroad running north and south, with a gradual rise in the terrain toward a saddle in the mountain ridge which opens on a plateau area near Chorwon. As I passed up the valley, the clouds were lowering, but beyond the saddle a glint of moonlight came through, indicating that the overcast was at least thinner there. I went through the pass into the Chorwon area, where I worked a couple of hours strafing supply columns and troops. There was just enough snow on the ground to disclose movement along the road. I wasn't aware of time or that I was receiving nothing on my radio. Ordinarily over enemy territory there is constant chatter on the radio channels, but in this case I was down low and didn't think it particularly unusual not to hear voices.

About one o'clock I started back down the pass, thinking I could get out the same way that I had come; but I ran into a wall of clouds. The ceiling had lowered until it covered the saddle. With mountain peaks on both sides I had to make a couple of quick turns and an emergency pull-up through the overcast. Climbing with full throttle, I made turns where I thought the valley ran, finally breaking out of the overcast at 12,000 feet.

The "lost procedure" in a combat area is to call out on a radio channel to a forward control post or a tactical air-direction center for a steer. Trying to make a call, I found that my radio dynamotor had ceased to function; my battery was down and I wasn't able either to transmit or receive. I consulted the E-6B computer, an all-purpose navigational aid which we had nicknamed "the confuser." In estimating the time that I had taken to make the emergency pull-up, my approximate ground speed as I was making it, and the distance that I had traveled, at the same time trying to make the radio calls and fly the plane, I found that the computer was exactly what it was called—a confuser. In exasperation I finally opened the canopy and threw it out. I then took a heading back toward Seoul in the direction in which I estimated it to be.

I was flying at 11,000 feet among brilliant stars in a crystal-clear night. Under me was a layer of white cotton clouds. It was a magnificent scene, and I enjoyed it—until I jerked myself back to the harsh realities: I could see no end to the overcast; I had no facilities with which to make a landing under instrument conditions; and a bail-out loomed ahead.

I estimated that I might be near my home base, but since Taejon is not far from the western coast, there was the possibility of a strong east wind blowing my parachute out to sea. I would live for no more than ten minutes in the cold water. Neither did I look forward to landing in guerrilla territory. But oddly enough my greatest worry was over abandoning my aircraft. Each plane takes on a definite personality and identifying characteristics—its trim, its tendency to yaw in a dive, its "feel" in landing. A pilot intimate with his plane can think ahead, plan his next move on what he knows are the capabilities and characteristics of his aircraft. I had flown many missions in Number 18. She flew a little left-wing-heavy, but knowing about it, I could easily compensate. The tension on her cables was perfectly in balance—for me anyway—leaving her controls neither too tight nor too loose. I felt that I knew her every mood and that she probably knew mine. To change to another plane now would be like suddenly dancing with a total stranger after a lifetime of dancing with your wife.

The only consolation I had was that, since it was a Korean aircraft, at least I would not have to make out the lengthy accident report required by the USAF. Lost above the clouds a few thousand feet above Korea and preparing to bail out, I sat there thinking of my acute aversion for forms; I hated forms so much that I'd taught Mike Bellovin to forge my signature on all routine papers. . . . Such were my world-shaking thoughts as I faced crisis.

Idly I began to check the stages of bailing out. Yank on the emergency release bar, and the clamps holding the canopy would unlock and the wind would whip it off. Then unfasten the safety belt and shoulder straps that secured me to the seat and remove the radio headset. Now the risky part: getting out. If I stood up and jumped, I'd get clipped by the tail; better to snake over the side. Safer yet, crawl out on the wing and let go. . . .

Then I thought I'd have another try at saving me *and* the plane together. I remembered a large pocket north of Taejon in which there were no high peaks. Prayerfully hoping that my estimated position was correct, I started to let down through the overcast. At a moment like this a pilot wishes he could reach forward with his foot and probe the clouds with his toes as a barefoot boy feels about in a creek bottom. The highest mountains in the area were about 5,000 feet; I decided to go down to 6,000 feet and see if I could break out. I did so, but I was still in the clouds. I went back up. I then thought perhaps it would be safe—considering the possibility of landing in guerrilla territory or floating out to sea—to let down again to 5,000 feet and make a quick pull-up if I saw a mountain. I started down, envisioning rocky peaks abruptly looming out of the clouds. But at 4,500 feet I suddenly came out in nearly complete darkness—into the pocket I had hoped for.

By this time I had flown over so much of Korea that I could usually find my way without a map. Even when above the clouds, catching only an occasional glimpse of the ground below, sub-conscious navigational instruments in the experienced pilot's mind keep him generally oriented. This particular night, however, the odds had been stacked particularly high against me. To get down I had needed luck or God's beneficence, and I had received both.

A few minutes later I sat in my stilled plane on the runway in front of the hangar. Instead of thinking of the mountain-peak death I had barely avoided or how near I had come to hitting the silk and leaving my plane, I was remembering how beautifully bright the stars had been above the white layer of clouds. Though lost above the clouds, those stars had given me a feeling of security and even of warmth. I knew why: when I was a child and the family would sit on the porch of a warm summer evening, my mother once explained to me that the stars are bright lanterns held by guardian angels. There is great consolation in the feeling that we are watched over. I felt it strongly, sitting there quietly on the runway.

xxi

We were in constant touch with our dual project at Cheju—the training program and the orphanage. Its coordinators at the start were Metcalf and Craigwell. With a dozen enlisted men and some Korean officers, they were conducting a ground school and landing practice for new cadets. When sufficiently checked out to be able to handle the F-51, these neophytes would join with us at Taejon, to be polished up in and for combat.

Mrs. Whang's work with the children went more slowly. It was handicapped, as it had been from the outset, by a lack of funds. On one visit she took me to the sick-room dispensary. Here the ill children were lying in rows on the floor, a single thin blanket under them and one on top. She explained that she could cover several children with one blanket. The image of rows and rows of little black heads sticking out from under the worn blankets stayed with me for many months. By the time spring came, the weaker ones had died off and the survivors had grown stronger.

But Mrs. Whang worked wonders. She made the rice soup suffice. She secured a sewing machine—*one* for a thousand children—and worked constantly on their clothes. To teach them democracy, she set up a system by which they elected an orphan mayor. She was ever conscious of their schooling needs, reaching out in many directions for paper, pencils, and scarce Korean schoolbooks. Under her urging they started a newspaper, and one little boy developed into an accomplished comic-strip artist, making the drawings with colored crayons and laboriously blocking in the

205

dialogue in pencil. All this, mind you, when they didn't have bread to eat, shoes to wear, or fuel to burn.

I rarely had to ask for contributions from the men. There was not one who did not have an abiding thoughtfulness and tenderness for our little charges. They gave so much that I was frequently called upon to write a letter back to a wife explaining that her husband was not spending part of his pay on some Korean beauty but was helping to keep a bunch of kids alive. In cases where I felt that this generosity couldn't be afforded, I tried to check it. The reply of one hard-bitten sergeant was typical: "Colonel, I only wish it was more!"

In the presence of so much death their kindness emerged with a fierce determination to preserve new life. They were an inspiration, and I wrote of them often to Mary, in part to indicate what this whole experience was doing for me. Her response was typical: she began bustling around Marietta for clothes, toys, and food packages that dropped out of the sky on Cheju like manna from heaven. George Metcalf's wife was doing the same in Wheaton, Illinois, and through a lady friend of Hal Wilson's packages started arriving from the Colorado Ladies of the Eastern Star.

At Taejon it became understood that, whenever there was a promotion, into the kitty went the difference in the first month's pay between the old salary and the new. Someone got hold of a Sears catalogue, and a council pored over it for likely items. Knowing how skimpy were bathing facilities on the island, they decided on camp-style rubber bathtubs. After the tubs had been ordered and received, and before they were sent on to Cheju, the purchasers heated water in pails and tried them out "just to make sure they work." The sight of grown men attempting to bathe in 2 inches of water in a collapsible tub was something like seeing a hippopotamus in a fishpond.

Even the winnings in the outfit's poker games were contributed to the orphans. While I never condoned gambling, I knew that it was inevitable in an outfit like ours. I settled for keeping the card games within limits which were principally sociable. After one game the players sent an emissary with a handful of money "for the orphans, sir." He explained that it was a percentage off the table; the men had agreed among themselves that thereafter 10 per cent of every pot would be levied. It helped.

Conditions were getting so crowded in the rickety building housing the children that the only answer seemed to be expansion. I tried my hand at outfoxing the quartermaster: I put in a requisition for sixty sixteen-man squad tents, figuring we could return them when facilities on the island were better developed. But someone caught on that sixteen times sixty amounts to more men than were ever in the 6146th Air Base Unit. The order was canceled—unquestionably with cause—and the children had to stay crowded in the old school.

Their numbers continued to grow because of the enemy's savage firing upon refugees. By driving them toward our lines, they could be used for cover and confusion. More lost and bewildered children came stumbling to us—singly, sometimes in a related pair, or in a band guided by an older child. Daily we would see evidence that the maternal instinct can be as strong in a tot as in a grown woman. We often saw a litle girl packing a younger brother or sister on her puny back while urging on others with patient firmness. Many were on the way to a rendezvous previously set by their parents in case of separation. Others whom we could identify as orphans we picked up, gave food and medicine —eye infections were particularly rampant now—and dispatched to Mrs. Whang in our own C-47.

Hal Wilson, a single man who professed to dislike children, became the butt of many a joke in regard to the orphans. Loving them as much as the rest of us, he nevertheless would look upon them with great uneasiness, almost as if they were creatures from some different planet. Whenever we had a particularly small one in tow, we would plop it in Hal's arms, tell him it was his turn at nursemaid, and then walk away from his cries of consternation.

Our C-47, originally merely a cargo aircraft, now carried the president of Korea as well as groups of orphans. Happily we had had it equipped by a maintenance depot with some airline seats. The Rhees had moved from Taegu to their residence in Pusan, where either Hal or I would on occasion pick up the President and fly him someplace he wished to visit. Through General Kim I had let President Rhee know that our C-47, except in special cases of emergency, was at his disposal. He obviously needed a plane, and we were proud to fly him. My admiration for the indomitable old man never lessened. Often it seemed that all that kept him going was the flame of patriotism alive these many years in his rugged frame. Nor could all their time of travail break Madame Rhee's serenity, humor, and graciousness.

By this time General Walker had been killed, and General Ridgway had assumed command of the UN forces. The Chinese Communists' supply lines, now stretched over hundreds of miles, were showing the strain of our constant air attacks. For the first time their advance faltered. The decision was made to stand. If there was to be no more retreat on the ground, we might be at K-5 for some time.

Now fifty-five enlisted men and eight officers, we set about making ourselves comfortable. Of the thirty quonset huts on the field, five or six were habitable. With the remains of the others we made livable permanent quarters for everyone.

Something there is that welds an outfit together—call it "spirit" or "purpose" or "personality." To Craigwell, Wilson, Bellovin and the others had been added Jimmy Gillespie—a boy with the rare freshness of youth still about him and yet a man fully prepared for combat or worse. When weeks before Jimmy had received his orders in Japan to join the 6146th Air Base Unit, he had found it difficult to do. He had chased us all over Korea. He had been mistakenly sent to Seoul days after we had left, from there north to Pyongyang, whence we had just evacuated, and finally to Taejon, where he caught up with us. Jimmy had been married a few weeks prior to coming overseas, and his young wife, no doubt not realizing how closely we lived with one another, sent him a ukelele. Representing the unit, Mike Bellovin wrote her in protest, claiming that listening to Jimmy on the ukelele was worse harassment than any the enemy had to offer.

It was horseplay and nonsense—but valuable to morale.

No one liked to be the first asleep, because he and his cot were likely to be carried outside. Awakened by the cold, he would have to tramp shoeless back through the snow. It was a good preventative for those who might want to go to bed early to lie awake in the dark thinking of home. There is nothing worse for morale than this kind of lonely longing.

I knew all about it from first-hand experience in two wars. I used to lie there thinking about my boys and how they had asked me to take them someplace—fishing, or to a circus, or to the zoo —and how I'd said too many times, "No, I'm too busy." Staring into the darkness of my tent, I'd think of the petty tensions that Mary and I like every other couple had sometimes felt. Now I wished ardently that I'd said, "I love you" to her a little more often. I wished I had taken my boys to the circus and the movies every time they asked. For if I died now, I'd never have a chance to make amends. So I used to say to fate or death or whatever it is that hovers over a fighting man, "Look, I'm not ready yet; I've got to go back and take my boys to the zoo."

While it sounds nice and even generous, this kind of thinking and praying ("God, let me live until my little boys are grown up") is a kind of wild search for a special excuse to live. A man feeling the imminence of death and the unknown casts about desperately for reasons why *he*, especially he, should be spared.

It does no good to lie awake at night with such thoughts. That's why I encouraged these jokes and horseplay, rough as they became at times. Laughter invariably drove away the tension. We developed a considerable reputation for congeniality, and Army officers going to and coming from the front lines took to dropping in on us.

One high-ranking officer, staying at our field overnight, once ordered a group of airmen to go to bed and shut up. Hearing about it, I went over and mildly suggested to him that it was too early for them to sack in. When he insisted that they must keep quiet, I answered politely that they had earned what little relaxation they were able to get. When the distinguished guest had gone to sleep, we gently carted him out into the snow. The cold soon awakened him. His language while dragging his cot and bedroll back to quarters was enough to heat up the whole barracks.

Loneliness and homesickness could be dangerously accentuated by letters about difficulties at home. I tried to keep my door always open for discussions that might help. Two sergeants, Dawson and Simon, were especially active in encouraging distressed boys to come to me for these talks. I knew all the men by name and in some cases the names of their families. The mere act of relating their sad tales seemed to release the pent-up bitterness, and some of the hurt went. If I could help with advice, I tried, though generally I could only let them talk it out and in so doing reach their own decisions. Ninety-nine per cent of their problems involved women—wives, fiancées, local girls of "ill repute." It got so that I yearned for a boy to come to me with a tale of woe about his father or his brother, such as: "My old man's got ulcers and I'm worried"—just for a change. But it never happened.

One of my sergeants who came from a Western state was married to a French girl whom he had met while serving in Europe during World War II. She evidently had her own private standard of morals, for he had had some trouble with her in the past. Now she was running wild. A friend and neighbor wrote this sergeant that his wife was entertaining a procession of men in their home in the presence of their ten-year-old daughter. Already at his wit's end, he next received the shattering news that she was divorcing him and demanding full custody of the child. While he didn't care about salvaging his marriage, the sergeant was frantic about the loss of his daughter and the atmosphere in which she would be growing up.

I contacted the Red Cross, which made a quick check on the

case and notified me that a "moral leave" of thirty days was justified for him to contest, if not the divorce, at least his wife's custody of the child. I got him on the first plane out, but at home he found that the divorce had already been granted. The wife had been given permanent possession of the daughter as well as most of their possessions. Being a resourceful man, he visited her at their former house and in the presence of witnesses (thus apparently avoiding a kidnaping charge) asked if the child would like to go for a drive. He thereupon drove her across the state line to his parents' home and put the little girl in their charge. Then, mind at rest, he came back to us in Korea. Whether his solution proved to be a permanent one I never found out. He didn't talk to me again about the matter.

Upsets over "Dear John" letters from fiancées soon passed after a period of surliness or despair. It was admissions of marital infidelity that carried a far deeper hurt. One errant wife wrote her husband that she had gone out on a drinking party with a group of friends. She had ended up in a tourist cabin with a man, where they had been caught in a raid. She knew that he would hear about it, so she wanted to tell him first and to assure him that it had never happened before, nor would it again. Her husband asked me to read her letter, which I took to be an honest, contrite, and distraught confession of a terrible error. He was livid with rage—until I asked if he had ever been unfaithful to her.

"Well—yes, once," he admitted, taken aback. It turned out that he had had an affair of some duration.

"Do you think she would have forgiven you if she had found out about it?" I asked.

"She might have. Yes, I think she would have—eventually." He paused. "But that's not the point. With a man it's different."

"Why?"

He shook his head. "I don't know."

"Then don't you think you could forgive her, since you feel she would have forgiven you?"

"No!" he snapped. Then he thought a moment. "Yeah, I guess I should." He smiled grimly before he left. "But it'll take a while!"

Another youngster came to my quarters and after some hemming and hawing said, "Sir, I guess you don't want me to tell you, but one of the men on the post has the clap."

"Has he had medical attention?" I asked.

"Yes, sir, but I thought you should know about it anyway. It seemed better to tell you than if you happened to see it on the report."

It was a peculiar statement, considering how the men stuck together and protected one another's interests.

"Is it you?" I asked.

"Yes, sir," he muttered, and then the story burst in a torrent of words. He had been married just before coming overseas and was deeply in love with his young wife. But one night he had been swept along by the group into doing something he didn't really want to do. Someone had suggested they visit a brothel; the others had agreed. Not wishing to appear "chicken"—or less masculine than the rest—he had gone along. He had been with an unclean woman ("I hated it," he said. "It was *awful!*") and had contracted gonorrhea.

The infection had been arrested, but his mind was in a torment. He began to cry, morally shaken by his experience. "What should I do, Colonel? I feel so sorry I'm about ready to blow my stack."

"Was it the first time you've done anything like this?"

"Yes, sir."

"Well, it's done. Learn from it. Not just that it's dangerous to consort with prostitutes—but that the act of infidelity is worse than the disease. The disease can be cured by drugs. But the damage you can do to something beautiful like your marriage is hard to repair. If you do it again, you may kill it entirely."

He looked surprised. These must have seemed strange words to a boy expecting a hygiene lecture from his commanding officer.

His eyes caught on my Bible, open on the table beside my bed, as he went out.

"Would you like to borrow it?" I asked.

"Thank you, sir." Picking it up, he went out quickly. It was a week before he returned it, with apologies for having kept it so long. He claimed that it had helped him enormously, that he had read long sections. I checked later to see if he had really read it or whether he had just been soft-soaping me. To my delight the Bible (a new one I'd recently received from home) was marked by fresh smudges and fingerprints not mine.

These interviews and intercessions were necessary because we lacked the services of a full-time chaplain. One came out on Sundays to preach to us Protestants, sitting on empty ammunition boxes in a large, breezy quonset hut, but the Catholics went to Taejon to their church, and the Jews caught airlifts over to an organization with a rabbi.

We encouraged the Korean Christians, having no minister, to join in our worship. Though they understood very little of the sermon, they would bow their heads when we did and do their best to sing the hymns in Korean.

Starting to chapel one Sunday, I invited a Korean officer to come along. He hesitated, and I wondered why.

"Are you a Buddhist?" I asked.

He shook his head.

"Protestant?"

He shook his head again.

"Catholic?"

No, not a Catholic either.

Baffled, I encouraged him to identify his faith. It had a long name—I could tell that right away. Finally, after many earnest but unidentifiable syllables, I caught the drift—he was a Presbyterian. I assured him that our services would do.

It was at Taejon that Miss Lee Meung Yeung joined us as secretary and interpreter. Highly recommended to me by the

Korean authorities, she was the daughter of a doctor who had become separated from her during a Communist advance and had fled south. Her perfect command of English, her intelligence, and her beauty were all highly appreciated by the men at K-5—until she began to get too curious.

In the evenings after missions she would ask us questions. Where had we flown that day? What targets had we bombed? What had we seen? In her quiet but persistent way she seemed to be seeking some special information. Yet she had come with such fine credentials. . . .

"Why do you want to know?" I asked her bluntly one night.

In answer she showed me a photograph of a modest two-story European-style house.

"This was my home," she said, "in Chorwon. You fly north, perhaps you have seen Chorwon? Perhaps you have seen my home? I want to know if it still stands."

I stood there, shifting uneasily from one foot to the other, saying nothing. There was nothing I could say. Chorwon was the important rail and road center north of Taejon that we had been bombing and strafing for days. There was nothing left of the town—not her house nor anyone else's. When I told her, she didn't say a word. She took the picture out of my hands and went away. She never asked another question about our missions.

Not long after, Miss Lee saved me from an extraordinarily embarrassing moment. I had given a mildewed parachute to our seven giggling mess girls with the suggestion that they make something for themselves out of the nylon. They appeared confused. Rather than try to explain such a touchy subject with gestures, I found a mail-order catalogue, pointed to ladies' undergarments in it, and then gestured to the parachute. The girls understood; or at least they departed with the parachute and in gales of laughter.

A week or so later Miss Lee came to me with a troubled expression on her lovely face.

"Colonel, the girls wish to show you something," she said.

"Fine, bring them in," I replied. We were all fond of these gay youngsters. Just seeing them brightened our days.

The troubled expression deepened. "They wish to show you what they made of that parachute."

"Good for them! I'd like to see."

"But Colonel, they're *wearing* what they made out of that parachute."

Then I heard giggles outside. Leaving Miss Lee as my deputy to examine and exclaim over the reincarnated parachute, I slipped red-faced out the back door.

Most of our missions now were east of Seoul in the vicinity of Wonju, where the First Marines were engaged. One morning Craigwell and I found a Red ammunition train there and dive-bombed it. Craigwell made the effective hit, and the train blew up with such a shock that my plane was tossed over on its back.

Righting the plane, I saw a great tower of smoke rising to what must have been 3,000 feet. Craigwell had disappeared. My stomach knotted. He had been even closer to the blast which had rocked me so; had it knocked him down?

I pushed down on my radio key, calling, "MacIntosh Two—MacIntosh Two!" No answer. "Can you hear me, Craigwell?" Still no reply.

Circling the towering gray pillar, I kept calling for a response which never came. My affection and respect for Craigwell had grown so that I couldn't bear to think of him going down. But as my frantic procedure continued to bring no result, I began to recognize that I must.

Then in one of the brief listening intervals (too brief, as it was straightway apparent!) a ground radio controller's voice sounded with weary patience: "Will you two guys stop blocking each other out? You're both all right, but you're hollering so much for each other neither of you can hear!"

It turned out that we had been chasing each other around the spreading column of smoke, each fearing that the other had gone down, without taking enough time to wait for the answering call. Flying back to base, I thought of how long Craigwell had been with me, how close we had grown, and how I wanted to see him go home in one piece.

Seoul—bombed-out, tortured, flattened Seoul—was recaptured once again by United Nations troops. I promptly called headquarters and asked permission for us to return to the field on its outskirts, Yongdungpo, where there were fewer runway hazards and where we could continue our training program. Permission was granted, but I was advised that it would take six weeks' work to get the field in operating condition again. I flew up immediately and, circling it, looked down to see what had happened to our former base, twice removed.

After we had left it the previous October, the Eighteenth Fighter-bomber Wing had laid a runway of 5,000 feet of steel planking over the grass we had been cultivating. Now, lowering gear and flaps, I went across it almost at landing speed. Our own B-26s had dropped 500-pound bombs on the planking in several places, rendering it useless, as the report had indicated. But to the north side of the field was a clear place with no craters which would do fine for a temporary strip until we could patch up the main runway.

Jubilantly I returned to Taejon and ordered preparations for the move back to what had been our best field. This was to be the least complicated of our hegiras, for now most of our maintenance equipment—engines and parts—was stored at Cheju. And even more important, in Taejon we were able to secure a locomotive and some boxcars to haul the bulk of our men and equipment, along with bombs, ammo, and fuel, in high style. Early in March of 1951, like a circus that has struck its tents, the first trucks pulled out, followed by the planes and finally by the biggest contingent, on the train.

We ferried the aircraft to Yongdungpo without incident and

started laying out our encampment. By the time the trucks arrived, we had planned our camp and surveyed the damaged strip. With the train's arrival we would be back in business at one of our favorite stands. I went down to the railroad station to meet it.

It didn't come. As time wore on, I waited with increasing anxiety. Then Cpl. Tom Cabanifs came hurtling through the door of the station so fast he pulled it off its flimsy runners. He was out of breath from having run a mile up the tracks. Our train had been wrecked.

xxii

It was a terrible accident. Two trains, one loaded with Korean troops, had collided head on just as our locomotive and boxcars were passing on the adjacent track. The wreckage exploded against our train. Cars had accordioned up and fallen off the track, many of them rolling down a 25-foot embankment. All three train crews had been killed, as well as 230 Korean soldiers. Many more were injured.

When I reached the site of the disaster, I saw a couple of my men helping in the swirling confusion. They said they thought the others also had escaped harm. It didn't seem possible, but going to our train, I found the rest of the outfit—uninjured.

Gratitude engulfing me, I went back to the jeep. There, unseen by the others, I leaned against it and gave way to tears—something I hadn't done for many years. I cried like a lost child. When I had myself under control, I went back to inspect the damage.

Our ammunition and gasoline cars were off the track. Again, unbelievably, they were upright. These two cars that the men had picked to ride in were the only two not totally demolished or severely damaged.

We worked through the night helping to evacuate the wounded. In the morning we were better able to examine what had happened to our equipment, and we found it almost intact. Bringing the trucks from the field, we began loading them and running a shuttle until all our matériel finally reached its destination. It seemed almost beyond belief that, surrounded by death and injury,

218

none of our personnel had been harmed. Having done all we could at the scene of the wreck, we sadly yet thankfully went to work setting up shop at Yongdungpo.

By this time we were slick, quick movers. We set up our tents adjacent to the flight line, using a technique of spacing them which we had developed through long and bitter experience. Our secret weapon was a 50-foot rope with knots tied at precisely calculated intervals. We stretched out the rope and quickly planted poles, each pole representing a specific tent. Lights cords, already cut to the correct length, were strung and plugged into a feed line to the electricity generator. Our living quarters were assembled almost as fast as they had been struck.

Our various moves had made us as practical as a fastidious housewife in the handling of our well-traveled gear. We had a half-dozen trucks with trailers attached. Each item of our possessions had a specific spot in a specific vehicle in which to be loaded (kitchen equipment in the "kitchen truck," etc.) and its place in the convoy would depend on the immediacy of its use. It was no fun being foot-loose transients, but at least we had become good at it.

Our initial task here at Yongdungpo was to put the runway in condition. The B-26 bomb hits in the pierced-steel covering were some ten yards across, and the twisted quarter-inch planking around the craters was impossible to straighten. Buildings within the area had been knocked down, and we used their debris for foundations in the craters and then packed dirt on top. The damaged sections of planking were replaced by others from farther down the runway. Without engineering tools this cutting and fitting had to be done with sledge hammers and chisels. Their rasping, clanging sounds filled our days and nights, and the job that had been estimated to take six weeks was completed in one.

In a burned-out hangar I noticed a steel water tank about six feet square lying among the twisted girders and blackened ruins. A flap of straw hung over an aperture in one end. Always aware of the possibility that guerrillas might be secreted around the field ready to snipe at night, some airmen and I approached the tank warily, wondering if it could be a hide-out.

A few feet away we could hear sounds inside. A Korean called in his language for whomever was inside to come out. The noises stopped. When no one obeyed, we tore off the flap, ready to fire. Four little boys were huddled in a corner like frightened foxes in a filthy den. Failing to convince them that we were friendly, we went away.

Thinking that a female voice might prove more persuasive, I sent our secretary and interpreter, Miss Lee, down to talk to the children. She knelt by the tank and spoke in gentle, persuasive tones to the children, but still they refused to leave their filthy refuge.

Some rations were set outside the tank; the next morning they were gone. This was repeated every few hours. Standing back at a distance, we watched the boys dart out, snatch the food, and jump back inside. We put some blankets by the hole; these they pulled in without even emerging.

Finally Miss Lee made them realize that we meant them no harm, and they came out. They were a pathetic sight. Rags hung on their emaciated little bodies. In the foulest of conditions, they obviously had not washed during the entire period of their containment in the tank. The oldest was about ten years of age, and the youngest six. I walked away, off by myself; I couldn't take it any more.

They had been living in that hole from the time the United Nations forces had left until we had come back; they had been in there when the B-26s had scattered bombs on the runway. To survive during those hard winter months they had gnawed on the roots of weeds and bushes that grew nearby. They had built fires along the edge of the tank to warm it and keep from freezing at night. Mentally they seemed to have reverted almost to an animal state, their eyes darting about wildly, their movements the swift, convulsive starts of fear.

The oldest boy had an eye infection which had spread down the side of his face. Dr. Kay gave him a shot of penicillin in the customary place. The boy burst into protest, pointing to his cheek. The interpreter explained that he was trying to tell us that he was sick in his cheek and not in the tender part of his anatomy where the doctor had stuck the needle.

We kept them around camp for several days until they were in fairly good health and then sent them down to Mrs. Whang to add to her population at Cheju.

It was becoming increasingly evident that the orphanage was going to need even greater assistance then we had originally thought as the demands upon it grew. I didn't feel that I could ask the men to contribute any more money than they already had. The Koreans, destitute themselves, had nothing to give. A Korean colonel on flying status received eight dollars a month. Several of my Korean officers' wives had sold their possessions in Seoul, one item at a time, just to get enough money to keep their families together.

On one of my flights to the island I had seen some two hundred of the orphans playing outside, each wearing a pair of shoes. I returned to the field with that small satisfaction anyway; the children didn't have to go barefoot outside in the cold, rainy weather. Yet the next time Craigwell and I discussed the orphanage's problem, he remarked right away, "We've *got* to get those kids shoes."

Apparently I had seen every pair of shoes the orphanage possessed on those two hundred children playing outdoors. In bad weather they could go outside only in shifts, having only one pair of shoes for every five or six children. They took turns wearing them. I passed that story around the base, not asking for more blood from these turnips but simply stating the facts. Three hundred dollars materialized from nowhere, and Craigwell flew to Japan, returning with more than six hundred pairs of shoes. He described it as "the happiest mission I ever flew in my life."

Then some genius suggested a highly original and illegal source of revenue.

There was no drinkable liquor available in Korea at anything short of stratospheric black-market prices. Some of the men had been made sick by drinking native whisky which was made in the afternoon, aged overnight, and consumed the next morning. (One bottle analyzed was found to contain a high content of uric acid; evidently the original ingredients had been fermented with urine.) The idea was simply to set up a club where we could sell decent drinks at a nominal price, reminding the imbibers between drinks that profits went to the orphanage and that, if they didn't pick up their change off the bar, every penny would go to a good cause.

It seemed like a plan good enough to try anyway—not larcenous and with double welfare aspects. The club would serve not only the men on the field but front-line troops passing through. I went to the men with it, making a final appeal for funds. I agreed to match the amount that they advanced to get our pub started. It came to six hundred dollars—enough to buy many cases of potables at the low rate current in Japan. The next trip on which our C-47 was scheduled to return from Tokyo empty we put the orphanage into business—that of running a bar.

It was an entirely irregular project that I would have neither recommended nor permitted under normal circumstances, but the situation on the island was far from normal. Our responsibility was to keep those kids alive by whatever means were open to us.

With our stock on hand to start us going, the club rapidly took shape. Korean workers made the counter, seats, and tables out of rocket boxes. Still we had no place to house our bistro; tents were in short supply, and no quonset hut was available.

But we had a friend.

We had been receiving a number of supplies through the port at Inchon. The port commander, a very agreeable brigadier general, had been kind to us on a number of occasions, often making trucks available to carry our supplies to camp. And he too had been having difficulty with men drinking native beverages. Now, in gratitude for his favors, I sent Mike Bellovin over to Inchon with a case of Scotch.

The General looked dubiously at the gift, asking what we wanted for it. Mike explained innocently that there were no strings attached—it was just a token of our esteem. The General remained suspicious, or at least interested. A few days later he sent his adjutant to call on us with a manner of casual curiosity.

I let it be known how badly we needed a quonset hut and explained why. I described the orphanage in great detail and the amount of money my men were pouring into it. The adjutant left after remarking noncommittally, but the following day trucks appeared bearing the dismantled sections of a quonset hut. These were unloaded without a word of instruction or explanation, and the trucks drove away. The General obviously was a man of heart.

The Korean carpenters, having recently finished building our tent frames, went to work on the new quonset. They not only assembled but decorated it. In went the counter, tables, and chairs. A small, wizened Korean civilian—not the bouncer type but a trustworthy and dedicated individual—was put in charge of the liquor. He always kept an abacus on the bar—not that he needed it much, for all our drinks sold for either a nickel or a dime, and no man was allowed to buy enough to get intoxicated. The choice of beverages was wide—not just Scotch or bourbon on the rocks but, for the exotic palate, grasshoppers, alexanders, and Cherry Heering.

The front lines now were along the banks of the Han River, not over five miles from the other side of Seoul. Infantry had first priority in the club; they soon were coming in and out of the place all during the evening. Each GI had to show justification for being away from his unit. If his outfit had just pulled out of the line, he received one drink free—"on the quonset," as we said. Our enlisted men had second priority, and then those from areas to the rear.

Though charging only a nickel for most drinks (we bought it by the case at a dollar a bottle), we made money hand over fist. Word of where the proceeds of the club were going spread fast. Many of the men would put down a dollar in script or sometimes even ten for one drink and say, "Keep the change for the kids." It was the happiest bar that ever existed. Not only were those boys drinking for the fun and relaxation of it; they were drinking for a cause!

There were two standing rules: no one was to get drunk, and it was to be an enlisted man's place only; no officers were allowed. (For the officers, so that they wouldn't brood or have hurt feelings, I had a little shelf of bottles in my tent. They could have a drink or two free of charge, as long as I was there with them.) The men maintained the club rules rigidly. If any man imbibed a bit too much, they told him to leave and not to come back that evening. As a consequence I never at any time saw a sign of drunkenness. Another understanding was that no neophyte unaccustomed to hard liquor was to be encouraged to take a drink. For the younger boys there were fruit juice and soft drinks. And the liquor drinkers were forcibly discouraged from making wise-guy comments to the fruit-juice drinkers.

Aside from the money we were making for the orphanage— by replenishing our stock we were able to send between five hundred and a thousand dollars to Cheju every two or three weeks —there were most satisfactory by-products. The number of man-hours available went up considerably. With the men staying on the base at night and not drinking the native rotgut, the general tone of health improved. The VD rate of my organization as well as of others in the area went down amazingly.

All in all, I could take some justifiable pride in being the biggest bootlegger in Korea.

I had a moment of panic one evening when a corps commander, a brigadier general, came by, prompted I'm sure by glowing tales of our pub. As I showed him around the post, pointing out the progress we were making, sounds of the evening's festivities began to emanate from the shiny quonset. He kept casting curious glances toward it while I tried desperately to attract his attention in other directions—"Now here is our power unit, sir . . . ," or "Our camp is so mobile we can strike it in an hour, sir. . . ." He might well have been surprised that a drag-tail outfit like ours had come into possession of a large, new quonset.

I was vastly relieved when his jeep left the field. At the same time I was sure that the kind General had heard or knew at least vaguely what was going on in that hut, but that his discretion had retained the upper hand over his curiosity. The abacus continued to click on the bar, and the money flowed in a steady stream to Cheju.

About this time my men paid signal honor to their bootlegging commander by means of an elaborate practical joke. I was honored because they worked at it so hard. It concerned my beloved old F-51, Number 18.

Hal Wilson was flying Number 17 at the time, and we kept up a running barrage of mutual disparagement of each other's plane. One morning I sensed that something was up from the slyly smiling American and Korean faces and from the surreptitious way in which people were slipping off somewhere. That afternoon I was summoned to the flight line, where I saw that the unit was lined up in formation behind some piece of broken-down machinery. On closer look it turned out to be an ancient, rickety Japanese biplane dating from decades past, with wings drooping and engine missing. On its fuselage was painted a large "18½," and it was rigged with simulated bombs. In a formal presentation Wilson bequeathed me the plane, declaring that it was obviously a superior aircraft to my Number 18. Then they all left me standing there with my gift, wondering how I was going to get the monstrosity off the field.

No present ever made me happier. If my boys undertook that many hours of extra labor to find that relic, haul it to the field, and fix it up, surely they must have loved me.

Meanwhile we were flying regularly from K-16, utilizing more Korean pilots all the time. While proficient on other scores, they had had no opportunity for extensive instrument training and were forced to stay on the ground in bad weather. This restriction irked them, but for the time being there was little help for it.

We ran daily missions through March of 1951, often conducting armed reconnaissance as far as 300 miles northward. Our normal procedure was to fly to Inchon and then up into the valleys and around the mountain peaks, searching out targets of opportunity. We found many. The Koreans were particularly delighted and enthused by hits on ammunition carts: it appealed to their love of fireworks as well as their determination to strike back at the despoilers of their homeland.

Instances abounded which lent fuel to their hatred. Flying north of Pyongyang one day, I saw a squad of enemy troops moving away from a farmhouse toward a creek bed. Turning around, I went down low to strafe across their path. As I passed the farmhouse, I saw something white out in the yard. Returning to come in lower, I saw that it was the bodies of the occupants of the house—five people in white Korean garments on which the blood showed, all stretched out dead. They had just been slaughtered by the troops they probably had housed the night before.

Those in high interception work or in big bombers normally lack close visual contact with ground forces. Our planes were sufficiently slow and could fly low enough for us to make out the faces of our soldiers and Marines. It was gratifying to see their mouths open in shouts of greeting, or to make a low pass over tanks in an advance column and have crews open their hatches and wave. It made for a sense of oneness against the beast.

That sense of oneness grew even stronger when I fully understood what extraordinary efforts the infantry made to rescue our flyers shot down near the front lines.

One spring afternoon I saw one of these rescues in full detail when I hurried to cover a fighter-bomber shot down in a patch of woods. Circling overhead, I watched the pilot get out of his cockpit, evidently uninjured, and run from the smoking plane. I stayed with him to scare off any enemy troops that might have spotted him as he scurried toward the road.

Jumping into a ditch, he started to move cautiously along it, looking for a way back toward our lines. His landing must have been observed from our line, for I saw an armored car come careening around a bend a mile away. Suddenly it began to fire at him. I couldn't believe my eyes and started to holler into the radio. Then I saw that it was firing over his head at a Chinese squad approaching from the opposite direction. When the car reached the pilot, a door opened and men jumped out and hauled him inside. It then wheeled around, still firing, and drove off to safety.

In April we received intelligence that the Communists were going to mount a sizable air armada. Since it was likely that they would strike one of our fields, we began to construct embankments of sandbags to protect the aircraft.

Running out of bags, we persuaded nearby Army engineers to send over a bulldozer and scrape troughs 6 to 8 feet deep in the earth, in which we parked our vehicles every night. It proved to be a questionable precaution. One night it rained heavily, filling the troughs with water and drowning the jeeps entirely. Only the tops of windshields were visible of our submerged weapons carrier, fire trucks, and ambulances. Dragging them out and getting them cleaned up was such a job that thereafter we let them take their chances topside.

The Communist counterattack came in April as scheduled. Planning to recapture Seoul, they approached the banks opposite our field and came within our artillery range. I counseled the officers not to show too much concern, as a number of the men were jittery. One sergeant broke down completely in anxiety and nervousness. He would sit in his work tent crying softly hour after hour. Finally we had to send him down to the training center at Cheju—no less a casualty than a man wounded from flying steel.

His cracking morale, while worse than that of most of the others, was indicative of the mounting strain. We were getting a number of replacements now—boys not long in the service. It was difficult for them to feel an identification with the organization, and some of the grizzled veterans treated them like raw recruits. I wracked my brain for some kind of a badge that would stamp and identify all members of the 6146th. The club was supporting the children pretty well, and we had a little spare money in our welfare fund. With this I sent to Japan for the loudest red-and-white sports shirts in the Orient for every man in the organization. They were allowed to wear them when they weren't working—in the mess, their tents, or the club, though not outside the area. It may seem like a trifling contribution to morale, what with huge enemy forces just across the river, but it helped. No other outfit had red-and-white sports shirts—you can be sure of that. Wearing one was a cocky badge of belonging. A new boy got a sense of who he was and, even more important, who his buddies were.

Another event which raised the morale of the men, or at least distracted them for a day, was the arrival on our field of General MacArthur on his way from Tokyo to Seoul.

There was some doubt that our runway could take an aircraft as large as his Constellation. General Partridge, now commander of the Far Eastern Air Force, arrived ahead of time for a check. I assured him that it was in good condition, though there were still a few mines around. He immediately asked to drive around the base, and in doing so he spotted a metal disk a foot in diameter with a steel cap on top. My hair stood on end as I thought of General MacArthur's Constellation rolling over a mine. And it surely looked like one.

Examination showed it to be only part of the drainage system the Japanese had installed during their occupation of Korea; but

228

General Partridge remained rather thoughtful going back to the operations hut.

General Ridgway was another in the receiving party. He wore a field jacket from which hung his unique trade-mark—two hand grenades—and he possessed the same impressive manner as Partridge and Timberlake, compounded of intelligence, strength, and understanding. When I asked if he would like something at the mess tent, he pulled a sandwich from his pocket, saying that he had come prepared; he had been on inspection trips with MacArthur before, and "the Old Man just doesn't know when to stop to eat!" He did want some coffee, though, and gulped his sandwich and hot drink at our crude table with the amiable simplicity and lack of pomp of any GI grabbing a quick bite.

MacArthur's plane landed safely, and he was among the first of his entourage to get out. He was wearing dark glasses, a heavy overcoat, and a muffler around his neck; but there was no mistaking that multibraided hat and the famous sharply defined profile. On his way toward Seoul, he stayed only long enough to rest a bit before hopping into a jeep. But watching him just those few minutes, I received the strong impression that here was a man shouldered with enormous responsibility that would have crushed most other men but that merely bent him down a little. Meanwhile my men, theoretically at work about the field, rubber-necked and ogled the General like a bunch of bobby-soxers admiring Frank Sinatra.

Compared to his, mine was a small responsibility. And it never did become one too heavy to bear. But I was getting tired in another way: emotionally.

I had stared at the miserable waifs climbing out of the water tank and then had turned away; another image had been added to the sum total of grief. A few days after on a road north of the field I had stumbled on the bodies of a mother and her two small children. She had been killed violently in some way, but there was not a mark on either of the children. Apparently after she had fallen, they had snuggled up to her warm body, and as it grew cold, they too had grown cold and died. And after that a fine, educated woman who had worked around the field, once a schoolteacher but now a penniless widow with two children to support, had been somehow caught in the mass of refugees between the two armies—I have no idea where she was going—and they also, all three of them, had been killed.

I can honestly say that, even after 250 missions in the air, I wasn't suffering from combat fatigue. But I was wrung out emotionally. If my body and my brain were still alert, my heart was tired.

xxiii

And now the Korean air force was spreading its wings and gaining favor with the UN forces. Korean pilots in ever increasing numbers were learning to handle the F-51. Their ground crews were becoming skilled and able; their radiomen were growing accustomed to American equipment. Properly equipped and uniformed, they were developing an *esprit de corps* which would further cement their ranks. Their allocation of aircraft, all F-51s, was raised to forty and then to seventy-five, which is group strength. Still, none of us anticipated that out of our little nucleus of die-hards, dragging our equipment from one muddy, crater-pocked strip to another, would grow the present powerful, jet-propelled air arm of South Korea's fighting forces.

As the ROK airmen became more proficient, my American boys were replaced through normal rotation. Their tenure had been lengthy and arduous; they deserved to go home. At every new departure I was brought a sense of how close our ceaseless gypsying had made us. Many among the original volunteers had revolunteered when their first tours had ended, doggedly sticking out conditions of working and living that even military career men seldom must face. Now, in the summer of 1951, we lived comfortably in permanent tents with wooden sides and floors, ate fresh vegetables and even meat occasionally, and had support all along the line. These boys had seen the job through; now they deserved to go home.

The added planes permitted more cadets to enter the program at Cheju Island, where their training would be gradually taken

231

over by members of the cadre of experienced Korean pilots and crewmen. The devotion to duty and the stern dedication of these Koreans had been another revelation to me. To learn all that they had from instructors who could not even speak their language had been a task requiring fortitude and persistence. Now the goal was achieved. They could look upon themselves—and back at their dead and injured—with respect.

Perhaps it was also getting time for me to go home, though I didn't realize it then. Little things to which I didn't give much thought might have suggested that changes had taken place inside me and that in some ways I was overdue for a change of scene.

For instance, there was the little matter of the cartoon. Sergeant Cuthbertson, an armament man who had been with me the whole while, was an accomplished cartoonist. During his free time he had drawn a picture of a tiger in the cockpit of an F-51 hurling bombs. Without asking what he intended doing with it, I suggested that it would make a good insignia for the ROK Air Force. He stubbornly refused to give it to them. Despite all his loyalty and hard work over the months, I came down on him hard, pointing out that his every minute on the field was for the benefit of the organization. When he still was reluctant to part with it, I pressed the point no further. That at least I am thankful for now, though I wasn't to understand until later why he had held back the drawing.

Then I almost shot a Korean child in my tent. Some of the men picked up a six-year-old girl in Seoul, where she was lying unconscious from lack of food. In the few days before it would be possible to ship her down to Cheju, she quickly regained health at the field. Staying with the mess-tent girls, she happily began helping in their work.

One night around four in the morning when Wilson was away, I became conscious that someone was in my room. In the moment between sleep and wakefulness I could hear breathing. Suspecting a guerrilla, I felt for my revolver and rolled over, ready to shoot. In the faint light of the small fire in the stove I saw the little girl, come to prepare my shaving water.

She jumped up, bowing. Then she took a can of hot water from the stove, poured it into a washpan, turned to bow again, and left. It was her way of showing respect for the boss of the camp. But I told the older girls I much preferred for her to stay in bed. Hers could have been a costly kindness.

Another event, both alarming and miraculous, took place on a flight with Metcalf and two Koreans northwest of Seoul. The pilot of a reconnaissance T-6 had spotted troops in a farm compound. He gave us the coordinates, and we started the run from 5 miles away, carrying in rockets and napalm. The best method of attack is to come in low and fast at a slight angle and ricochet the napalm off the ground so it will splash in a wide area rather than stick in one spot. But this way a pilot rarely gets a close look at his target.

Coming down from 500 feet to 300, I had my bomb switches on, the target lined up, and everything in readiness for a perfect pass. As I approached the farm target, my thumb was poised over the bomb-release button; yet for some reason I couldn't push my thumb down. It was an involuntary hesitation. In the split second before passing over the target I saw not troops but a woman surrounded by children. To me it is a miracle that my thumb froze over the button: the Good Lord interceded as I was about to take more innocent lives.

I called to the others not to drop. Wheeling tightly, I headed back over the compound to break off their attack if they should not have heard me. They had, and another terrible mistake was avoided by what can only have been an intervention of Divine Will.

Another day, strafing in the same area, I looked down to see a child of twelve run out of a house—run in such terror that her spindly legs seemed to pull her ahead of my roaring plane. Again I was blessed by seeing her soon enough so that she might live.

Once before I had not been so blessed, and the child I machine-gunned from the air will remain in my mind forever.

An ever increasing concern about my pilots developed in me. Each new mission extended the already long odds against them and might be their last. Craigwell had flown most of his missions at my side; I dreaded having anything happen to him. He was too fine a man and officer to meet the fate that steady risk must eventually impose. When he reached 180, I told him that he had done much more than his share, and would be replaced. Today, I am happy to say, he is one of the country's outstanding jet pilots.

Jimmy Gillespie had over a hundred missions. I had seen him wounded in the face when flak splintered his Plexiglas canopy; I had watched him parachute from a plane with a dead engine. Any day now might see that warm exchange of letters between him and his young wife terminated by a sad one from me.

Hal Wilson had turned over our C-47 to a new pilot, Captain Erickson, and was back in his F-51 again, flying with his usual dauntless skill. But the change-over made me uneasy: if he went down in flames, I would never be able to forgive myself for acceding to his wish to get back into combat. These feelings were intensified when Captain Choi, one of our best Korean pilots, did not return from a flight over Kaesong.

For myself, I at no time believed that disaster would prevent my return to Mary and the boys. I frequently expressed this confidence; yet the paradox was that I recognized I could be wrong. This was manifest in many different ways. Perhaps the most apparent was my reluctance to have my picture taken while readying for a mission. Our personnel on the base had cameras, and Armed Forces photographers were often around. I tried, not always successfully, to avoid being snapped before a take-off. If I met my death, I didn't want an issue made of it by someone's pointing to a newspaper photograph and saying, "Look—here's Hess just before he got it."

I recognized the possibility that I might not go on indefinitely from another indication—my growing feeling about beautiful days. Spring weather in Korea is delicately lovely. The earth begins to turn a bright green, the air seems especially fresh, and a gentle breeze blows. I was reminded of spring back in Marietta. And I would think, "If it is going to happen to me, I hope it won't be on such a day as this. Better if it's rainy or cold—but not on a clear, sunny day when I know how good it is to be alive."

My constant hope was that I might live long enough to see the orphanage established on a secure basis. Mary, always in my thoughts, could carry on for both of us at home if the worst happened. If I met my end over here, at least our sons would be provided for until grown. There was no such future apparent for the children now at Cheju and for others who would join them there. They deserved so much more than a steady diet of rice soup, a few ill-fitting, cast-off clothes, and a battered dormitory for a home.

The fund-raising club was so illegal that I could not expect my successor to sanction its continuance. To my own boys, who had given so generously to keep these kids alive, I could only say that a man never stands so close to God as when he has a child by his side. But some kind of steady support had to be provided for that pathetic flotsam cast upon the shores of rocky Cheju Island if they were to have any of the chances in life assured to my Alan and Larry. I don't remember ever having prayed for cash—cold cash—before, but I did now. "Let me see them given some means of sustenance," my plea tolled incessantly through my mind. It still does.

In his *Essay on Man* Alexander Pope declares, "Oh, blindness to the future! kindly given, that each may fill the circle marked by Heaven; who sees with equal eye, as God of all, a hero perish, or a sparrow fall." I could trust that His infinite mercy would somehow find its way to our sparrows. I believed that it would in those dark hours, and I was determined, though I knew not how, to continue my own puny efforts on behalf of the children even after I left Korea.

In May Don Nichols, my invaluable source of "inside dope," came to tell me that it might not be long before I would be sent home. I ridiculed the idea. Neither General Partridge nor General Timberlake had even mentioned it, although they frequently asked how I felt and what I planned to do. I had always replied that I intended to remain here until we had won the war. Working with the Koreans, seeing them happy and seeing them grief-stricken, the conviction had grown in me that it was as much my country and fight as it was theirs. I had talked often with Koreans, high and low, of their emerging identity as an independent people, of their 4,000-year identity as a nation, of the pride that should be theirs, of their throwing off the decades of subservience and embracing freedom. Though stretching a historical parallel, I had even equated their present struggle with our own American Revolution.

Mike Bellovin, who had been with me longest and who perhaps knew me best, was the only one who ever voiced doubts about my physical condition. But I would answer that I did not feel combat fatigue in any way. And there still remained so much to do. . . . So I laughed off Don Nichols's suggestion that I would be going home.

Then General Timberlake called me to his headquarters at Taegu. Thinking that it was some matter of coordination or instructions, I flew the morning's mission, refueled, and went down to the scene of our arrival from Japan.

A year had turned K-2 into a huge, fully operational base. Eight-thousand-foot paved runways had supplanted the former cowpaths of half that length. There were permanent buildings in place of our tents and ramshackle huts, and the population was up to several thousand from our handful. Troop-carrier aircraft were all around, and jets drilled the air. It was a scene which bespoke efficiency and power and top fighting pitch; but it awakened in me a bit of nostalgia for the dismal, barren spot where we had landed as "Bout I" and where the fighting ROK Air Force had been born.

In his office General Timberlake began with compliments about the thoroughness with which the Koreans had been trained and spoke in glowing terms of the future of their air force, which so short a time before had been on the verge of being disbanded entirely.

He then told me flatly that my tour was ended.

I had flown 250 missions. It was against Air Force policy for one pilot to accrue so many while there were others who had none. I was to be sent home at once for reassignment. He ended with a broad smile, a crushing handshake, and congratulations: I was to be awarded the Legion of Merit.

Outside I had mixed feelings: a sense of relief, yet a heaviness of heart. I felt that the job was not yet done, and to be thus abruptly removed from the scene was a little like having a rug jerked out from under me. And I was tired—terribly, suddenly tired as never before.

The news had preceded me back to camp. One by one the Koreans came to my tent to talk, and much was said without many spoken words. A few attempted to be jovial, but jokes fell so flat that they soon ceased. While I knew that the work would go forward in good hands under Col. Kim Shin Kim, it was difficult for me to talk of this future in which I would take no part.

Before his death Captain Choi had lived in the tent next to mine. Somewhere he had picked up an ancient Chinese beheading sword, elaborately worked but with a dull edge which suggested that it had belonged for many years to some Manchurian palace guard. I had admired it, and now his fellow pilots presented it to me in his memory. Today, whenever I see Larry or Alan using it, striking a rather alien note in a cowboys-and-Indians game, the years roll back. Once more I see it hanging on the wall of Choi's quarters alongside his flying helmet—a juxtaposition that always intrigued me.

Of all the Koreans, it was most difficult to part with Dr. Kay Won. Having worked with both the orphans and our field personnel, he was closely linked to my two divergent interests. He gave me a promise, unnecessarily, that he would continue to look after the children's medical needs—a promise he is still faithfully fulfilling today.

Colonel Kim flew me to Cheju. A flight of F-51s met the C-47 and escorted us in. After parting with the officers and men at our post, I went over to the orphanage.

The children were assembled outside, all in their clean and mended best. Stepping forward, the leader of the Boy Scouts asked me to inspect the troop. I walked along the file in its makeshift uniforms, my face aching with the weight of a forced smile. The days of my own membership in a similar yet so different group in Marietta returned vaguely to mind. I gave them the salute (was it two fingers or three?), which they snappily and proudly returned. I went quickly over to make conversation with Mrs. Whang.

She had prepared a little program. The children sang and performed folk dances with astonishing delicacy and grace. Afterward they presented me with little cards, pictures, and albums they had prepared. On my last tour of inspection with Mrs. Whang I thought their facilities somewhat improved. They had more blankets, more clothes. Their food shipments consisted of more than six bags of rock salt. But with the growing number of charges their needs would inevitably mushroom. Leaving, I did not know if I would ever see them or Mrs. Whang again, but I pledged that I would work to the best of my ability to keep money coming. God has allowed me to keep that pledge.

That night back at K-16 before returning to Taegu, en route to Japan and home, I made farewells to the whole group at the field, military and civilian. The men presented me with, of all things, an embroidery. It was Cuthbertson's cartoon—the F-51 with Korean markings for "By Faith I Fly" and "18" on the fuselage, with the caption "The Flying Tiger of Korea." He had given it to the Koreans to prepare for me, as had been his intention all along. And I had criticized him harshly for his reluctance to

238

give it to the squadron as an insignia. I was as deeply touched as I was shamed, but I never had a chance to apologize to Cuthbertson. I only hope he reads this.

One token of regard that moved me as much as any came from an old "papa-san" who had joined us in Taejon. When we left K-5, he had asked through the interpreter if he could come along with us to work for nothing, if necessary. I had said no, feeling that he should not leave his family even if there had been room to transport him, which there wasn't. Several weeks later he had showed up at Yongdungpo, having given his family every cent he had earned with us and walked all the way, sleeping in the fields at night.

Around ten o'clock he appeared at my tent with some wilted flowers in his hand. He had gone miles into the country to collect them. Tears in his eyes, unable to speak English, he held out the small, dusty bouquet. Taking it, I knew that no one had ever received a better tribute. Time had already withered and crumpled its petals, but when I looked at them, I felt—or hoped I felt—some of his own pervading humility—an echo of the small but steady voice of humanity.

The morning of departure, on the way to the flight line with Colonel Kim, I tried to avoid looking at my plane. Number 18 had become such a part of me that I knew I was abandoning an old friend. An explosion across the river drew my glance, and I had to go over and touch it. The Korean letters for "By Faith I Fly" had grown nicked and dim with the passing of each day and each mission. Looking at them, I wondered if any crusader had ever had a worthier talisman. Surely none had ever hung up his shield and weapon with deeper acknowledgement than I.

I don't like good-bys. I've had to say them to so many people. It seems as if my life is just a long series of good-bys. I had purposely avoided any formal leave-taking now. But as I walked toward the flight line, I saw that the men had drifted down there—all of them. I shook hands with a few, trying to smile. Some of

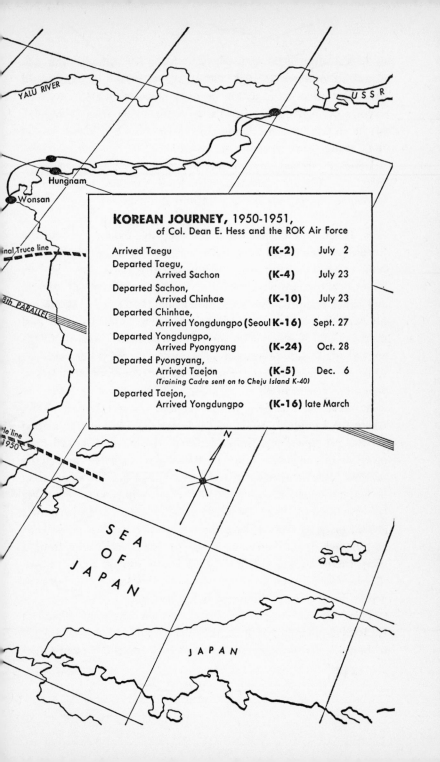

YALU RIVER

USSR

Hungnam

Wonsan

KOREAN JOURNEY, 1950-1951,
of Col. Dean E. Hess and the ROK Air Force

Arrived Taegu	**(K-2)**	July 2
Departed Taegu, Arrived Sachon	**(K-4)**	July 23
Departed Sachon, Arrived Chinhae	**(K-10)**	July 23
Departed Chinhae, Arrived Yongdungpo (Seoul **K-16**)		Sept. 27
Departed Yongdungpo, Arrived Pyongyang	**(K-24)**	Oct. 28
Departed Pyongyang, Arrived Taejon *(Training Cadre sent on to Cheju Island K-40)*	**(K-5)**	Dec. 6
Departed Taejon, Arrived Yongdungpo	**(K-16)** late March

inal Truce line

38th PARALLEL

le line
1950

N

SEA
OF
JAPAN

JAPAN

us would meet again stateside, and for a few minutes the talk would be loud and excited, and an ember of the old fire would glow. But then we'd go our separate ways, each with his own feelings of inadequacy and disappointment that the "old days" of the 6146th and the fighting ROK Air Force couldn't be entirely revived over a couple of drinks.

I looked at the solemn faces, Korean and American, once more. I made my one-word speech—it was my old nemesis: "Good-by"—and blindly climbed into the plane.

In Taegu in the morning I was taken to a theater where the Korean air force had prepared a celebration. Many cadets had been brought in from an academy recently started in Chinhae. Some local orphans were there too. Prior to a program of dramatic and ballet performances two children hung a large wreath around my neck. I gave them an Oriental obeisance, bowing slightly and drooping my shoulders with my palms together. Ordinarily this is an Oriental mark of respect of a junior for an elder, but the audience seemed to recognize my deep feeling for what those youngsters represented.

At noon, on President Rhee's request, I was taken to Pusan, where the President, Madame Rhee, and I walked in the garden for the last time. At a simple lunch of baked fish I basked once more in the radiant vitality of this old man. Tired though he certainly was, he actually looked and sounded much younger than he had during the dark days of the Pusan Perimeter. In discussing the economic plight of Korea, he sadly admitted that his country at that moment did not have the resources to care for its orphans and homeless children. For them he must seek help from a sympathetic world and from God. Then he smiled: the truth was that he did not even know how he was going to pay the Japanese printer for the latest shipment of Korean won.

Then his staff began arriving, and soon afterward American Embassy representatives headed by Ambassador Muccio. It proved to be for a surprising ceremony—to award me the Korean Order

242

of Military Merit, the country's highest of its kind. Only six had been previously presented to Americans, generals all of them, including Ridgway, Stratemeyer, Partridge, and Timberlake. On the wall behind President Rhee I saw a painting of a woman with a child in her arms fleeing from a burning village. As he pinned on the medal I felt that I deserved it only if I had helped in some small way to keep that fire from spreading any farther.

Paper work, the dreadful routine of forms and files, is not usually very interesting, much less moving. But at Taegu, where I submitted my final reports on the 6146th Air Base Unit and on my work with the ROK Air Force, I found it just that. The records of my pilots, dead and alive, were in those papers, the numbers of our planes, the names of our fields. Just the name of Mike Bellovin alone. . . . I gave Mike the highest effectiveness report I had ever given a man in the service and still did not think I'd done justice to his contribution.

That night there was another gathering in Taegu: members of the Fifth Air Force staff, Korean Minister of Defense Chin, the Korean army chief of staff, Air Chief Kim, and some of his flyers. The next morning Hal Wilson, with Colonel Chung as copilot and Ray Engel as crew chief, flew us to Tachikawa Air Base in Japan in our C-47. At FEAF headquarters General Crabb asked for a briefing for his staff on the Korean air force. This was to conclude my official contact with it, so I ended the talk by requesting that authorizations be made for increased complements of aircraft and equipment—hollering to the end!

Now I was through. All that remained was a final get-together with friends who had come from Korea to see me off and remnants of the team now in Japan.

Red Varner, one of the original volunteers, was there, as were Craigwell, who also was preparing to go stateside, Hal Wilson, George Metcalf, and several of the Korean flyers. Looking around the table trying to make conversation, I wondered how many of these might die before this conflict was resolved. I felt that I was walking out on them—and then suddenly felt that I would stay with them in some fashion as long as they fought and flew against the enemies of freedom. To that path I would remain committed. I had not finished the course I had chosen, right or wrong, on that long-ago Sunday in Ohio.

"Oh, Lord, Thou hast seen my wrong, judge Thou my cause," cried Jeremiah. Could I not ask the same?

a final word

Today, though many miles removed from the Korean scene, I am doing essentially what I did then: dividing my time between the Air Force and the orphans.

I have remained in the Air Force instead of going back into the ministry for two reasons. First, I believe that opposing communism or any kind of totalitarianism must be the full-time job of at least a few Americans, and that I have been well prepared for the task. And second, I have been able to serve the Korean orphans better by remaining in the Air Force than had I returned to the ministry. "Operation Kiddy Car" and what little I accomplished on Cheju Island for the children received considerable attention in the United States, with the result that I was able to raise ten thousand dollars for the orphanage in the first year after my return from speaking engagements and public appearances.

But I have high hopes that with God's help and that of many generous Americans this will prove just a beginning. The Korean children on Cheju Island are, for the time being, safe from starvation and Communism. But while conditions at the orphanage are adequate, they would never meet United States orphanage standards. We have added a few quonset huts to the old frame building, and we are now receiving subsistence sums from orphanages and private organizations in the United States. But the island orphanage must be regarded as only a temporary and inadequate refuge for the thousands of Korean children who need our help. With part of the money I raised Mrs. Whang has purchased a piece of land outside Seoul for the ultimate erection of a permanent orphanage on the mainland. On this land is a small rock quarry, and it is our plan that the older boys will help to quarry the rock for the building of their new home.

But I hope and pray that this will be just a beginning. In some practical way I want to dedicate what remains of my life and energies not only to those destitute children in Korea but to the war orphans of the world. Toward this end I have taken a first humble step: the organization of a five-man group called "Hope, Incorporated," whose one and only purpose is to focus attention on the distressed children of the world, to plan and raise money for them, to feed and clothe them, and to assure them of a future.

It is an enormous task and an ambitious plan, yet I have faith that much can be accomplished. There are already successful organizations operating in the field. Furthermore, I have seen with my own eyes the touching generosity of American boys in Korea giving almost more than they had to give. Recently the Korean ambassador in Washington told me that his government had estimated that American GIs, hardly the wealthiest group on this globe, had given more than nineteen million dollars in money and gifts to the people of his country. Where there is that kind of compassion and generosity there must also be hope for a better world.

For now, at least, this, along with my regular Air Force duties, must be my work. But I cannot deny that from time to time I think with longing of a little frame church in the quiet Ohio countryside—perhaps the one at Paw Paw, with its single-ringing bell and its oak-shaded cemetery. Perhaps when I am older, I shall once again be its minister—if I feel myself qualified and if the good and simple people of that farming community will accept me in spite of all that I have done in an airplane.

Washington, D.C.
June 1, 1956

246